THE SPOT

PART III
Styles

CONTENTS

To Justine, Jared, Leah, Chloe, and Sasha
—E.D.

To my parents
—S.B.

Third Printing, 1989

Published 1984. Revised edition 1988.

This book was set in Baskerville by Black Dot and printed and bound by Halliday Lithograph in the United States of America.

Library of Congress Cataloging-in-Publication Data

Diamond, Edwin.
    The spot: the rise of political advertising on television / Edwin Diamond and Stephen Bates. —Rev. ed.
        p.   cm.
    ISBN 0-262-04095-6.   ISBN 0-262-54049-5 (pbk.)
    1. Advertising, Political—United States. 2. Television advertising—United States. I. Bates, Stephen, 1958-
II. Title.
JF2112.A4D53 1988
659.2'9320973—dc 19   88-2941
                                        CIP

THE SPOT

The Rise of Political Advertising on Television

Revised Edition

Edwin Diamond and Stephen Bates

The MIT Press
Cambridge, Massachusetts
London, England

PART IV
Effects

INTRODUCTION

In 1948 Harry S. Truman announced his determination to bring his presidential reelection effort to the villages and towns of America. He was able, by his own estimation, to log 31,000 miles in three months and shake the hands of some 500,000 voters. Scarcely four years later, Dwight D. Eisenhower sat down in a New York City studio to film three dozen television commercials, for which the voters were brought to him—a few days later an enterprising agent for Rosser Reeves of the Ted Bates advertising agency rounded up a group of tourists waiting to see the show at Radio City Music Hall, and took those "typical Americans" to a studio where their questions for Eisenhower were filmed, to be joined to Ike's answers. With that bit of splicing into a series of spots, called "Eisenhower Answers America," a new era of media campaigning began.

Dating from Rosser Reeves and Ike, political advertising on television represents a form of persuasion a little more than thirty years old. In that period the short (thirty- or sixty-second) political commercial, or polispot, has developed both distinct rhetorical modes and distinct visual styles. The polispot has also grown to dominate U.S. political campaigns, especially in national presidential elections and in the megastates. For example, of the $67 million in campaign funds that Ronald Reagan and Walter Mondale each spent in 1984, almost half went into "paid media" —political advertising, mainly on TV—and the same ratio is expected to hold in the 1988 election. In New York in 1982 a rich unknown named Lewis Lehrman, who had never run for public office before, spent close to $10 million to run as the Republican-Conservative nominee for governor. His aggressive polispot campaign gave him statewide recognition (from zero to ninety percent) and the nomination. In the general election Lehrman almost won the governorship.

Despite the importance of the polispot form, however, little has been written in any orderly fashion about the recent rise and present role of political advertising and marketing in American politics. Every four years magazine and newspaper articles appear, summoning up fears of campaign manipulation and behind-the-scenes image-makers. Those few books that have touched on political advertising have fed the popular iconography of media mercenaries who sell candidates like soap. We have found these old fears to be groundless and/or exaggerated. The real state of affairs is probably more serious: a new form of political communications has appeared, one that depends on high technology and big dollars and that may be turning elections and campaigns into a kind of spectator sport, a television entertainment, something to watch and enjoy but not necessarily to participate in by voting. In order to present that argument, our account is divided into four parts. Part I shows how media strategy fits within the wider campaign, using a case study from the 1984 campaign of John Glenn, and discussing the 1984 Reagan-Mondale race as well as the emerging patterns for 1988. Part II is a narrative of the role of television and polispots in the presidential elections from Eisenhower-Stevenson in 1952 to Carter-Reagan in 1980. The emphasis is on description and the presentation of representative spots from those campaigns, both in the text and in illustrations. Part III is our analysis of the major persuasive techniques and the visual styles of the polispot form, based on textual and visual examples from campaigns for mayor, governor, congressman, and senator, as well as president. Part IV brings together the political narrative and the media techniques in order to explain how polispots work and to assess the actual (as opposed to the fanciful) effects of television campaigns.

Our findings are based on two primary sources. First, we conducted extensive interviews with nineteen of the leading media managers in the country. Along with these question and answer sessions some media managers allowed us to watch them at work, and others arranged for screenings of their videotape collections of polispots, accompanied by their commentaries. We thank them for their help: Roger Ailes, John Deardourff, David Garth, Robert Goodman, Charles Guggenheim, Michael Kaye, Arie L. Kopelman, Malcolm MacDougall, Scott Miller, Joseph Napolitan, Barry Nova, Daniel Payne, Gerald Rafshoon, Rosser Reeves, David Sawyer, Tony Schwartz, Stuart Spencer, Robert Squier, and Ken Swope. In addition to the interviews and screenings with the media managers, we talked with other communications specialists, scholars, archivists, consultants, political candidates, and elected officials. We thank them too, and especially F. Christopher Arterton, James David Barber, Becky Bond, Walter Dean Burnham, L. Patrick Devlin, Ed Dooley, Dick Dresner, Albert Eisele, Jack Flannery, John Florescu, Curtis Gans, Kay Israel, Martin A. Linsky, Andrew Litsky, Eddie Mahe, Bill D. Moyers, John F. Nugent, J. Gregory Payne, Raymond K. Price, Jr., Robert Shrum, Jane Smith, Douglas Watts, Lewis Wolfson, and Stephen C. Wood.

Our other source of primary materials is the polispots and other political television materials in the archives of the News Study Group now at the Department of Journalism at New York University. This collection, begun in 1972 at MIT, now numbers some 850 commercials, from "Eisenhower Answers America"

(1952) to samples of the high-tech campaign of 1988. The News Study Group archives were organized and administered from 1980 to 1984 by Jack Link, whose untimely death deprived us of a lively and inquiring friend. Barry S. Surman prepared and photographed storyboards and stills for the illustrations. In addition to our own reporting, interviewing, and analysis we consulted reports, articles, campaign memoranda, books, public opinion polls, and political memoirs.

For administrative assistance, we thank Eva Nagy of the Department of Political Science at MIT and the staff of Harvard's Institute of Politics. We also thank Ann Fryling, Karlyn Keene, John O'Sullivan, Paul E. Schindler, Jr., Cynthia Schmechel, and Polly Smith. Final responsibility for the argument and the analysis rests, of course, solely with us.

THE NEW MEDIA AGE

PART I

RONALD REAGAN: MORNING AGAIN . . . AND THE MORNING AFTER

CHAPTER 1

Eight p.m., and David Sawyer and Scott Miller settle in to work for their client, John Glenn, U.S. senator from Ohio, candidate for the Democratic party nomination for president, genuine national hero. It has been a long day, and Sawyer and Miller must be conscious of time. Though it is October 1983, with the presidential election still one year away, candidate Glenn trails Walter Mondale in the early maneuvering for the nomination. Mondale has already won important endorsements; the AFL-CIO, the National Education Association, and Democratic party leaders such as Governor Mario Cuomo of New York have come out for him. If activists dominate the party caucuses and closed primaries, then Glenn must get "the mandate of the people" in the open primaries—demonstrate his ability to attract those moderates (Democratic and Republican) and independents who will later be needed to win the general election. Glenn's pragmatic answer to Mondale's institutional lead at this point in the campaign is media (as Mondale's would be if the situation were reversed).

That is why Sawyer, a forty-seven-year-old former filmmaker, and Miller, an ex-advertising copywriter who helped create some of the most acclaimed Coca-Cola ad campaigns ("Coke Is It!" "It's The Real Thing!"), are working late. They are the communication strategists for the Glenn campaign, hired to create his television advertising and to help make his mandate. They don't have much time.

Tonight, with the telephone at last silent and the conferences out of the way, Sawyer and Miller have two assignments. First, they will review the campaign's "early media," a Glenn television commercial made for airing during Saturday night prime time on the CBS network. Next they will prepare an "instructional" videotape of Glenn's speaking style, to be played for the candidate in his Washington office in strict privacy.

Sawyer's involvement in political campaigns goes back to the late 1960s, and he has submitted to enough reporters' interviews to be sensitive to what may be written that can hurt him, or his candidate. Inevitably there have been news stories about the media mercenary in politics only for the hefty fees (upwards of $15,000 to $25,000 a month, plus the advertising industry's standard fifteen percent commission of the hundreds of thousands of dollars paid for television commercial time). A few days earlier a newspaper article had referred to Sawyer as Glenn's "voice coach," a description that pained the consultant. More important, Glenn himself had been stung by a Mario Cuomo comment about the candidate's "celluloid image." The barb of course cut two ways. While Glenn is a certified national hero, he has had a hard time parrying the charge that he hasn't accomplished all that much in the two decades since his Mercury orbital flight. "Mr. Glenn's candidacy is still firmly bolted atop the rocket that lifted him into orbit 21 years ago," Howell Raines wrote in the *New York Times* on this very day that Sawyer and Miller are working late. Moreover, as a hoped-for consensus candidate seeking to occupy the middle of the political road, Glenn has tried to avoid taking too many specific policy stands in his early campaign. His opponents, especially Mondale, have homed in on Glenn's fuzziness.

Clearly Glenn must offer some substance in his advertising. His commercials can't look too stylized. His demeanor on the stump can't seem too staged. Images, celluloid or real, can't be too prominent in the campaign. And Sawyer in any event says he doesn't believe slickness works in political advertising. The audience voter, he says, has grown too sophisticated to be taken in. "They have been watching television for years," he says. "They have been exposed to paid political advertising, to news, to speeches. There is no way you can manipulate them, not now."

But just as clearly some communications strategy has to be followed. It is the way of the political world now, for any office bigger than village selectman. Aristotle argued that the ideal state ought to be no larger than a few thousand in population, so that citizen and magistrate could know each other. Madison in *The Federalist Papers* recognized that citizens would organize into factions and counted on the size of the American republic (with its population of three million) and on the federal system to prevent any single faction from gaining ascendancy. Today, in David Sawyer's view, technology has reunited the 230 million people of the republic, drawing together the voters and their leaders. Face-to-face meetings with everyone are no longer possible, but substitutes are available. All during the summer and fall of 1983 the public opinion specialist William Hamilton worked with Sawyer and Miller, polling voters on their opinions of the candidates (as were Peter Hart for Mondale and Richard Wirthlin for Ronald Reagan). Sawyer's associate, Ned Kennan, a social psychologist by training, convened representative samples of the electorate for small meetings called, in the marketing trade, focus group interviews (FGIs). In FGIs lasting as long as three hours, people expressed their feelings about their own lives and their attitudes about the country and its leaders, about family, friends, work, goals. The findings of this research became the basis of Glenn's first television advertising spots. True enough, critics might complain about the prominence of media mercenaries in the campaigns, about the high-tech marketing of candidates, about the manipulation of the hapless voter. But Sawyer saw it all as *greater* democracy and choice; polling, attitudinal surveys, and television would together achieve the Aristotelian goal. "We can now engage in a genuine dialogue with the voter," Sawyer told us, "and we can measure the impact we are having."

Reaching for "Hot Buttons"

The offices of D. H. Sawyer & Associates were then at 60 West 55th Street in New York; in 1986 they moved to sleek new offices. DHS & Associates, like a score of similar firms across the country, is equipped to do time-buying, FGIs, advertising, and all the other tasks of the modern political campaign. Its work is substantive, though it must necessarily deal in appearances too. During the fall of 1983 Sawyer and Miller were involved in what John Carey at the University of Pennsylvania called the metacampaign—the campaign within the campaign. The metacampaign is waged not so much to win public support as to convince the big contributors, party workers, reporters, and the other attentive political elites of the actual campaign's credibility. If the metacampaign succeeds, money and volunteers will flow in; the press and the opinion makers will promote the desired positive image. In the campaign of John Glenn this would mean the appearance of a winner to Mondale's loser image, even though Mondale might in fact be leading in the public polls.

Metacampaigns and media politics begin so early, require so many specialist talents, and cost so much that their very prominence often obscures the fact that this is a relatively new development in American politics. The Mondale strategy was until very recently the exclusive path to victory—a traditional old politics campaign of organizational loyalties, institutional endorsements, and party identification. Glenn, by contrast, started out as a new politics campaigner. Sawyer may have been exaggerating when he told us, that autumn night, that the Mondale versus Glenn race was a "battle for the soul of the Democratic party." But it did begin as a contest about where the muscle and bone of modern electoral politics were and a test of how much could be achieved by media and advertising. Certainly, when it started, no one could say with assurance how it would turn out.

Sawyer holds a Scotch whisky and ice in a glass. Miller is sipping Coke from a can. Sawyer went to Milton Academy and studied Chaucer at Princeton. Miller, as it happens, is from a small town in Ohio, just like Glenn. Sawyer is dressed in the manner of an Ivy League executive about Manhattan: gray suit, oxford shirt, muted silk tie. Miller, thirty-eight, is wearing blue jeans, a blue denim jacket, and boots; with his reddish-blond hair and bent nose he looks like a New York City plainclothes detective. Sawyer made independent documentaries, including one nominated for an Academy Award, before going into the political communications business fourteen years ago. Miller joined Sawyer in 1976 to moonlight in political campaigns, while still holding down his creative job for Coca-Cola and other clients at the McCann-Erickson advertising agency in New York. Those campaigns for Coca-Cola remain as close to his consciousness as the can of Coke in his hand. Miller did the Mean Joe Greene television spot in 1978, an ad so popular that it spawned a TV movie. Many people who don't drink Coke—somewhere, someone said it's not "good for you"—can still remember today that old Mean Joe commercial as an emotional experience. Why were we moved by it? Why should a thirty-second commercial pitch on an ephemeral medium, for what is, after all, a trivial product, affect us so? And what might that have to do with the advertising campaign of John Glenn and the choice of the next president of the United States? Sawyer had spoken of a type of commercial that touches us personally, that hits what marketing specialists call our "hot buttons" of emotional response. Soft drink commercials on television are usually full of frolicking and fun: people playing with dogs, Frisbees, children; handsome young couples nuzzling; above all, folks smiling while consuming the product.

Coca-Cola usually does its commercials that way and so does Pepsi-Cola. The trade calls them life-style commercials. We the viewers are supposed to associate all the good feeling and all the good living with the drink—and reach for it. The Mean Joe spot, however, went against this frothy wave of advertising.

Joe Greene was a large, menacing-looking (and black) football player of the champion Pittsburgh Steelers teams of the 1970s. He served on the defensive line where the toughest physical combat takes place. Even if much of the audience didn't know this background, the commercial makes it clear:

VIDEO   AUDIO

Camera up on close-up (CU) of grim Greene, limping slowly down tunnel from field toward locker room; words "Mean Joe Greene" superimposed on picture.

Cut to kid (white, about age nine) standing in tunnel, bottle of Coke in hand.

Kid [sound on film (SOF)]: "Mr. Greene! Mr. Greene! . . . I just want you to know: I think—you're the greatest!"

Cut to Greene, grimacing.

Greene [SOF]: "Yeah. Sure."

Cut to kid, offering bottle.

Kid [SOF]: "Want my Coke? It's okay. You can have it."

Cut to Greene, sighing. He takes it, drinks greedily.

Greene [SOF]: "Okay. Thanks."

Cut to kid, who hesitates, waiting for autograph or some sign of recognition.

Music, lyric under dialogue: "A Coke and a smile/Makes me feel good/Makes me feel nice."

Finally kid turns to leave, reluctantly.	Kid [SOF]: "See ya, Joe."
Cut to Greene, suddenly animated. He grabs his game jersey and tosses it.	Greene [SOF]: "Hey, kid! Catch!"
Cut to kid, beaming, catching shirt.	Kid [SOF]: "Wow! Thanks, Mean Joe!"
Supers fill screen: "HAVE A COKE AND A SMILE . . . COKE ADDS LIFE."	Music swells.

Undeniably, we feel good after seeing this thirty-second playlet. "A transition has taken place," Miller explains, gesturing with his own can of Coke. "The world is an unhappy place: your boss doesn't appreciate you, or your spouse, or your parents, or your kids." But in the miniworld of "Mean Joe and the Kid," "an emotional exchange occurs"—between adult and child, hero and audience, black and white. The black man still cares, with all the burdens he has had to bear. The kid can still dream of bright tomorrows, when he is a man and a hero. We all can still hope. We begin to feel good about ourselves and the world. Our hot button has been touched. And the medium of this human exchange, its symbol, is Coke.

At this point, in our view, the transitional picture gets murky. Some people, at some level of cognition, will associate their good feelings with Coke and go out and purchase the drink. Others will savor the spot—and continue to drink 7-Up. Memorable advertising, we know, often wins prizes but fails to move goods. No one has been able to encapsulate the successful marketing of products, let alone political candidates, in one surefire formula. "Ninety percent of my advertising doesn't work, and ten percent does," a bit of Madison Avenue apocrypha has an executive complaining. "But I don't know which ten percent." None of this stops advertising and marketing people from trying to find the ten percent that works. And Sawyer and Miller admit to no self-doubts. As Coke is the common ground for "Mean Joe and the Kid," so too in the Sawyer-Miller 1984 scenario is Glenn to be the common ground for Americans: the hero symbol who makes us feel good. An observer may doubt whether the public will buy the product. But if Sawyer and Miller are worried, they aren't showing it this night.

A Narrow Window of Opportunity

Sawyer and Miller have finished editing and are screening their first Glenn commercial on a videoplayer in a conference room; the shelves on the wall are stacked with cassettes. A file of survey research, thick as the Manhattan phone book, sits on Sawyer's desk. As much as possible has been done to discover the hot buttons of the contemporary American voter. For weeks now, Sawyer and Miller have been studying the Hamilton polls and the Kennan FGIs. Voters have been telling the researchers that they feel oppressed by events: the economy swings, incomprehensibly, between highs and lows; the nuclear weapons buildup outpaces the efforts at arms control; Dioxin, toxic waste, and acid rain seem to threaten the air they breathe and the land they live on. They feel unappreciated, misunderstood. Above all the characteristic American confidence in a plentiful future—the belief that our kids will have it even better than we did—has been reversed. As the Reagan eighties reach midpoint, Americans are telling the Glenn researchers that they believe things will be worse for their kids than they have been for them.

These same Americans also have much to say about the putative leaders of the country. Walter Mondale, for example, comes across as honest and likeable—"Heck, I like him too," says Sawyer. The FGIs reveal that while many Americans consider Mondale a traditional politician, they also believe that the current troubles of the nation are moral rather than political. Mondale, as the Glenn strategists have been reading the research in late 1983, is identified with the discredited past and with the waffling policies and big spender approaches of the Jimmy Carter administration "that got us into all this trouble in the first place." The immediate beneficiary of this disenchantment with Carter and traditional Democratic party policies has been, of course, Ronald Reagan. In the FGIs that Sawyer and Miller have in front of them, Reagan appears as the "stern father," in Sawyer's phrase, who in 1980 administered the bitter medicine we all knew we needed to take. We were too soft, too permissive, too lazy. The Japanese were producing better cars and TVs. The Russians—even the Iranians—were pushing us around. A typical Reagan voter, a blue-collar worker on an assembly line, might say in his focus group, "I've been a Democrat, and I was making $20.50 an hour. But I wasn't working that hard, and we weren't doing that good a job. We needed to be shaken up." He approved of Reagan's attacks on "welfare bums." (When he lost his job, and when his unemployment benefits seemed threatened, he may have felt differently.) Reagan may have been right for 1980 and for today, though even that was beginning to be questioned. But he had not been all that fair to the poor, the black, and the dispossessed. Indeed, some of the research uncovered voter fears of impending social upheaval, especially in the northeast (real-life mean—and mad—Joes would throw rocks rather than jerseys). It was, in short, time to move ahead.

If Mondale represented policies of the past and Reagan those of the present, then that left one direction for John Glenn. What would be more apt for the first American to go into orbit than to identify with the future? It seemed perfect for Glenn as a communications strategy. But when people were asked in their FGIs what they knew of John Glenn, they would offer "former astronaut" and little else. Glenn may have become, post-astronaut, both a successful business executive (good enough to become a rich man) by the late 1960s and a U.S. senator by 1974. Yet few people knew that. One of the first tasks of DHS & Associates would be, as Sawyer explained, "to help fill in the gaps in the candidate's record." If Glenn was being positioned in the political marketplace as a leader for the future, then his early advertising had to tell people what he had been doing the last twenty years.

Still Glenn's past contained the major edge that DHS & Associates would be extremely reluctant to lose. When the men and women in the focus groups expressed their pessimism about the state of the country, they also recalled a time when, they said, things were good, when the country was on the move, when it was possible to believe in themselves and in their leaders. That time, according to Sawyer, was the early 1960s, with the mythic John F. Kennedy in the White House. In all the surveys, Kennedy's presidency was remembered (or misremembered) with pride as a time of Camelot and Can Do. He promised to get Americans on the moon before the Russians, and we did it. He scared the steel barons into line. He faced down Khrushchev in the Cuban Missile Crisis (never mind Castro and the Bay of Pigs).

With this research Sawyer and Miller began shaping the words and images for Glenn's first advertising. A camera crew went to Ohio to tape Glenn delivering a speech at a school; the crew followed him to a factory visit and a county fair. In Newton, Iowa, Glenn and his wife Annie met with some thirty voters assembled by the Glenn campaign at the Izaak Walton League lodge. Glenn is standing in front of a fireplace and an American flag. The Iowans are seated on folding chairs. The questions and answers are spontaneous. Glenn gives long "untelevision" answers; to the first question about nuclear arms, he says he has a five-point program—and explains each point. The emotional hot point—the human exchange—is clearly intended to be the appearance of Mrs. Glenn, who until a few years ago had a major debilitating stutter. She is asked what kind of man, and potential president, her husband is, and she replies quietly, exerting control over each word: ". . . He knows about war . . . he has been in two. He doesn't have to watch late-night television to know about war. . . . He will work hard and keep his promises. He cares about the poor . . . the people without anything to eat . . . he cares about the en, nnnn, envir, enviro . . . let me try that again. He cares about the *environment*. He cares about the handicapped. I ought to know. I'm one. I was one of them, and he helped me. I could go on and on. . . ." Glenn then comes to his wife's side and says, "Well, I guess I have one vote here. . . ." "Annie," he explains, "used to be an eighty-five percent stutterer, which means that she couldn't get out eighty-five percent of all her words without stuttering. . . . You don't know what it means to Annie to get up and give a speech like that."

Sawyer had two crews at the Izaak Walton lodge shooting about two hours of the exchange; then, back in New York Sawyer's editors cut the material to thirty minutes. Meanwhile other researchers obtained NASA film and news stock of Glenn's orbital flight and his return to a joyous national welcome. The Walton lodge material was shown on statewide Iowa television only, on the evening of October 19. On that night several thousand Iowans were invited to some seven hundred house parties around the state to see the program. Glenn had been having severe staff problems with his Iowa state campaign, and the house parties were intended to be an "organizational tool" to attract volunteers. While the Iowans saw the Walton lodge material, the Ohio tapes together with the historical footage were edited into a four-minute, thirty-second spot for national exposure. The political realities of Glenn's situation—his strategists' conviction that he had to create his mandate at the very beginning of the nomination process, in Iowa and New Hampshire—had dictated an early start. "We have," said Sawyer, "a very narrow window of opportunity." The shorter spot, called "Believe in the Future Again," first aired on CBS at 8:55 p.m. EST, October 15, 1983.

In "Believe" the spot makers positioned Glenn as the common ground, the link both to a patriotic heritage and to a confident future. "He shows he has no fear," Miller says. The political present is ignored: no specific Glenn votes in the Senate are mentioned. The transition point, the emotional exchange, occurs with the evocation of John F. Kennedy and the space program's triumphs. That was the time when, the commercial implies, America had the right stuff. Glenn has it now, to lead America to greatness again:

VIDEO	AUDIO
. . . Cut to Glenn in space suit, walking by camera, waving; cut to extreme close-up (ECU) of Glenn's face seen through visor of helmet, as he prepares for blast-off.	Announcer [voice-over (VO)]: "They call him one of the true American heroes."
	Mission control voice, as heard inside Mercury capsule [VO]: "Godspeed, John Glenn!"
Cut to rocket lifting off; cut to Glenn inside capsule, moving slowly in weightlessness.	Announcer [VO]: "Hurtling through space at five miles per second, as the whole world held its breath.
Cut to John F. Kennedy, walking in front of Glenn; then Kennedy and Glenn in motorcade (black and white footage).	"He represented America in one of its finest hours, fulfilling the pledge of a young president full of hope and courage and faith in our future.
Cut to various shots of Glenn campaigning.	"Astronaut, Marine officer, successful businessman, senator—a lifetime dedicated to excellence, dedicated to this country."
Cut to Glenn outdoors, talking to voter, then walking off and shouting.	Glenn [SOF]: "Got one vote today!"

Cut to Glenn and his wife in motorcade, waving; then cut to various shots of Glenn with voters.

Announcer [VO]: "This is the message he takes forward, with his wife Annie by his side. Talking about what we *can* do, not what we can't. Not just promising what he'll do for you but telling you what we can do together."

Cut to Glenn at outdoor rally.

Glenn [SOF]: "This is a time to set a new direction. It's a time to begin setting goals again for this country. It's a time to challenge the American people—"

Announcer [VO]: "This is John Glenn."

The air time for "Believe" cost $35,000—a real bargain, says Sawyer—and the fund-raising trailer at the end brought in some $5,000 in contributions. This was a bonus; "Believe" basically had been designed to begin the metacampaign aimed at the attentive political audiences. As Sawyer explained, Glenn, by being first with his message, was attempting "to frame the campaign with his chosen themes." The media campaign itself came next, in January, with a $3 million series of spots intended to accentuate the differences between Mondale and Glenn. The spots depict a Mondale who is a tool of big labor and other special interests, whereas Glenn is framed by such words as "independent," "honest," and "courageous."

Every four years presidential campaigns produce a vogue word, like *credibility* (much used in the first post-Watergate election of 1976) or *momentum* (George Bush was said to have it, briefly, in 1980). For 1984 *framing* was favored. Glenn's attempts to frame

1984: JOHN GLENN

Glenn ID Commercial

"Godspeed, John Glenn!"

"Fulfilling the pledge of a young president"

"John Glenn for president"

the campaign reflect an understandable concern for taking the initiative and presenting his candidacy and the race in his own terms. A frame, however, also implies setting rather than substance. The Glenn candidacy had a series of major problems with the substantive part of the campaign—the contents of the frame.

There was, most of all, the matter of his fuzzily defined demeanor. Who, exactly, was John Glenn? As his detractors saw him, Glenn was a not very bright, retired Marine colonel. Barry Nova, a New York advertising man, did the media and advertising when Glenn first ran for the Democratic nomination for U.S. Senate in 1970. Nova is now a business executive in Greenwich, Connecticut, out of advertising and politics ("I don't even go to Madison Avenue any more," he says). Glenn, Nova now says, was a "great astronaut and a valid national hero" but also "shallow of thought . . . an egocentric." There was also the matter of Glenn's erratic ability to communicate his goals. In 1970 Nova found Glenn "pedantic in speech," and declared he didn't know what his candidate stood for and didn't think the Ohio voters knew either. Some thirteen years later, media managers still worried about Glenn's speech-making abilities, and Nova said he still didn't know what Glenn stands for.

Walter Mondale, for his part, also had an early framing strategy, one intended to prevent being engulfed in Glenn's elaborate media launching. Throughout 1983 Mondale consistently raised the most money of any candidate from private sources. He entered 1984 with some $9 million—to Glenn's $6 million—and, under the terms of campaign finance law, got an additional $3 million in federal money, an allocation based on the amount of money raised privately (through the convention, each candidate could spend $24 million). With money and organization in place, Mondale's framing strategy called for attack. A perfect metacampaign event provided the stage for one execution of this strategy. During September and October of 1983 the New York

State Democratic party held a series of candidate forums through-out the state. Governor Mario Cuomo, the leading Mondale supporter in the state, served as host and interlocutor.

On September 26 in Syracuse Cuomo caught Glenn by sur-prise, asking Glenn to tell the audience how he differed from Mondale. The automatic pilot locked into place. Glenn said that while he had been going around the country discussing his own views, he was not going to characterize the views of another candidate, drone, drone, drone. Two days later in Rochester, Cuomo pitched the readied Mondale the same question. Mondale replied in forceful detail, ticking off traditional Democratic party policies that he had supported and Glenn opposed; score a big win for Mondale.

Glenn came better prepared for the final candidates' meeting at Town Hall in New York City. One of the three designated questioners, the Duke University political scientist, James David Barber, asked Glenn in effect if his orbital flight wasn't something of a stunt, like Evel Knievel hurtling the Snake River Canyon on a motorcycle. Barber had voiced a legitimate concern of voters, asking if Glenn possessed sufficient knowledge of political affairs, if he had the right stuff to be president. But the reference to the stunt man was maladroit. The crowd began hissing Barber before he had finished. Glenn forcefully talked about his military service, his fighter pilot missions in World War II and Korea. "I was not doing *Hellcats of the Navy* on a movie lot"—a reference to a Grade B Ronald Reagan-Nancy Davis movie—"when I was doing 149 missions." To rising applause, Glenn declared how proud he had been to represent the United States as an astronaut and to show the world what America could accom-plish. Hot buttons tingled.

This may have been the high point of 1983, and of his cam-paign, for Glenn. In the early fall of 1983 he was leading Mondale thirty-nine to thirty-three in some polls; by the end of the year the figures showed a startling reversal, with Mondale being fa-vored over Glenn forty-three to twenty-nine as the institutional endorsements and organizational strengths of the Mondale campaign began to pay off, at least in the popularity polls. Mondale's old politics approach brought victory in the Iowa party caucuses on February 20. In New Hampshire's first primary on February 28, Senator Gary Hart emerged with an unexpected win. In both contests Glenn was a disappointing also-ran.

In the Iowa-New Hampshire stage of the 1984 campaign Glenn had framed his issues, re-identified himself, introduced his theme of leadership for the future, and attacked Mondale in negative ads—Sawyer preferred to call them contrast ads—as the candidate of the special interests. Glenn had used his astronaut image and the bulk of his campaign capital, and the voters rejected him. In mid-March he withdrew.

What happened? As we shall see repeatedly in the narrative that follows, electoral politics involves much more than the media plans of any one candidate. In 1984 it's clear that Mondale's initial organizational successes and Hart's early "momentum" provide some explanation for Glenn's faltering trajectory. But John Glenn himself must answer too for his sputtering campaign. His television ads were in our opinion excellent—on the whole better than any of the spots for the other Democratic primary candidates, and as good as any primary spots we encountered in our research. They helped "blow a hole," in Sawyer's words, in the notion of Mondale's "invincibility." But the real Glenn, as opposed to the videotape Glenn, couldn't exploit that hole. Hart, whose media also positioned him as the candidate of the future, was able to move into the breach—even as Glenn failed to stir those Iowa and New Hampshire voters who came to take his measure. Some of them, on meeting him, were to declare that there was "no there there."

Hart's Stumbles, Mondale's Beef

Gary Hart, the cool, enigmatic senator, became Mondale's chief rival. Hart's rise and fall had a meteorlike quality—though his wilder trajectory wouldn't occur until three years later, on the eve of the 1988 race, in the company of a sometime model and prospective starlet named Donna Rice. Hart was 46 in 1984; he had managed George McGovern's disastrous 1972 presidential campaign. In 1974 he won election on his own in his home state of Colorado. Hart called himself the presidential candidate of "new ideas." Handsome, rangy in his cowboy boots, he looked a lot like Warren Beatty, and in fact often spent time with the actor. Hart became a viable alternative to Mondale, in the press accounts at least, when he won a not-so-close second in Iowa, 16 percent to Mondale's 50 percent, and from there achieved an unexpected win in New Hampshire.

Hart's media man was Raymond Strother, a Texan who had attended LSU and had done a number of Louisiana statewide races. Hart was his first presidential campaign client. In 1983 Strother had approached Hart. When the senator asked, "How would you portray me?" Strother replied appropriately to a candidate professing "new ideas": "The messenger should become the message." Hart and his aides screened samples of Strother's Louisiana work, and liked what they saw. The financially strapped Hart campaign also liked Strother's offer to work without a fee, taking only 15 percent of the campaign's expenditures for TV and radio time—instead of the usual 15 percent plus a sizable fee.

Two months remained before the Iowa caucuses, and the campaign had nothing on television. Strother needed to make commercials quickly and cheaply. He screened a film of Hart's, shot the previous year on a Colorado mountain. Hart's comments on specific issues were far too long for thirty-second spots, and so Strother used a computer graphics device that created the effect of turning pages: it peels one image up, over itself, and off the screen. This covered the splices where Strother cut Hart's comments. Hart's face filled the center of the screen, surrounded by a grid that seemed to disappear behind the image. At the bottom of the screen was Hart's name in computer-style letters—a reinforcement of the "new ideas" strategy. Hart had been called an "Atari Democrat," in recognition of his economic emphasis on postindustrial technologies rather than smokestack America. Now his ads looked like a videogame display. The page-turning spots helped Hart make an impact on Iowa. Hart's Iowa "success," in turn, helped the campaign raise money, which bought TV time for the ads in New Hampshire.

But commercials caused the Hart campaign to stumble on the eve of the Illinois primary. Strother made an ad that linked Mondale to Edward "Fast Eddie" Vrdolyak, a leader of the "white" faction of Chicago's Democratic party (the other faction belonged to Harold Washington, Chicago's first black mayor). As the video showed pictures of Vrdolyak and Mondale, the announcer said: "Eddie Vrdolyak has decided that Walter Mondale will be your candidate for president. Gary Hart and a lot of people who think for themselves stand in the way." The spot was designed for the Chicago TV market, with its large black audience.

Attacking a candidate on the basis of his supporters is as old as politics; the coming of the polispot only helps dramatize this form. A Lyndon Johnson commercial in 1964 told viewers that the Ku Klux Klan had endorsed Barry Goldwater—and accompanied the charge with shots of Klansmen and cross burnings. Hart himself, in ads aired a few weeks earlier, had tried to tie Mondale to "the Washington insiders and special interests." Hart's problem lay with his own insiders. Hart had not seen the Vrdolyak script; when he did, he vetoed the ad. Hart believed it would be a mistake for a presidential campaign to get embroiled in Chicago's roughhouse racial politics, and he had said as much in a newspaper interview. But by then the ad was already on the air—at the instruction of campaign poller Pat Caddell.

At this point, the Friday night before the Tuesday primary, Strother knew killing the rest of the spot's schedule would be difficult. More than that, Strother believed the change in strategy would become *the* campaign story through Tuesday. Strother recommended leaving the ad on for the weekend and pulling it

1984: GARY HART AND WALTER MONDALE

**Hart Page-Turning
Commercial**

Denim jeans and Atari
graphics

Mondale ID Commercial

In presidential suit and
tie

Monday. The campaign manager, Oliver "Pudge" Henkel, concurred, and he passed the recommendation to Hart. But Hart was adamant: the ad had to be canceled. Meanwhile Hart refused to answer reporters' questions about the ad's attack on Mondale. "Why should I have to?" he said. 'They're not my ads. I didn't want them produced, and I didn't want them on the air." It was answer enough for the voters, but the TV stations had programmed their weekend schedule on computers, and the programs couldn't be changed. As Strother had feared, the Hart campaign's confusion over the ads became the story of the final days, conveying the message that Hart couldn't run his own campaign. Mondale said he wondered how a man who couldn't even get his own ads off the air could handle the presidency. (Campaign manager Henkel later remarked that winning the presidency is easier than canceling a TV ad on a weekend.) Caddell's polls had shown Hart eleven points ahead; by Sunday night, as the Vrdolyak spot story dominated the news, Hart was nine points behind Mondale.

While Hart's video attack on Mondale backfired, Mondale's video attacks on Hart seemed to hit their target. Mondale's spots had their roots in focus groups held after New Hampshire. The groups had found strong support for Gary Hart across the board—except on one issue. When asked whom they would be more comfortable with in a foreign crisis, Hart or Mondale, strong majorities chose the former vice-president. The result was Mondale's red phone ad: Camera up on a red phone—presumably the White House–Strategic Air Command link, an image that the media managers have called upon from the early days of the missile age—as the voice-over speaks of the presidency as "the most awesome, powerful responsibility in the world. . . . The idea of an unsure, unsteady, untested hand is something to really think about." The ad reinforced what the press was saying about Hart. Mondale won Illinois by five points, and went on to win the nomination.

In the general election, Mondale faced a far tougher battle. Even the best-tuned strategy would hardly have guaranteed victory, given the generally optimistic mood of a middle-class electorate in an America not at war and enjoying economic good times. Moreover the incumbent was well-liked and at ease with the demands of a media campaign. Mondale, on the other hand, was clearly uncomfortable with television. "I never warmed to TV," Mondale would say later, "and it never warmed to me." From a technical point of view, the Mondale media effort was competent enough. Time-buying is one of the technologies of the mass media campaign, and the Nielsen measurements showed that Mondale's time-buying operation bought more viewers per dollar than Reagan's did. A Mondale spot on CBS on October 4, for example, drew a 19.0 rating—the best political rating of the month—whereas a Reagan spot rated an 8.8 on NBC the following night—the worst of the month. The Mondale problem was not advertising technique but political judgment.

The Mondale campaign tried out a variety of media experts and media themes. Richard Leone, who had a background in New Jersey politics, was Mondale's senior media adviser, and a young Texan named Roy Spence produced the spots. The campaign tried to hire David Garth, a leader in the field (see chapter 14). But Garth demanded full control of the Mondale media campaign, and the candidate's inner circle of loyalists from his Minnesota days—known as "The Norwegians"—wasn't willing to delegate that much authority. The campaign then turned to David Sawyer and Scott Miller, available after the Glenn debacle. DHS created more than a dozen spots for Mondale; the campaign ultimately used only one of them, in which a roller coaster plunges down a steep slope. The voice-over says, "Nineteen eighty-two. Reaganomics sinks our country into the deepest recession and unemployment in fifty years." Screams echo in the background, and then the closing graphic fills the screen: "If you're thinking of voting for Ronald Reagan in 1984—think of what will happen in 1985."

Another Mondale theme was fairness—urged on the campaign by Pat Caddell, who had joined Mondale after Hart's demise. One well-conceived ad combined an economic message with the fairness theme. The camera shows business types in dark suits marching from the U.S. Treasury building into limousines; the voice-over identifies them as "profitable corporations that pay no taxes, defense contractors on bloated budgets, foreign interests who make money on our debt. . . . You're paying for their free ride." A series of spots tried to create an image of the Other America excluded from the Reagan prosperity. One, aimed at liberal hot buttons, showed elderly women, dignified but frightened, talking quietly about proposed cuts in food stamp aid for the poor. "I just want enough to get along," one says to the camera. "That's all I ask." Another showed a farmer saying, "I guess if I had enough money, maybe I could be a Republican." The theme of Reagan's "unfairness" never caught on. One trouble was that the definition of the Other America was too narrow. Voters might shake their heads compassionately at the plight of the elderly woman on food stamps, and then cast their vote for Reagan anyway. A better strategy might have been to include blue-collar and middle-income people in the Other America excluded from the Reagan bounty.

When candidates fall far behind, they turn to so-called negative or attack spots (we treat this inevitable progress—or, actually, descent—in more detail in chapter 14). At the campaign's end the Democrats' chosen anti-Reagan theme was the threat of nuclear war as well as Reagan's reputation as a too relaxed, no-hands president. One spot dusted off the red phone from Mondale's primary ads. The voice-over talks ominously about "killer weapons in space" with "a response time so short there'll be no time to wake a president."

Reagan's Winning Ways

In retrospect it's hard to believe that Reagan's reelection effort was ever in doubt. Try as he did, Mondale couldn't link Reagan to the mounting federal deficit, the greatest burden of Reaganomics to the country. The national debt simply wouldn't stick as a campaign issue: it was too abstract—no one could look outside the window and see the beast labeled "deficit" hunkering down on the front lawn. On the other side, Mondale was identified as the candidate advocating the need for a tax increase, and that homed in on almost every voter's immediate vision. While it was said that Mondale was promising April 15 for everyone, Reagan offered up Christmas morning with bright presents under the tree.

It was late May when the first flight of Reagan ads aired. "It's morning again in America," begins the mellifluous voice of Hal Riney, one of the hottest ad men of the 1980s (Gallo Wines, later Bartles and Jaymes). A series of lush shots follows —families, a parade, a wedding, and, over and over again, American flags. "Americans are working again," Riney says in one ad, "and so is America." Another spot shows workers refurbishing the Statue of Liberty, and closes with the graphic: "President Reagan: Rebuilding the American Dream." A few of the spots take an indirect dig at Mondale; Riney asks, "Why would we ever want to return to where we were less than four short years ago?" In most of the "Morning Again" ads a small photo of Reagan appears at the end, next to an American flag.

A member of Mondale's media staff termed the ads "a Hollywood feel-good campaign." The slickness was a conscious decision, according to Reagan's media director, Douglas Watts. "We wanted high production values," he told us. For one thing, "Nancy Reagan demanded them." Mrs. Reagan had collaborated with White House aide Michael Deaver to oust Peter Dailey, the Los Angeles advertising producer who had created Reagan's 1980 ads. Dailey's work, Mrs. Reagan believed, looked amateurish and unpolished (that had been Dailey's intent; he feared slickness would remind voters of Reagan's Hollywood days.) In Dailey's place the campaign ultimately created its own ad agency by borrowing talent from Madison Avenue agencies. The Tuesday Team, as the group was called, was headed by

James Travis, the president of the agency Della Femina, Travisano. Aside from Hal Riney, team members included Phil Dusen-
berry, who had produced Pepsi's Michael Jackson ads, and
Ron Travisano, who had created the singing cat ads for Meow
Mix.

Besides the "Morning Again" spots, the Reagan campaign aired
a half-hour film on September 11 which further drove home the
simple themes of optimism and patriotism. One thirty-second
sequence showed Air Force One, the Statue of Liberty, the White
House, and eleven shots of American flags. Another sequence
showed Reagan eulogizing the men who fell at Normandy Beach.
But Reagan's best spot of the period waved flags only metaphori-
cally:

VIDEO	AUDIO
Camera up on a grizzly bear. It lumbers across a hilltop, crosses a stream and forges through underbrush.	(Under announcer, a drum plays incessantly, like a heart-beat.)
Cut to a slightly blurry image of the bear (shot through a diffusion filter). It walks slowly along a ridge, silhouetted against sky. It looks up, stops suddenly, and takes a step backward. The camera pulls back to show a man standing a few yards away, facing the bear. He too is silhouetted. A gun is slung over his shoulder.	Announcer (Riney) [VO]: "There's a bear in the woods. For some people, the bear is easy to see. Others don't see it at all. Some people say the bear is tame. Others say it's vicious and dangerous. Since no one can really be sure who's right, isn't it smart to be as strong as the bear? [Pause.] If there is a bear."
Cut to closing graphic: "President Reagan: Prepared For Peace."	

Riney had created "Bear," working up a storyboard that used magazine cutouts. The spot was filmed in Oregon, using a bear trained to stop, look up, and step backward when it walked into a hidden wire. Tests showed the spot achieved an extraordinarily high recall rate. Many viewers missed the Soviet allegory but got the message of peace through strength. According to Watts, the ad attracted two demographic groups whose views often diverge: women liked the peace-through-strength appeal, and blue-collar men warmed to the macho theme.

The Reagan campaign also reminded viewers of Mondale's April 15 "promise." "Tax Vignettes" showed a hard-hat laborer at work, a woman in a kitchen, and a farmer in the field, while the announcer said that Mondale expected people to put in a bit more overtime, to stretch the family budget farther, and to spend a few more hours in the fields—in order to pay higher taxes. On election day, November 6, the voters pulled the lever for December 25. Reagan won 59 percent of the popular vote, to 41 percent for Mondale. In the electoral college, Reagan won 49 states; Mondale held only his home state, Minnesota, and the District of Columbia.

The media campaigns directed at the voters in 1984 weren't nearly as bad as critics claimed, nor were they as good as the media makers sometimes boasted. Both Mondale's and Reagan's spots were a sideshow to the election. Much more important in shaping the outcome were incumbency, a voting class that saw itself enjoying peace and prosperity, and the candidates' debates that initially stirred and then allayed apprehensions. The voters loved Reagan in November as much as they had the previous January. The TV advertising was largely background music to the affair.

1986–1988: Accentuating the Negative

More to the point, though, Americans aren't likely to live through a presidential race (or senatorial or gubernatorial campaign) *un*accompanied by political advertising—at least not in the

1984: RONALD REAGAN

Reagan's Bear

"There's a bear in the woods"

"Some people say the bear is tame. Others say it's vicious and dangerous"

"Since no one can really be sure who's right, isn't it smart to be as strong as the bear?"

lifetimes of today's registered voters. If anything the polispot sounds are growing louder and more discordant. The 1986 midterm elections earned the title "The Year of the Negative" in the *Washington Post*. The columnist Charles Krauthammer echoed Spiro Agnew: "Political advertising has reached a nadir of nattering negativism." The humorist Mark Russell suggested that a political consultants' association name their award for the best polispot "The Sleazy."

One especially vicious 1986 race was that for Senate from South Dakota. The Republican incumbent, James Abdnor, ran a spot attacking the Democratic candidate, Congressman Thomas Daschle, for having invited Jane Fonda to testify before the House Agriculture Committee. Fonda, the Abdnor ad says, "has been identified with more radical causes than almost anyone in America"; worse, she "writes and speaks against eating beef and pork, our state's biggest farm products." The Daschle campaign responded with an ad that shows a room full of actors playing cigar-smoking political consultants. "We'll distort the farm thing, confuse 'em with Fonda, all the usual liberal stuff," one says. "When we're finished," another says, "Daschle's mother won't vote for him. [Pause.] Let's go tell Jim."

In Maryland, meanwhile, Republican Senate candidate Linda Chavez's spots attacked her opponent, Barbara Mikulski, as a "San Francisco-type liberal." The line resonated not only with the Democrats' sometimes-rowdy 1984 San Francisco convention, but also with San Francisco's reputation as a city of gay men and lesbians (Mikulski was unmarried). In Nevada, Democratic Senate candidate Harry Reid's spots attacked the Republican, Jim Santini, for inconsistency on various issues. In response, Santini's ads labeled his opponent "Dirty Harry."

In truth, the attack ads of 1986, although memorable, hardly predominated. The majority of polispots were mild and frequently interchangeable. One consulting firm, Greer & Associates, designated its various client-candidates as "Georgia's man," "Washington's man," and "Connecticut's [Christopher] Dodd." One Greer

client was praised for "standing up for Wisconsin," another for
"standing up for us," still another for "stepping up to the future."
Most of all, 1986 was costly: candidates for the House and the
Senate spent more than $400 million, nearly 25 percent of it on
television.

Almost before the '86 payments had cleared the campaigns'
checking accounts, the first TV dollars in the 1988 presidential
election were being spent. In April of 1987 former Arizona
Governor Bruce Babbitt, one of the contenders seeking the
Democratic nomination (seven at the time), ordered a quarter-
million dollars worth of commercials in Iowa. No matter that it
was still eleven months before the first delegates to the Democratic
convention would be selected. The race—to the White House for
the candidates, and to the banks for the consultants—was on. It
was the earliest-ever start for presidential commercials.

By summer's end the candidates had begun to line up media
advisers. Vice-President Bush, for example, signed up Roger Ailes,
the media manager who played a prominent role in Richard
Nixon's 1968 campaign. Babbitt's initial spots were produced by
three non-Washington companies that specialized in product,
rather than political, advertising: WFC Advertising of Phoenix, the
Magus Corporation of Philadelphia, and Papanek & Young of
Hollywood. Missouri Congressman Richard A. Gephardt hired
Doak, Shrum & Associates of Washington. Governor Michael
Dukakis of Massachusetts hired a Boston-based consultant, Daniel
Payne. Illinois Senator Paul Simon hired David Axelrod, a former
Chicago Tribune reporter who had run Chicago Mayor Harold
Washington's media campaign in 1987. Senator Bob Dole of
Kansas hired James Travis, a Tuesday Team alumnus. Pat
Robertson, the television evangelist of the Christian Broadcast-
ing Network, assembled a team of experienced media people
in-house. Going against the tide, as usual, wasd the maverick
Gary Hart. When he reentered the Democratic race in Decem-
ber opf 1987, he said he had no media consultants, pollsters,

staff, or money. It would be, he said, "unlike any campaign you have ever seen."

At least for the other candidates, the 1988 campaign promised more attention than ever to the political advertising arts. A fund-raising letter on behalf of Dole presented recipients with a choice. Which commercial would they rather see the campaign air: one on the Reagan-Republican record, or one on Dole's vision for the future? If it seemed that ordinary people were being treated as media experts, there was some basis for this regard. In the spring of 1987 the Babbitt campaign taped its first TV commercials at a farm outside Des Moines. A member of the film crew approached the farmer and, speaking slowly, asked if he had any hookups for "*eee*-lectricity" close by. The farmer smiled and said: "Don't you worry, boys. We've got a 220 over there for your lights, and the generator packs can run over here." His place had been used for on-location polispots before.

Most of what we observed in the 1980s—the pervasiveness of television, the skills of the political ad people, the clash between the old politics and the new politics, the growing sophistication of the viewing public in Iowa and elsewhere—fits in with developments that began when the broadcast advertising arts first came to American politics. To understand the seemingly dominant role of political ads today, we must begin with the circumstances of their introduction four decades earlier.

1952–1980

Part II

THE RADIO AGE AND THE BIRTH OF SPOTS

CHAPTER 2

In the beginning, there were no commercials. And, for a while, no one demanded any. The first radio station in the United States, KDKA in Pittsburgh, went on the air in 1920. Owned by Westinghouse, its programming—live music, theater, sports, and speeches—was offered solely as a means to sell more Westinghouse radio sets. By late in the decade corporate America had discovered the airwaves, but only for generating so-called "tradename publicity." Listeners could tune in the *Maxwell House Hour*, the *General Motors Family Hour*, the *Cities Service Orchestra*, and the *Ipana Troubadours*, among others. No direct advertising was allowed. Indeed, there was to be no description of the product, much less any mention of price. The sponsor advertisers, said NBC president Merlin Aylesworth in 1928, were content with "the goodwill that results from their contribution of good programs."

The contentment didn't last, and neither did broadcasters' fastidiousness about products and prices. By the 1930s short, punchy commercials, called "spot announcements" or simply "spots," were commonplace. The broadcast historian Erik Barnouw credits two factors for the change in policy: the 1929 stock-market crash, convincing business executives that "resolute salesmanship" was now needed, and the creation of a new network, the Columbia Broadcasting System, whose survival seemed to require breaking the rules. These developments gave advertisers the upper hand in their dealings with broadcasters. If George Washington Hill, the storied head of American Tobacco (and the model for the Sidney Greenstreet character in *The Hucksters*) wanted to promote Cremo five-cent cigars in specific, even graphic, terms, CBS would let him. "Between blaring numbers of the Cremo Military Band," writes Barnouw, "its announcer shouted: 'There is no spit in Cremo!' "

Political campaigns also discovered that radio time was for sale. In 1924 both presidential candidates, Democrat John W. Davis and Republican Calvin Coolidge, bought radio time for speeches (but not for spots). The Republicans spent $120,000 on radio, the Democrats, $40,000, and Coolidge won. Four years later the first political spots appeared, when the GOP organized some 6,000 "Minute Men" all over the country to present brief radio talks on behalf of the Republican ticket. Scripts were sent in advance, so that the same talk was given nationwide on a particular day. The Democrats meanwhile permitted engineers to carry out an experiment. Pictures of New York Governor Al Smith's announcement of his presidential candidacy were carried live, from Albany to Schenectady (fifteen miles) by a new process called television. Smith's unsuccessful candidacy featured two other innovations: a radio play based on the candidate's life and the first five-minute speeches via broadcasting.

Television went nowhere for two more decades, but political operatives intuitively understood the power of moving images. In 1934 the muckraker and Nativist Radical Upton Sinclair became the Democratic candidate for governor of California. Businessmen and conservatives, who regarded Sinclair's program to end poverty as a Bolshevik plan to redistribute the wealth, were horrified. The Republicans hired Lord & Thomas, a top ad agency, and also retained the California political consulting firm, the first in the nation, of Whitaker & Baxter to fight Sinclair. Whitaker & Baxter produced phony newsreels of staged events. In one, dozens of bedraggled hoboes leap off a freight train, presumably having arrived in the Promised Land of California. Explains one bum: "Sinclair says he'll take the property of the working people and give it to us." In another, a bearded man with a Hollywood-Russian accent explains why he will vote for Sinclair: "His system vorked vell in Russia, so vy can't it vork here?" The bogus newsreels were shown in California movie theaters, between features, thanks to Louis B. Mayer, head of MGM Studios and a power in the California Republican party.

Except for their physical location in theaters, these Republican newsreels would serve as a model for television spot advertising when TV became a dominant national force, overshadowing radio and indeed killing off the theatrical newsreel. Just as movie programming gathered a captive audience for Whitaker & Baxter's phony newsreels, so did television programming collect crowds for the advertisers' brief spots. Of course it took time for television to become that dominating force, and it took time before the spot became the dominating form of TV advertising. World War II delayed television's commercial development until the late 1940s, and only then, as it became apparent that television would be a bigger, more lucrative enterprise than radio—emblematically, radio's *$64 Question* quiz show became the *$64,000 Question* on television—did the networks assert economic control over the airwaves. As it happened, 1952 was a year of change for television, as well as for the advertising spot. The year 1952 also transformed the way Americans elected their presidents—a change directly related to the twin developments of television and the TV spot.

The Desilu Revolution

In the election of 1948 the victorious Harry S. Truman could boast: "I traveled 31,000 miles, made 356 speeches, shook hands with a half million people, talked to 15 or 20 million in person." Truman's predecessor, Franklin D. Roosevelt, had used radio to become the Great Communicator, a role half forced on him — confined as he was, with his polio-withered legs, to a wheelchair — and half seized by dint of his wonderful, assured, commanding radio voice and manner. Truman, with his flat, sharp Midwest accent, about as pleasing as the sound of chalk squeaking across a blackboard, had a low opinion of broadcasting. "My own experience is all in personal contact," he allowed. His campaign did produce a single short spot, with the candidate urging people to vote; records do not indicate whether it was shown in movie theaters or on TV. When, at a news conference after the election, a reporter asked Truman whether TV had boosted his campaign, the other reporters present burst out laughing. Truman said television had been of some use, and added that he was sorry it hadn't reached more people.

Developments in the next four years helped TV reach a far larger audience. A transcontinental cable, inaugurated experimentally in 1951, permitted nationwide TV networks to form. The number of sets fast proliferated, to an estimated nineteen million in 1952. By then some forty percent of American households could be reached by TV, with the percentage rising to sixty-two percent in the populous northeastern areas. Programming began to fill with faces soon to be familiar — Milton Berle, Ed Sullivan, Arthur Godfrey, Dave Garroway, and the cast of the golden age comedy classic *Your Show of Shows*, among them Sid Caesar, Imogene Coca, Carl Reiner, and Howard Morris. One of the fastest climbing programs on the new A.C. Nielsen ratings was *I Love Lucy*, starring forty-two-year-old Lucille Ball and her husband, Desi Arnaz.

Millions of Americans watched Ball play the zany, calamitous Lucy Ricardo on CBS Mondays at 9 p.m. EST, but the situation comedy manufactured more than laughs. *I Love Lucy* was produced by Ball and Arnaz's own corporation, Desilu Productions, and co-owned with CBS. As such, *I Love Lucy* marked the beginning of a major change in the structure of television. At first, following the precedent established by early radio, television programs were sponsor owned and sponsor controlled. Advertising agencies generally supervised and sold the shows, incorporating the sponsor's name into the title (*The Goodyear Television Playhouse*). But network executives, notably William Paley, the founding father of CBS, were not satisfied with merely renting out the airwaves; they wanted program control for themselves. So the networks, in concert with producers like Desilu, gradually eased sponsors out of programming during the 1950s. Increasingly, if advertisers wanted to be heard—aside from Procter & Gamble owning daytime soap serials, or IBM underwriting a prime-time special— they had to buy thirty- or sixty-second advertising units.

While some sponsoring companies and advertising agencies may have deplored the passing of the good old days, one Madison Avenue adman in particular, Thomas Rosser Reeves, Jr., couldn't have been happier. Rosser Reeves was born in Danville, Virginia, in 1910, the son of a Methodist minister. He came North to make his fortune in advertising in 1934 and did so well that he retired a millionaire several times over at the age of fifty-six. We talked to Reeves one summer afternoon in 1983, in his co-op apartment overlooking Gramercy Park in New York City. He explained his enthusiasm for spots, his philosophy of the USP—unique selling proposition—and his role in helping elect a president with the first TV spot campaign. (Reeves died in January 1984.)

In the 1950s Reeves was dean of the hammer-it-home school of advertising, the prince of hard sell. The most effective selling method, Reeves felt, was USP. Whereas most ads use words like "best," "biggest," "brightest" interchangeably, Reeves's theory was that the most effective ads boldly stake out a claim untouched by the competition. A long-standing ad slogan developed by Reeves, for instance, boasted that M&Ms melt in your mouth, not in your hand. Though a skeptic can argue that the phrase on examination doesn't mean much, Reeves would hold that it is memorable, it is unique, and it is so attached to M&Ms that no other candy would dare make a similar statement. "The USP leaps out at you!" Reeves wrote in his book, *Reality in Advertising*. "And the result is not only usage pull but high penetration as well."

Reeves and the Ted Bates agency, where he worked, gave the USP hard-sell treatment to a number of products: Anacin (the spot showed animated hammers bashing away at cerebrums), Rolaids (holes burned in cloth by stomach acid), Colgate Dental Cream with protective Gardol (baseballs hurled toward the viewer), and Bic Pens (ballpoints shot from rifles and crossbows). Reeves once told Thomas Whiteside of *The New Yorker* that the sixty-second Anacin spot cost the client $8,400 to produce and "made more money [for Anacin] in seven years than *Gone With the Wind* did for David O. Selznick and MGM in a quarter of a century." Reeves added of his own role: "Not bad for something written between cocktails at lunch."

Ted Bates was the hottest agency in New York in the early 1950s. Quite simply, Reeves said, the reason was television. "Nobody else knew what to do. The advertising agencies didn't know how to write copy. Everyone was floundering around." The Bates agency, however, had begun working with TV almost from its start as a commercial medium. "There were so few TV sets it was idiotic," Reeves recalled. "We didn't make money on it." The agency did gain experience, however, and gradually, said Reeves, an understanding that they were onto something big. "We discovered that this was no tame kitten; we had a ferocious, man-eating tiger. We could take the same advertising campaign from print or radio and put it on TV, and, even when there were very few sets, sales would go through the roof." In the process Bates got the jump on the competition: "It was like shooting fish in a barrel."

One of the Bates group's discoveries was that spots could help reduce the risk for advertisers—and ad agencies. Because many programs in the early days were produced by agencies, the agency would find a sponsor and buy network time. If the program was a hit, the advertiser's announcements in and around the program would reach a large audience. If the program flopped, the sponsor would lose money, and the agency might lose the account. In the transitional period between the old sponsor system and the new network system, Reeves saw an opening: why not wait until some other agency created a hit program, letting them take the risks, and then buy spot announcements before or after the hit? "We walked in, seized all the great spots, sewed them up for sponsors, put them in the contract, worked out the techniques, and took over," said Reeves.

Television spots, Reeves had learned, could sell consumer products. Why couldn't they do the same for a politician? In 1948 he tried the idea out on Thomas E. Dewey, the governor of New York and Republican candidate for president against Harry S. Truman. "This could be a very close election," Reeves recalls saying. "I can pretty much tell which states are going to be close. If you would start two or three weeks before election day, and saturate those critical states with spots, it could swing the election." Dewey dismissed the suggestion, according to Reeves. "I don't think it would be dignified," said Dewey, whose small stature, black moustache, and stiff manner had earned him the invidious title, "little man on the wedding cake." So Reeves sat back, and watched Dewey lose. Effective use of TV by Dewey, Reeves says now, could have made the difference.

In 1948 there were fewer than half a million TV sets in the nation. In 1952 there were nearly nineteen million. If the idea had been a good one in 1948—and Reeves was confident that it had—it was better still in 1952. A number of people outside the Bates agency also gave some thought to joining TV and politics. One of them was Dewey. The New York governor, after all, had grown comfortable with Madison Avenue. The Republican party, especially in New York State, had traditional ties with the big advertising agencies: both were apostles of free enterprise, and both, at least in the first half of the century, drew from the same ranks of white, Protestant, upper-class males for their leaders. Among the agencies closest to the Republican party was Batten, Barton, Durstine & Osborn; Bruce Barton, a BBD&O senior partner, helped Dewey deal with the new medium.

Barton appears as a figure in the popular culture of the near past well worth studying for an understanding of both advertising and politics. He had been an informal adviser to Calvin Coolidge and Herbert Hoover in the 1920s; he had served as a GOP congressman from New York City briefly in the 1930s, worked on publicity for Alf Landon in 1936, and advised Dewey in his first presidential race in 1944. Four years later BBD&O formally got the Republican National Committee account. The historian John E. Hollitz found in Barton's papers, in the archives of the State Historical Society of Wisconsin, some reasons why Barton enjoyed such a long, productive career. BBD&O had handled advertising for two of the packaged goods giants, General Mills and Lever Brothers. When the product is cereal or soap, the audience is large and undifferentiated. Barton had done well by the giants; he believed that the same approach would work in politics. Candidates, he thought, needed to seem above "the plane of partisan politics." They needed to be "humanized" in order to appeal to "the great silent majority of Americans" (Barton used the phrase in 1919, some fifty years before Richard Nixon would popularize it). In 1924 Barton was warning Coolidge: "The radio audience is very different from the assembled crowd. The radio audience tires quickly and can walk out on you without your knowing it." Barton also wrote a life of Jesus Christ, *The Man Nobody Knows*, that was a best-seller in 1925. Barton introduced readers to a secular Jesus, a go-getter in the 1920s American style, a super-salesman who could "translate a great spiritual conception into terms of practical self-concern" with methods "not unlike those used now" for overcoming "unreasoning resistance to a helpful idea, service, or product." As such, wrote Barton, "Every one of His conversations, every contact between His mind and others, is worthy of the attentive study of any sales manager."

But even an advertising expert who knew the real Jesus could be sorely tried in a political campaign. Dewey's close circle of advisers and his Albany staff kept Barton and BBD&O from getting access to the campaign or the candidate. The political crowd, in a refrain from the gut to be repeated in many campaigns since, didn't think the ad agency men knew the ins and outs of politics. Barton, not one to turn the other cheek, delivered his own indictment of the shortsightedness of the cronies and hangers-on—a counterrefrain also heard often in the years since. In February 1948 Barton wrote Dewey about the governor's circle of advisers and speechwriters: " . . . Albany does not think about the United States; it thinks about Jews and Catholics, and the CIO and the AF of L and of . . . God knows what." Barton advised Dewey to "forget about all the racial and economic groups to whom platforms make their separate appeals and simplify and clarify the whole thinking of the people. . . ."

Dewey listened, but not until two years later. His 1950 campaign for reelection in New York included a touch of the General Mills–Lever Brothers approach to addressing society as a mass. The governor, aided by BBD&O, held an eighteen-hour "talkathon" on television. Voters congregated at camera locations all over the state to ask questions, with Dewey answering from a studio. The production captivated the critic John Crosby, writing in the pro-Dewey *New York Herald Tribune*: "Dewey threw the script away. . . . He spoke extemporaneously; he moved from spot to spot, picking up state reports and documents; he sat on the edge of his desk (never once did he sit behind the desk); he scratched his head, put his glasses on, took them off, wiped them. Essentially, though, he answered questions—hundreds of them. . . . He answered them in awe-inspiring detail, spouting figures and facts without hesitation." During the program, a

Dewey aide lamented that a great statesman should be forced to undergo such theatrics. A BBD&O man shrugged and quoted Jimmy Durante: "Dem's da conditions dat prevail." Dewey won by over half a million votes, and analysts attributed a hundred thousand votes to the TV finale. Dewey had seen the picture-tube light.

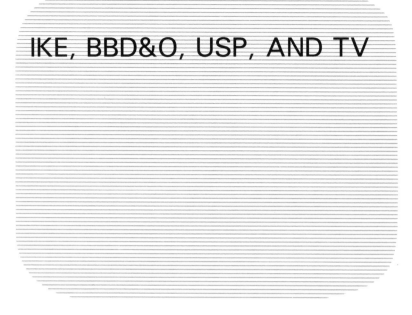

IKE, BBD&O, USP, AND TV

CHAPTER 3

In 1952, after twenty years of Democratic party rule, the country seemed to agree with the Republican slogan, that it was "Time for a Change." American troops were engaged in an indecisive, bloody war in Korea; at home, the New Deal machinery of reform sputtered. Truman decided not to run again. On the Republican side, Dewey, a two-time loser, hardly stirred the party faithful. A fresh start seemed called for, and both Democrats and Republicans reached outside the party ranks to find their candidates.

It was April when Truman announced he would not run, leaving the field wide open and only a few months to go to the Chicago convention. Estes Kefauver, the Tennessee senator, came to Chicago with the greatest number of delegates. Kefauver had delivered some televised speeches in the primary campaign, but he told *Newsweek* that TV is "very expensive." Otherwise, the Democrats did virtually no advertising, though the party did hire the Joseph Katz agency of Baltimore and New York to help stage the Chicago convention and lend a hand with TV-radio speeches. But the Democrats back then didn't believe, deep in their hearts, in the advertising arts. Madison Avenue was, well, *Republican.* Moreover the Democratic party in convention was largely made up of powerful satrapies: Tammany Hall in New York, Boss Hague in New Jersey, the Kelly-Nash machine in Chicago, the labor bloc from the AFL and CIO, southern senators with their loyal delegations.

In the convention the assembled satrapies drafted the ostensibly reluctant Adlai Stevenson, governor of Illinois. A Princeton man, he had served in the State Department in Washington, acquiring the reputation of an "internationalist." Stevenson delivered an eloquent acceptance speech, televised live. Unfortunately most of the country was in bed by that time. The convention schedule had been upset in part by the presence of the new factor in politics, television. The Massachusetts delegation discovered that, by demanding a roll call on a vote, each delegate would have a few seconds in the camera's eye, to be seen by the folks back home. Other delegations followed suit, and the convention came to a standstill. That set the pattern for the Democrats' misadventures with television in 1952.

Eggheads and Miscues

Stevenson needed TV. A spring poll found that only a third of voters knew who he was—this for a man soon to be running against General Dwight D. Eisenhower, adjudged by the same polls to be the most admired living American. Trying to generate familiarity—what would come to be called name ID—Stevenson made heavier use of TV in the earlier stages of the campaign than the Republicans and hired ad agencies to help out. In addition to the national committee's arrangement with the Joseph Katz agency, the Stevenson volunteers' organization contracted with Erwin, Wasey Co. of Chicago. The Milton Biouw agency also worked for the Democrats, and radio executive J. Leonard Reinsch of the Cox stations, who had advised Truman on broadcasting, helped Stevenson with his television style.

Stevenson was no TV star. Columnist Marquis Childs uncharitably described him as "a short, stocky, almost bandy-legged man whose appearance was hardly calculated to win the mass television audience." In fact Stevenson was attractive, in a Princeton gentleman's way. More than any other feature, his distinguishing marks were his balding head and donnish manner (the term "egghead" was coined as a put-down of Stevenson and his intellectual followers). Ike too was balding; but while Ike came off as sincere and likeable, Stevenson often seemed aloof. If Ike was everyone's father, then Stevenson was everyone's brother-in-law, and a smart one at that. Still, Stevenson was a literate, meticulous speaker, and in 1952, the year that television arrived as a political tool, the Democrats formulated an advertising strategy ideally suited to the radio age. They put almost all their TV money, $1.5 million (or nineteen out of every twenty dollars they had to spend on the medium) into eighteen half-hour segments for speeches by Stevenson, Truman, and other Democrats. The air times they bought were Tuesday and Thursday nights, between 10:30 and 11:00 p.m. They did this well in advance, in May, so as not to have to pay preemption charges (the salaries of the stars, writers, and directors whose program was being preempted; for programs already filmed, say the *Jack Benny Show*, these costs could run as high as $80,000). By using late-evening time slots, they also saved money. And, they theorized, the regular time slots would build a steady audience, switching to the Democratic speeches from habit.

The drawbacks of the Democratic advertising plan gradually became apparent. The evening speeches attracted an average audience of 3.8 million, in all probability an audience of people already committed or leaning to Stevenson. William Paley, the founder of CBS and a broadcast presence for six decades, once remarked that in his experience he found "the cheapest things often turn out to be the most expensive, and the most expensive things turn out to be the cheapest." So too in politics. As Democratic National Committee Chairman Steven A. Mitchell would tell the House Elections Committee after the November debacle, "We chose the more economical and apparently less effective method. . . ."

The bargain basement time slots created some, but not all, of the Democrats' difficulties. Stevenson contributed too. He would get so involved in his speeches that he missed his time cues. As he built to his rhetorical climax, the televised Stevenson would abruptly fade, in midsentence, to be replaced by the station's next program. It was, for a man who took such care in writing his speeches, inexcusable, and it happened repeatedly. Time cues weren't a problem in filmed, edited commercials, and Stevenson's spots were generally tight and focused, conveying the major themes of the campaign. Several Stevenson spots advertised the candidate's courage—the man who would "talk sense to the American people." In one, a demure woman speaks in a monotone about how "excited" she is about Stevenson. Another, no more animated, uses a man who could be the woman's suburban husband:

VIDEO	AUDIO
Medium shot of thirtyish, dark-haired man, standing behind podium; podium has on front "ADLAI E. STEVENSON" and a check mark, as if from a ballot.	Man [VO]: "You won't get up and turn your television set off, will ya, if I start talking about politics? Don't get me wrong—I'm not a politician. I just get excited about politics once every four years. And I'm really excited this time. I can't get over this man Stevenson. There's a man with real courage. When I think of

what he believes in—and what he has the backbone to say—

"Well, for example, he said that he'd resist any special privileges for pressure groups—and he told *that* to labor unions in Detroit. And another time, he said that he wouldn't stand for special privileges for any special interests, including veterans—and he told *that* to the American Legion. That took real courage. And about tideland oils—Stevenson believes they belong to all of us—and he told *that* to the governor of Texas. Oh, he may lose Texas, but he sure stuck to his guns. He hasn't sold out for *any* special votes.

"You know, it takes courage to be a great president. But in my book, it takes even greater courage to be an honest candidate.

"You're right—my vote's for Stevenson."

In 1960 John Kennedy picked up on this "blunt truth technique" (as a public relations consultant had termed it), discussing his Catholicism before a hostile audience of Protestant ministers; in 1980 John Anderson also used the technique, telling gun owners that he favored handgun control. In 1952, though, the blunt truth was that the Democrats were strapped for money, unconvinced about the efficacy and dignity of spots, and critical of the Eisenhower advertising campaign. The Democrats thus bought only $77,000 in air time for their spots.

The Stevenson election-eve telecast was a fitting end to the campaign. The program begins with Vice-President Alben Barkley gamely trying to put a positive light on the Democrats' minimal TV budget: "Ladies and gentlemen, since the Republicans have occupied the last thirty minutes over these facilities, and will occupy thirty minutes after we have finished, I presume it would be fair to say that the Democratic speechmakers constitute the wholesome meat between two slices of stale bread." Barkley then introduces President Truman, who speaks slowly and calmly. His words, though, are anything but calm. The election "may decide whether we will find lasting peace, or be led into a third world war." The Republicans have tried "to spread confusion and discontent" with a "campaign of fear and deception." After Truman finishes giving 'em hell, the program cuts to Stevenson and running mate John Sparkman ("The men you will elect president and vice-president of the United States when you go to the polls tomorrow"). The two men sit together at a desk in a living-room set, surrounded by two of Stevenson's sons (the third, the announcer explains, is on Marine duty at Quantico), Mrs. Sparkman, and the Sparkmans' daughter. Stevenson starts with a question for his teen-age son: "Well, Gordy, what do you think of the campaign by this time?" The son, trembling, standing with his hands clasped awkwardly, says, "Well, if the strong feeling for you by the universities is any indication of your national strength, I'd say you're in." Stevenson laughs hollowly. "I hope," the son adds. "*You* hope," says Stevenson. Asked what he thinks of the campaign, Stevenson's youngest son replies, "Well, I like watching television more than being on it." Sparkman notes that he and Stevenson haven't seen each other since August 16. "Has it been that long?" asks Stevenson. "Certainly has," says Sparkman. "Sixteenth of August." Stevenson shakes his head. "Goodness."

After a bit more small talk, Stevenson talks sense to the American people one last time before the election. He is low-key, thoughtful, realistic: "I have said what I meant, and meant what I said. I have not done as well as I would like to have done, but I have done my best." As Stevenson reaches his peroration, the sound fades down. He has run out of time.

Merchandising Eisenhower

Meeting in July, after the Democrats, the Republicans chose General Dwight D. Eisenhower in a draft about as real as Stevenson's. If the Republican delegates had been allowed to vote their souls, they would have chosen Robert A. Taft, the senator from Ohio. But Taft's isolationist record convinced the party's internationalist wing that he wasn't electable. The Eastern Establishment liked Ike, and that chorus included the powerful voices of Henry R. Luce, owner-publisher-editor of the Time Inc. magazines; John Hay Whitney, owner of the *New York Herald Tribune*; and the party's 1944 and 1948 nominee, Thomas Dewey. After getting Ike, the party leaders, for geographic, ideological, and demographic balance, named as the vice-presidential nominee Richard Nixon, the young (thirty-nine) junior senator from California, the nemesis of Alger Hiss and Communists in government.

The Eisenhower-Nixon ticket probably would have won, whatever campaign strategy it employed and whatever the Democrats did. It was time for a change. But Bruce Barton, for one, was worried. He peppered Eisenhower's staff with advice. After one early Ike speech reminded Barton of Tom Dewey's cadences, the adman wrote the General: "Beware of those boys. . . . Dewey is a three-time loser. He has never thought about the United States. All New York politicians think about is Jews, Negroes, Labor, Farmers, etc. — pressure groups. . . ." Barton also suggested that Ike use notes instead of written-out speeches; this would give the impression of "talking to people as one frank, unassuming American to his fellow Americans." Later in the campaign Barton held up the example of Bishop Fulton J. Sheen, who appeared as host and homily-presenter on the popular early 1950s show, *Life Is Worth Living*—"one of the most spectacular successes on television," Barton declared. "Monsignor Sheen . . . uses no manuscript; just stands up and talks, and from time to time illustrates his point by writing on the blackboard." Suppose Ike were to use a similar technique, Barton suggested, talking "to the people whose income is $5,000 a year or less. Let's write that on the blackboard, $5,000."

Barton's concerns eased a bit when both the Republican National Committee and Citizens for Eisenhower-Nixon gave their advertising accounts to BBD&O. Ike developed a strong liking for BBD&O president Bernard "Ben" Duffy, an ebullient child of Madison Avenue; the campaign's goal, Duffy once remarked, was "merchandising Eisenhower's frankness, honesty and integrity, his sincere and wholesome approach." Duffy and the General became friends. "You are telling me things I ought to have been told from the start and that nobody told me," Eisenhower supposedly told him. Unlike Dewey, Ike came to the election without a retinue of advisers; the newcomer listened to newcomers, like Duffy. Inexperience bred innovation, including a willingness to take a gamble on a new medium. The official campaign plan, meanwhile, was also urging Ike to take a gamble. Written by the Republican National Committee's director of public relations, a former journalist and PR man named Robert Humphreys, the plan emphasized the potential of television: "Both Republican candidates have warm and winning personalities. . . . They . . . would normally be welcome visitors in almost one hundred percent of the living rooms of America. Obviously the thing to do is to gain entrance for them into the homes of America by every means possible so that the warmth of their personalities can be felt." Humphreys urged the Republicans to move away from formal, televised speeches, which "by their very nature, cannot impart the real warmth of personality with which both candidates are endowed. Therefore informal, intimate television productions addressed directly to the individual American and his family, their problems and their hopes, are necessary to make the most of the ticket's human assets." Finally, Humphreys thought that broadcast commercials of a minute or less had a place, albeit a limited one: "The use of radio and TV station-break 'spots' during the last ten days of the campaign is a must for stimulating the voters to go to the polls and vote for the candidates." At an August 7 meeting of campaign strategists, the plan was approved.

Still, Republicans worried. In 1948 Dewey had seemed like a sure thing; might not the Democrats, victors in the past five presidential elections, manage to pull off another upset? A stereotypical gathering of Republicans—some oilmen sitting around a table in a country club not far from Watch Hill, Rhode Island, in the summer of 1952—shared their concerns and decided to give Rosser Reeves a call ("I had some oil interests at the time," Reeves modestly recalled during our interview). As Reeves remembers it, one of the oilmen, James Snowden, fretted that "Time for a Change" notwithstanding, the Democrats had an effective slogan: "You Never Had It So Good." What, Snowden wondered, could Reeves create for an alternative Republican slogan? "Ike doesn't need a slogan," Reeves says he replied. "He needs a strategy." Snowden invited Reeves to come talk to him and his friends. So, as New York admen and clients often do, they met for lunch at the Racquet Club on Park Avenue. "I said Ike ought to use spots," Reeves recalls. "These oilmen, they didn't know an advertising spot from Alpha Centauri, so I explained the whole theory. 'This is a new medium called television. It's so powerful that it's changing the whole media structure of the world.' " Spots—the strategy Dewey had rejected—could win the election. The oilmen told Reeves to work on it; the money for such a spot campaign could be found, if Reeves would put it together.

Reeves then asked a former Bates associate, Michael Levin, for help. Levin, then with Erwin, Wasey & Co., agreed to write up a campaign advertising plan. Levin closeted himself for a weekend with Samuel Lubell's *The Future of American Politics*, a highly respected analysis of the time, and emerged with a plan, confidently entitled "How to Insure an Eisenhower Victory in November." In its recommendations for advertising, the Levin plan closely followed Reeves's views: "It has been proven over and over in the course of radio-TV experience in this country that spots are the quickest, most effective and cheapest means of getting across a message in the shortest possible time. It is recommended that $2,000,000 be spent in three weeks on this campaign. . . . The spots themselves would be the height of simplicity. People . . . would ask the General a question. . . . The General's answer would be his complete comprehension of the problem and his determination to do something about it when elected. Thus he inspires loyalty without prematurely committing himself to any strait-jacketing answer. . . . Putting the spots on for only a three-week period gives the following advantages: (1) It gives maximum effectiveness of penetration and recall without becoming deadly to the listener and viewer. (2) It delivers this maximum just before election. (3) It occurs at too late a date for effective Democratic rebuttal."

Reeves also wrote his own memo to the Eisenhower team, laying out the "no risk" strategy of advertising time buying he had evolved: "A big advertiser . . . puts on a one-hour television show. It may cost him $75,000—for that one hour. Immediately after, another big advertiser follows it with another big expensive show. Jack Benny! Martin and Lewis! Eddie Cantor! Fred Allen! Edgar Bergen and Charlie McCarthy! Or dozens of other big-time stars. THESE BIG ADVERTISERS SPEND MILLIONS—WITH TOP TALENT AND GLITTERING NAMES—TO BUILD A BIG AUDIENCE. But—between the two shows—comes the humble 'spot.' If you can run *your advertisement* in this 'spot,' for a very small sum *YOU GET THE AUDIENCE BUILT AT HUGE COSTS BY OTHER PEOPLE.*" As much as cost efficiency the spots approach appealed to Reeves because of simplicity. As Reeves listened to the various speeches made throughout the spring and

summer of 1952—by General Douglas MacArthur, as well as
Eisenhower and Stevenson—an insight gnawed at him. "Ike made
a speech in Philadelphia, and he covered thirty-two separate
points. I sent a research team down the next morning. We got
a thousand people to interview, as I recall it, and said, 'Did you
hear Ike's speech?' Then we said, 'What did he say?' Nobody
knew. Well, no advertising man would be surprised. You cannot
write an advertisement that says thirty-two things about the
product and expect the audience to remember. Ike should have
taken one of those issues and really wrung it out."

Reeves took the Levin plan and his own memo and ideas to
Walter Williams, national chairman of Citizens for Eisenhower-
Nixon. Ike himself, Reeves insisted, had to appear in the spots.
Williams was wary. So was Sherman Adams, manager of the
campaign and Eisenhower's closest political adviser. But Reeves
had some allies. One was Alfred Hollender, a friend of Ike's and
a veteran broadcaster (who later headed the television department
of Grey Advertising). Another was Jock Whitney, owner of the
New York Herald Tribune and a major Republican fund raiser.
These high-powered Ike boosters met with Reeves for dinner in
a private room at "21," the premier Manhattan watering hole
of the ad business. Hollender explained that the Citizens were
"planning to raise millions of dollars and they don't know how
to spend it." Reeves allowed as how he did. He got the account.

Although the Bates agency was given a piece of the GOP ad
budget, Reeves did most of his work on a six-week leave. "I had
to," he remembers, "because some of my clients were Democrats.
Come on—I didn't want to go out of business." In a room of
the St. Regis Hotel off Fifth Avenue, Reeves intensively reviewed
Ike's positions and rhetoric, scrutinizing speeches, articles, and
background papers. Reeves remembered the multitheme Philadelphia talk, and its lack of penetration. He winnowed points
of the speech down to about a dozen major issues. But that was
still too many. The Eisenhower campaign needed a single,
straightforward focus, Reeves felt. So he visited the public opinion

analyst, George Gallup, and asked him what issue was particularly troubling the American people. There were three, answered Gallup: corruption, rising taxes and inflation, and the Korean War. Three issues was still too many, Reeves grumbled. The campaign needed *one* theme; it needed USP. But Gallup stood his ground.

Reeves settled for the Gallup three of Korea, corruption, and cost of living. He was told to have the scripts written and cleared in about two weeks' time, so Ike could film them on September 11. That was less time than Reeves had hoped for —and far less time than commercial clients normally gave agencies—but he dutifully set to work. The scripts, he insists, came almost entirely from Eisenhower statements. "I did not put one single word into Eisenhower's mouth," he says. "I took those out of the speeches that he had already made. So you see I *was* an honest operator in this." Getting the scripts approved meant meeting with the clients, only instead of three or four men from Lever Brothers, commercial style, there was the entire Republican National Committee—"a real pain in the ass. It was a giant committee, and you had to meet them whenever they were passing through New York."

On September 11 Eisenhower and Reeves met for the first time at the Transfilm, Inc., studio on West 43rd Street in Manhattan. Reeves wanted Ike to do the spots without glasses, but the General's nearsightedness meant he couldn't read the cue cards. So the scripts were hand-lettered headline fashion on poster board and held close enough so that Eisenhower could read them without squinting. Twenty-two scripts had been written and approved. Reeves had thought filming that many, with delays and retakes, would take most of the day. But Eisenhower was breezing through them one after another. So Reeves commandeered a typewriter and began writing additional scripts as quickly as he could. He'd had two weeks to write his first scripts; now he churned out another twenty or so in a couple of hours. Each script was reviewed by the candidate's brother, Milton Eisenhower, read quickly by Ike, lettered on the giant cue cards, and filmed. Eisenhower sat fidgeting between takes, remarking at one point, "To think that an old soldier should come to this!" By the end, though, Ike had joined in the spirit of the day, writing one script himself (Reeves generously calls it the best of the lot). When Ike walked out that evening, all forty scripts had been filmed. Each was a brief response to a hypothetical question.

Now that the Eisenhower answers were in the can, the questions had to be filmed. Reeves wanted a diverse group of people. The original plan had been to send camera crews all over the country, to tape a random sampling of Americans. Someone—his name is lost to history—hit upon a money-saving idea that Reeves quickly embraced. On two afternoons Bates employees mingled with the tourists at New York's Radio City Music Hall. Those who looked like "everyday Americans" were asked to come to a film studio. There they recited questions from cue cards. The result was a selection of "people from different sections of the country—real people, in their own clothes, with wonderful native accents," Reeves later recalled. The tapes were edited, an announcer voice-over was added, and the spots were completed. The format for all of the brief spots was the same: a humble citizen, his eyes raised as if gazing at a giant, asks a question; then cut to Ike's succinct answer.

VIDEO	AUDIO
Slide: "EISENHOWER answers AMERICA," with oval photo of Eisenhower. In fine print at bottom of screen: "A POLITICAL ANNOUNCEMENT PAID FOR BY CITIZENS FOR EISENHOWER."	Announcer [VO]: "Eisenhower answers America."

Cut to dark-haired woman.	Woman [SOF]: "The Democrats have made mistakes, but aren't their intentions good?"
Cut to Eisenhower.	Eisenhower [SOF]: "Well, if the driver of your school bus runs into a truck, hits a lamppost, drives into a ditch, you don't say his intentions are good; you get a new bus driver."
Cut from opening slide to black man in plaid shirt and sportscoat.	Man [SOF]: "General, the Democrats are telling me I've never had it so good."
Cut to Eisenhower.	Eisenhower [SOF]: "Can that be true when America is billions in debt, when prices have doubled, when taxes break our backs, and we are still fighting in Korea? It's tragic and it's time for a change."
Cut from opening to middle-aged woman, holding sack of groceries.	Woman [SOF]: "I paid twenty-four dollars for these groceries—look, for this little."
Cut to Eisenhower.	Eisenhower [SOF]: "A few years ago, those same groceries cost you ten dollars, now

twenty-four, next year thirty—that's what will happen unless we have a change."

Cut from opening to well-dressed couple.	Man [SOF]: "Mr. Eisenhower, are we going to have to fight another war?"
Cut to Eisenhower.	Eisenhower [SOF]: "No, not if we have a sound program for peace. And I'll add this, we won't spend hundreds of billions and still not have enough tanks and planes for Korea."
Cut from opening to balding man in suit.	Man [SOF]: "Mr. Eisenhower, do all the taxes we pay get to Washington?"
Cut to Eisenhower.	Eisenhower [SOF]: "Not when dozens of tax collectors have to be fired or quit because of graft and corruption. That's why I say, it's time for a change."
Cut from opening to elderly woman in hat.	Woman [SOF]: "You know what things cost today. High prices are just driving me crazy."
Cut to Eisenhower.	Eisenhower [SOF]: "Yes, my Mamie gets after me about the high cost of living. It's another reason why I say, it's

time for a change. Time to
get back to an honest dollar
and an honest dollar's work."

Reeves would be the first to admit the spots were artless. "Unlike a lot of my competitors, I never tried to make *interesting* commercials . . ." he once said. "When you put a commercial on the air one night and you have twenty million people looking at the screen, how the hell can they *help* seeing what you put on?"

"This Isn't Soap Opera"

The spots were supposed to be the Eisenhower-Nixon ticket's secret weapon, but Eisenhower inadvertently mentioned them to reporters two days after the filming. Worse, Reeves began to worry that a leak had sprung in his agency, that someone was giving material to the press. In early October he grew certain: the Stevenson campaign high command distributed copies of the Levin plan to reporters. A Stevenson spokesman attacked the "high-powered hucksters of Madison Avenue" and their "super colossal, multi-million dollar production designed to sell an in-adequate ticket to the American people in precisely the way they sell soap, ammoniated toothpaste, hair tonic or bubble gum. They guarantee their candidates to be 99 and 44/100 percent pure; whether or not they will float remains to be seen." Stevenson himself picked up the theme, fresh at the time, that Madison Avenue was trying to sell a candidate the way it sold soap: "I don't think the American people want politics and the presidency to become the plaything of the high-pressure men, of the ghostwriters, of the public relations men. I think they will be shocked by such contempt for the intelligence of the American people. This isn't soap opera, this isn't Ivory Soap versus Palmolive."

While the Democrats complained, the Republicans went about getting the spots on the air. The production costs of the spots,

$60,000, had been paid for by the Eisenhower campaign committee. Money for time had to come from elsewhere. The budget for televising speeches had been set before Reeves arrived, so a separate, special finance committee was created. Local Republican organizations were also encouraged, in a special flyer printed by the Citizens Committee, to borrow the film prints and air the spots themselves. As a consequence, Reeves later said, "We have no idea how much was actually spent." Another hurdle then appeared: some TV executives refused to show the spots, arguing they were not fit for a presidential campaign. Carroll Newton of BBD&O pressured Frank Stanton at CBS and Joseph McConnell at NBC, and the networks backed down. One radio network, however, stood firm. Westinghouse president Joseph E. Baudino said the Westinghouse stations had a policy against accepting spots for political candidates; campaign issues, he said, could not be discussed adequately in one minute—again, an objection that would become familiar. The Eisenhower admen bought time slots (with the advice of executives at A.C. Nielsen, the ratings firm). Of the forty ads Reeves and Eisenhower had filmed, twenty-eight were used; they appeared in mid-October in forty states, with the heaviest schedules run in the states considered critical to the election—New York, New Jersey, Illinois, Massachusetts, Michigan, Maryland, Indiana, California, Pennsylvania, Texas, and Connecticut.

While the spots were the major innovation in the 1952 campaign, the Republicans tested a variety of other television formats. In May the Republican Congressional Committee aired a paid program called "The Case for a Republican Congress." The show presented its case dramatically, putting the Democrats on mock trial. Republican congressional leaders starred while professional actors portrayed the Democrats. The Republicans also used filmed cartoons. "Korea—The Price of Appeasement" featured a satanic Oriental brandishing a blood-covered sword. Another, "Ike for President," featured a jingle ("You like Ike! I like Ike! Everybody likes Ike!") and animation by the Disney studios. At the same

1952: EISENHOWER VS. STEVENSON

Eisenhower Commercial

"Eisenhower answers
America"

"I paid twenty-four dol-
lars for these groceries—
look, for this little"

"A few years ago those
same groceries cost you
ten dollars, now twenty-
four, next year thirty—
that's what will happen
unless we have a change"

Stevenson Commercial

"I'm excited about voting
for Governor Stevenson
for president. I think he is
a new kind of man in
American politics"

time the Republicans pushed and hauled at the traditional, radio-age paid political speech, reshaping the form for television. BBD&O decreed that each Eisenhower speech had to be no more than twenty minutes long for a thirty-minute slot. The rest of the time would be filled with film of Ike moving through the adoring crowds. The entrances were planned, shot by shot, with Mamie Eisenhower playing a supporting role. The visible use of Mrs. Eisenhower in the campaign was calculated, not only as an element of Ike's fatherly image but also to remind voters that Stevenson was a divorced man, heretofore a major taboo in American politics. The traditional radio form also was used to carry a televised speech, late in the campaign, by Senator Joseph McCarthy. Stevenson, said McCarthy, had to answer for his "aid to the Communist cause." Twice, by accident or intent, McCarthy referred to Stevenson as "Alger" instead of "Adlai." Candidate Nixon also used Alger Hiss in his speeches. In an October 13 TV address Nixon attacked Stevenson for having been a character witness on Hiss's behalf. Nixon emphasized that he didn't want to imply that Stevenson was a fellow traveler, merely that he had been duped. "If Stevenson were to be taken in by Stalin as he was by Alger Hiss," Nixon said, "the Yalta sellout would look like a great American diplomatic triumph by comparison."

On election eve the Republicans stretched the new medium to its limits in a fast-moving show overflowing with fast cuts and on-location footage. Film clips of Korea, Alger Hiss, and Julius and Ethel Rosenberg—the convicted "atomic spies"—depicted the Democratic record; clips of Eisenhower with soldiers, with his family, and with Winston Churchill suggested the Republican alternative. The show switched from city to city—including San Francisco, New York, Cleveland, Los Angeles, Seattle, Philadelphia, and Baltimore—letting Eisenhower supporters have a word, via TV, with the General. "I'm Irene Costello," said a woman standing on a San Francisco street. "I pound a typewriter, and I've been crusading plenty." A Korea veteran said, "Well, all the guys I knew out in Korea figure there's only one man for the

65

job, General, and that's you." Between these segments came quick breaks to Nisei for Eisenhower-Nixon, Tykes for Ike, and various other supporters. The program ended with Ike and Mamie cutting a victory cake.

Did They Like Ike or Ike's Ads?

Just as Rosser Reeves in 1948 thought Dewey might have won with television spot advertising, so Reeves thought in 1952 that Eisenhower would have won without TV and spots. At the time Reeves urged the Republican National Committee to undertake a survey to assess the spots' impact. The committee refused; they wanted people to think Ike's charisma, not his TV, made the difference. Reeves ultimately agreed. "It was such a landslide that it didn't make a goddamn bit of difference whether we ran the spots or not," he told us. Along with many commentators, Reeves judges the TV campaign "only an interesting footnote to history." It is much more than that. The 1952 Eisenhower spot campaign first raised the major, disturbing—and continuing—questions about politics, advertising, and television. Should presidential campaigns be run by marketing principles and admen, or by political tactics and party professionals? Do thirty-second or sixty-second spots ignore issues and content in favor of image and emotion? Does the best man win, or the most telegenic performer? Can money buy enough media to buy elections? Every four years since 1952 these questions have reappeared, and each campaign since has provided enough contradictory answers to keep at least some of them alive and unresolved.

CHECKERS

CHAPTER 4

The TV campaign of 1952 may not have played a decisive part in the Eisenhower-Nixon victory, but it did initiate a process that changed electoral politics. Truman-style whistle-stop tours were about to become history. The radio age was ending. All signs showed that longer set speeches played to the already convinced, to smaller TV audiences, to audiences more and more quick to grow restless (as *Arthur Godfrey* and *Lucy* were setting the thirty-minute standards of performance). Television had dealt a mortal blow to the traditional political speech, though it took an election or two before the older form buckled and sank practically out of sight, no longer a centerpiece of presidential campaigns, to be replaced by quick spots, short productions, and fast-paced telethons and specials. How strange and ironic, then, that perhaps the most effective piece of political advertising of our times was a traditional radio talk delivered on television toward the middle of the 1952 campaign, just as the spot was becoming king. We refer of course to Checkers.

Richard Nixon gave his Checkers speech on national television on the evening of September 23, 1952, from the stage of Los Angeles's El Capitan Theater, which had been converted into a television studio by NBC. Over the years Checkers has taken on the dimensions of a myth, which both Nixon's detractors and Nixon himself, in his book *Six Crises* and later in his memoirs, helped construct. Some people, for example, believe that Checkers, the Nixon family cocker spaniel, actually appeared on the broadcast, hence the name. Others, their memories better—only Mrs. Nixon was present on stage with Nixon—still denigrate the candidate for his "tastelessness," trotting out as he did references to his wife Pat, daughters Tricia and Julie, family dog Checkers, family car 1950 Oldsmobile, family finances, family debts, even family closet contents (no minks, just Pat's "respectable Republican cloth coat"). Most everyone, enemies and supporters alike, agree that Checkers melodramatically saved Nixon's threatened position on the Republican ticket, when hundreds of thousands of supporting calls overloaded telephone switchboards in the greatest single demonstration of television's reach before or since. The facts about Checkers deflate much of the mythology of both critics and supporters; they make a better story about the advertising and political arts as well.

The story began on September 18 with a page one headline in the pro-Stevenson *New York Post*: "SECRET NIXON FUND!" Inside, the jump headline elaborated: "Secret Rich Men's Trust Fund Keeps Nixon in Style Far Beyond His Salary." There was enough truth in the allegation to make it worrisome, but enough missing context to make it unfair. Such funds were standard among politicians of the time, a way of doing aboveboard political work with political contributions rather than a government salary. There was nothing secret about it. Stevenson, it was later learned, had a fund too, one that was bigger than Nixon's. But the story mushroomed. Nixon later related in his *Six Crises* (1962) that a kind of ad hoc conspiracy kept the fund story alive—Democrats looking for a vote-getting issue; scandal-minded reporters who, if not secret Stevenson lovers, then revelers in wrongdoing; finally, and more sinister, the "they"—Communists? Communist supporters? Comsymps?—who wanted to harm "the work I was doing in investigating Communist subversion in the United States." But still later in his 1978 memoir *RN*, Nixon dropped the Communist explanation and offered a more sophisticated, and heartfelt, analysis. What really kept the fund story going, he finally acknowledged, was General Eisenhower.

The fund story broke on a Thursday, Nixon feelingly explains, but the presidential candidate didn't talk to his running mate until late Sunday night—and then Ike said he wasn't committing himself to Nixon because "in effect people will accuse me of condoning wrongdoing." In the time between Thursday and Sunday, what's more, the *New York Herald Tribune* published an editorial declaring that "the proper course of Senator Nixon in the circumstances is to make a formal offer for withdrawal from the ticket. How this offer will be acted upon will be determined by an appraisal of all the facts in the light of General Eisenhower's unsurpassed fairness of mind." Nixon got the message. "The fat"—his fat—"was in the fire," he writes in *RN*; the *Tribune* wouldn't have published the editorial unless it reflected the views of "people high in the councils of the Eisenhower campaign." The General's lieutenants wanted to dump Nixon. As Garry Wills shrewdly observed, "the Establishment was at work." Nixon had been put on the ticket for "balance"—to attract the Taftites, the westerners, the conservatives who viewed with suspicion the New York internationalist crowd, the pinched minds who didn't even like Ike. "He was there to draw the yokels," writes Wills. "If there was any doubt about his ability to do that, no one would feel compunction at his loss: Ike was too valuable a property to be risked. . . ."

Eisenhower and his advisers were letting Nixon twist slowly, slowly in the wind. But Nixon was no patsy. In his phone call with Ike on Sunday night, he pushed for an announcement "one way or the other. . . . There comes a time in matters like this when you've either got to fish or cut bait. . . . The great trouble here is the indecision." That is the version in *Six Crises*. In *RN*, his postpresidency memoirs, Nixon reports his words to Eisenhower this way: "There comes a time in matters like this when you either got to shit or get off the pot. . . . The great trouble here is the indecision." Ike remained noncommittal. Nixon, no yokel either, knew what to do. At thirty-nine, he was not about to commit hara-kiri. He met with advisers William Rogers, the genial lawyer, and Murray Chotiner, the political infighter (high road and low road). "Everyone present agreed," Nixon later wrote, "that somehow I had to get an opportunity to tell my story to millions rather than to the thousands who were coming out to hear me at the whistle-stops. There was only one way to do this—through a national television broadcast." Thomas Dewey called with advice. "I don't think Eisenhower should make this decision," the man who used to abhor television said. "Make the American people do it. At the conclusion of the program, ask people to wire their verdict in to you in Los Angeles." Nixon agreed. The Republican National Committee and the Senatorial and Congressional Campaign Committees purchased a half hour for $75,000 from NBC. "My only hope to win," Nixon remembers, "rested with millions of people I would never meet, sitting in groups of two or three or four in their living rooms, watching and listening to me on television." Getting their support required that the broadcast "must not be just good. It had to be a smash hit—one that really moved people, that was designed not simply to explain the complicated and dull facts about the fund to the people, but one that would inspire them to enthusiastic positive support." The story Nixon had to tell was necessarily a personal one. Eisenhower had said, "Tell them everything you can remember. Tell them about any money you have ever received." That meant a complete public accounting of, as Mrs. Nixon remonstrated to her husband, "how little we have and how much we owe"—on national television. It was, Nixon wrote, a "humiliation." No wonder, then, Nixon's histrionics during Checkers, his haunted, tense face, the viewers' feeling that Nixon was about to cry on camera. He was entitled. As Garry Wills writes, "No one who knows the full story can suspect Nixon of acting, or blame him for the tension he felt and conveyed—it would be like blaming a recently flayed man for 'indecent exposure.' " It is no wonder too that Nixon's anger at Eisenhower grows with each retelling of the story.

The Fighter Bloodied But Unbowed

But Nixon wasn't so ground down that he lost his bearings the night of the broadcast. His own accounts stress his sense of "kinship with Teddy Roosevelt's description of the man in the arena, whose face is marred by dust and sweat and blood." Nixon pictured himself as a solitary fighter, jotting down his thoughts on postcards, working through Monday afternoon and evening on his speech in a suite in the Ambassador Hotel in Los Angeles, leaving the hamburgers from room service untouched. At the studio he continues the portrait of one man fighting on alone: "I had ordered that no one was to be there during the speech except for the director and the technical crew. We arranged for reporters to watch on a monitor in a separate room." One of those reporters, however, did some poking around and wrote a somewhat different picture of the man in the arena. The reporter, James A. Kearns, Jr., worked for the *St. Louis Post-Dispatch* (which Nixon considered blatantly pro-Stevenson). Kearns's version is that the Nixon speech was rehearsed and produced by Edward A. "Ted" Rogers, on leave from a Hollywood advertising agency and former production supervisor of *The Lone Ranger* (appropriately enough), *Beulah*, and *Mystery Theater*. According to Kearns, Rogers worked with representatives from BBD&O and Kudner (who flew to Los Angeles in the crisis to whip Nixon's script into shape). At the studio Kearns reports, "the TV experts had Nixon sit at the table, then stand next to it, and then do the same thing again and again. Under their deft prompting, the candidate practiced posing with his right hand on the table, then with his left hand in a trouser pocket. . . . Mrs. Nixon, nervously clasping a handkerchief, was carefully coached to keep a relaxed pose in her chair, her head turned at a certain angle, her face arched in a close-mouthed smile. The dress rehearsal, with the star going doggedly through the directed motions, continued almost to the moment of curtain time. In the last minute the coaches ducked behind an off-stage screen."

Nixon, for his part, reports the same scene: "Ted [Rogers] showed me the set. I asked him to remove a small vase of flowers because I thought it looked out of place. After a brief lighting and sound check, we were ushered into a small room at the far side of the stage." Whichever version is correct—and probably one man's brief lighting and sound check is another's careful rehearsal—Nixon is the sole source of what happened next: ". . . only three minutes before we went on the air. I was suddenly overwhelmed by despair. My voice almost broke as I said, 'I just don't think I can go through with this one.' 'Of course you can,' Pat said matter-of-factly. She took my hand, and we walked back onto the stage together."

The rest is on film, for each of us to judge. "My fellow Americans," Nixon began, "I come before you tonight as a candidate for the vice-presidency and as a man whose honesty and integrity have been questioned." Nixon quickly went through the Price Waterhouse audit of the fund, and the opinion about its legality by the law firm of Gibson, Dunn and Crutcher. This biographical first section—the first of the speech's four parts as Nixon saw it—was intended to lay to rest questions about his financial status, and Nixon listed everything he owned and every debt he owed. "Pat doesn't have a mink coat," he said. "But she does have a respectable Republican cloth coat, and I always tell her that she would look good in anything." Then Nixon talked about his dog:

VIDEO

AUDIO

Nixon, unsmiling, rubs his face, as though this is a particularly painful admission.

Nixon [SOF]: "One other thing I probably should tell you, because if I don't they will probably be saying this about me, too. We did get something, a gift, after the nomination. A man down in Texas heard Pat on the radio mention the fact that our two youngsters would like to have a dog, and believe it or not, the day before we left on this campaign trip we got a message from Union Station in Baltimore, saying they had a package for us. We went down to get it. You know what it was? It was a little cocker spaniel dog, in a crate that he had sent all the way from Texas—black and white, spotted, and our little girl Tricia, the six-year-old, named it Checkers. And you know, the kids, like all kids, loved the dog, and I just want to say this right now, that regardless of what they say about it, we are going to keep it."

Checkers behind him, Nixon moved into his second section, his counterattack against Stevenson. The third section praised

1952: CHECKERS

"My fellow Americans, I come before you . . . as a man whose honesty and integrity have been questioned"

"Pat doesn't have a mink coat. But she does have a respectable Republican cloth coat"

"Folks, he is a great man, and a vote for Eisenhower is a vote for what is good for America"

Eisenhower, and the fourth asked the audience to send letters and wires to the Republican National Committee in Washington to indicate whether they thought Nixon should remain on or step down from the ticket. Thirty plus years later, the speech stands up sturdily, whether studied as masterful political rhetoric or watched as soap opera intended for the "yokels." Yet Nixon thought he had failed, that the whole effort was a disaster. Ted Rogers had crouched beside the camera in front of Nixon. Using hand signals, he cued Nixon on how much time was left. "I saw him when he held up one hand for five minutes," Nixon remembered, "and then three fingers. By that time I was so wrapped up in what I was saying that I didn't see his signal for 'ten seconds,' 'five seconds,' or 'cut.' I was still talking when time ran out, standing in front of the desk with my arms stretched out toward the camera. Suddenly I saw Ted Rogers stand up, and I realized that I had gone overtime. I couldn't believe it. I hadn't even given people the address of the Republican National Committee so that they would know where to send their telegrams. I felt almost dazed. I took a few steps forward and my shoulder grazed the side of the camera. I could hear Ted Rogers saying that they had waited until what sounded like the end of a sentence and faded the picture although I was still talking. . . . Pat embraced me, and I could only say, 'I'm sorry I had to rush at the last; I didn't give the National Committee address. I should have timed it better.' " The speech had been aimed at swamping the committee back in Washington with cards and calls—so that Eisenhower and the Eastern crowd would be forced to keep Nixon on the ticket. But Nixon, like some scrambled egghead, an Adlai Stevenson, hadn't delivered the punch line.

No matter. Over nine million sets were tuned to Nixon that night, according to Nielsen, almost half of America's television households. Astoundingly, perhaps as many as one million citizens were moved to send a letter or wire supporting Nixon—no one knew the count for certain because cards and calls went everywhere. Many viewers were further moved to send small contributions as well, enough to cover the costs of the program. Eisenhower had watched with Mamie in Cleveland. His first words were to Arthur Summerfield, the former Chevrolet auto dealer and chairman of the Republican National Committee, which had put up some of the $75,000 for the telecast. "Well, Arthur, you certainly got your money's worth tonight," Ike said. When Nixon flew to Wheeling, West Virginia, to meet—finally— with Eisenhower, the younger man reports that Ike hurried up the steps of the plane and into the cabin. "General, you didn't need to come out to the airport," said Nixon. Eisenhower, grinning, replied, "Why not? You're my boy!"

Nixon's version, however, conceals some of the General's own marshaling of strategy. Eisenhower had not commanded the victorious Allied armies on charm alone. The day of Checkers, Bruce Barton sent a note to Ben Duffy about Eisenhower's projected response to the Checkers speech. "The General must be expertly stage managed," Barton said. He suggested that Ike watch privately with Mamie, wait for fifteen minutes after the speech, and then come out with a "spontaneous" handwritten memo that would say: "I have seen many brave men perform brave duties. I have seen them march up to the cannon's mouth not knowing whether they would live or die. But I do not think that I have ever witnessed a braver act than I witnessed tonight. . . . " Barton wrote this assessment for Ike to deliver, of course, before anyone had seen the speech. The BBD&O connection apparently paid off. Immediately after Checkers, Eisenhower did indeed discard his prepared speech and come out of a private room with new notes. He declared in part: "I have seen many brave men in tough situations. I have never seen any come through in better fashion than Senator Nixon did tonight." Nixon was back on the ticket and in politics to stay, to play a major part in the next three decades of American public life. So too with television.

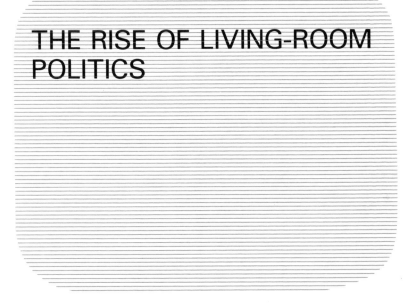

THE RISE OF LIVING-ROOM POLITICS

CHAPTER 5

Not long after the 1952 election RCA, a major manufacturer of television sets, took out full-page newspaper advertisements, declaring that "television has brought their government back to the people!" True, the Eisenhower-Stevenson campaign had been televised to the nation's living rooms, but the people were not all that enamored of the new visitor. Eisenhower's inauguration, the beginning of the first Republican presidency in two decades, attracted a television audience half the size of that viewing another program aired the same week—the *I Love Lucy* episode in which Lucy Ricardo goes to the hospital to deliver Little Ricky. The experiments with political television in the 1954 congressional races did little to excite otherwise engaged voters. Some candidates produced spots half the length of "Eisenhower Answers America." Ten seconds long, the scripts sometimes made Ike's seem encyclopedic. Minnesota gubernatorial candidate Orville Freeman, for instance, used this spot in 1954:

VIDEO	AUDIO
Block letters: "FREEMAN FOR GOVERNOR."	Sound effect: alarm clock [two seconds]
	Announcer [VO]: "Minnesota needs a wide-awake governor! Vote for Orville Freeman and bring wide-awake action to Minnesota's problems."
	Repeat alarm clock sound effect.

As with any new technique, there were bound to be errors. Thomas Stanley, candidate for governor of Virginia in 1954, bought a time slot in order to be "interviewed" by one of his campaign managers. They finished their script a minute early; as a contemporary account described it, "Stanley solved the problem by grinning apologetically and shaking his manager's hand vigorously for sixty long seconds." Still, thanks more to Lucy Ricardo than to Thomas Stanley or Orville Freeman, television entered the 1956 campaign firmly entrenched. Now there were twice as many TV sets—nearly forty million—and four times as many TV stations as in the preceding presidential year. "The choice for a candidate," wrote Walter Goodman in 1955, "is no longer *whether* to use TV, but how to use it and how much of it he can afford."

Politics Comes to Madison Avenue

In many ways 1956 was a replay of 1952. As before, Ike was hugely popular. This time clearly it was not time for a change. The Democrats did what they could under the circumstances; they argued that change was coming regardless, that a second Eisenhower administration would turn into a Nixon presidency.

Eisenhower's health had slipped badly over the past year. In September 1955 he had suffered a serious heart attack; nine months later, he fell victim to ileitis. At sixty-five, Ike suddenly seemed an old and sick man, placing new importance on his running mate. For his part Nixon was nearly as unloved as Ike was beloved. Harold Stassen started a dump Nixon movement among moderate Republicans. When the movement failed, it remained for Stevenson and the Democrats to run against Nixon. Ike was too popular to be attacked directly; Nixon had no such shield, and Ike's health gave the Democrats their opening.

BBD&O again handled the Republican National Committee account. Carroll Newton, the time buyer from 1952, was put in charge. The National Citizens for Eisenhower Committee hired Young & Rubicam and the Ted Bates agency. A Republican party spokesman, L. Richard Guylay, minimized their actual role; they were, said Guylay, "technicians." But the Democrats saw in Madison Avenue another issue safely distant from Ike. In his acceptance speech at the Democratic convention, Adlai Stevenson returned to the theme he had used in 1952: "The men who run the Eisenhower administration evidently believe that the minds of Americans can be manipulated by shows, slogans, and the arts of advertising. This idea that you can merchandise candidates for high office like breakfast cereal—that you can gather votes like box tops—is I think the ultimate indignity to the democratic process. . . ."

Despite Stevenson's criticism the Democrats planned some merchandising of their own. The party had about $8 million set aside for advertising Stevenson as well as congressional candidates. But in 1955 when the Democrats started talking to ad agencies, no one wanted their business. By the end of the year the Democrats were getting desperate, and advertising industry leaders were shuffling their feet and glancing at one another, embarrassed. It might, they feared, look like some sort of conspiracy to keep the Democrats from the White House, to the detriment of the agencies' public image. A group of executives met to discuss the matter. The advertising trade association began calling members, trying to find an agency for the party. There was talk of putting together an outside task force of talented people from various agencies so that no one agency would have to work with the party, in much the same way ad agencies share public service work for TB or Easter Seals. The Democrats refused; they wouldn't accept charity from Madison Avenue. The Democrats had been cold-shouldered in part because, as *Printer's Ink* magazine explained, "big agency men don't want to alienate the Republican businessmen who head many client companies," and in part because of Madison Avenue's Republican bent.

Finally, party chairman Paul Butler found a small agency called Norman, Craig & Kummel—Democrats, at that—who were willing to do the campaign. Chester Herzog, a thirty-four-year-old account executive whose credits included Blatz Beer, headed the Democratic effort. He gathered a half-dozen talented, Democratic copywriters, on temporary leave from other firms, and set to work. Nevertheless, after all that searching the Democrats, like the Republicans, minimized the importance of the admen. Walter Craig, a former vaudeville actor and agency partner, echoed Guylay: "To most politicians and their traditional public-relations men, TV is something new and completely strange. They don't know its mechanics, or how to evaluate and use it. They need experts to lead them through its labyrinth."

The Republicans by and large planned to repeat the formula of 1952. The advertising schedule again would be concentrated close to the election. "I think our use of TV right up to the last minute of the '52 campaign helped people make up their minds," said BBD&O president Ben Duffy. The agency started buying up time segments a year early, saving preemption costs for longer segments, as well as locking up the best times before the Democrats got organized. As in 1952 many of the Republican TV productions would star Eisenhower, with one difference. In 1952 Ike had gone along reluctantly with the TV appeals, sharing the old Dewey notion that spots were "undignified." This time Eisenhower announced, early in the campaign, his intention to run primarily on television; now it was the old-fashioned whistle-stopping that appeared "unseemly" for a sitting president.

BBD&O did introduce one innovation in 1956. Half-hour speeches had worked well in 1952, but even then there had been some adverse reaction from viewers, angered at the temporary disappearance of a favorite show. The day of the thirty-minute political speech was past, Guylay stated flatly; even Lincoln's second inaugural couldn't hold a prime-time audience when up against a popular sitcom. The Republican solution was a new, in-between form, the five-minute spot. "Hitchhikes," they were called—free rides on somebody else's audience, just as with Rosser Reeves's shorter spots. Run between popular programs, they would be as effective as spots in holding onto a presumably restless audience; they would be long enough to provide more information than a spot (and perhaps reduce some of the criticism of huckster brevity and simplemindedness). The admen had to convince networks and sponsors to lop five minutes out of their shows, but that could be done—if not by appeals to good government and democracy, then by threatening to preempt the entire program which candidates at the time had the right to do under FCC regulations. Finally, hitchhikes were bargains, costing around $10,000, whereas a half-hour program could cost $60,000 for air time plus $20,000 or so for preemption.

The series of Eisenhower five-minute hitchhikes was called "Your Government and You." It began October 15 with a talk by the president, who sounded like a barker promoting all the good acts ahead in the carnival:

VIDEO   AUDIO

Eisenhower addressing   Eisenhower [SOF]: " . . . Your
camera.   administration will try dili-
                                         gently through the next three

weeks to explain its record of achievements, the problems before it, and the policies by which it proposes to solve them. You will hear your Secretary of State, John Foster Dulles, tell of the spirit that impels us in achieving peace and the record we have made as a nation in our united effort for peace. You will hear your Secretary of the Treasury, George Humphrey, tell how his department has checked the galloping inflation, cut taxes, balanced the budget, and reduced the debt. You will hear your Secretary of Defense, Charles E. Wilson, tell how we have saved billions of dollars on the Armed Forces, reduced our manpower requirements, and still provided a more secure defense. You will hear your Secretary of Labor, James Mitchell, tell how employment, wages, and income have reached the highest levels in history. You will hear your Attorney General, the Secretary of our new Department of Health, Education and Welfare, and other Cabinet officers tell what we have done to combat monopoly, to extend Social Security for seventy million Americans, and other accomplishments of this Republican administration. I am proud of the record, and I think you will be proud of it, too. So let me ask you one thing. Whenever you can, listen to this series, and talk the facts over with your family and friends. Then make up your mind as to how *you* will vote on November 6. . . ."

The Republicans also used short thirty- and sixty-second spots again. One features Eisenhower, surrounded by the aura of the presidency:

VIDEO	AUDIO
Camera up on CU of presidential seal.	Announcer [VO]: "The President of the United States."
Cut to medium shot of Eisenhower clad in three-piece suit, standing behind desk; behind him are bookshelves and American flag.	Eisenhower [SOF]: "You decide the future of America for four years this coming election day. We in the Republican party pledge ourselves to continue our

> program of peace, security, and prosperity, that has made our party the party of the future."
>
> Announcer [VO]: "Vote for your future. Vote Republican."

The Republicans produced a few films that required program preemption. Unlike the 1952 efforts, which were mostly straightforward speeches, these 1956 campaign films embraced television production values. "People don't like looking at one guy's face all the time," Republican party chairman Leonard Hall said. "You've got to have action." One half-hour show featured Ike talking for all of sixty seconds; the rest was devoted to film and other spokesmen. The Republicans also produced a fifteen-minute TV film for use in congressional campaigns, "These Peaceful and Prosperous Years." As described in a prospectus to Republican congressmen, the telefilm followed "an average American family going about their daily living under a Republican era of peace. . . . The family is seen at home with the housewife enjoying her modern work-saving conveniences; the father enjoying the recreational opportunities afforded by his earning capacity, and the two children, teenagers, doing the things children of this age bracket enjoy doing. . . ." The film closes with an announcer saying, "Give Ike a Republican Congress," followed by Ike and Mamie singing a duet, "God Bless America."

Similarly soporific was "The People Ask the President," aired on October 12. An announcer told viewers that the questioners are "your neighbors." Eisenhower began, as he often did at his regular news conferences, with an announcement; then he took questions from the group. One man, a New York garment worker, asked about the "big shots" who populated Ike's Cabinet ("eight millionaires and a plumber," the joke went). Ike bristled: "Now,

I have three or four very successful businessmen in the Cabinet. My friend, the Defense Department is spending something like forty billion dollars a year of our money. Most of that goes into . . . procurement of things—tanks and planes and guns and ammunition and all of these modern weapons. Who would you rather have in charge of that, some failure that never did anything or a successful businessman?" That was the program's toughest question. Others ranged from neutral ("I wonder if you could tell us what sort of a man Vice-President Nixon is?") to fawning (from an auto worker: "Some fellows feel that the Democratic party is on their side. I happen to know that you are on their side even more so . . . and I wish, Mr. President, that you would explain and enlighten my buddies back home as to your stand on labor unions. . . ."). A black minister, perhaps unintentionally, reminded the audience about Stevenson's status as a divorced man: "My intricate problem as a pastor . . . runs throughout the nation . . . torn and broken homes. The beauty of your home, with your wife by your side helping you go forward, the union of your home, your children, your grandchildren, a real home life, is what America needs as a pattern and as a philosophy." On October 24 Ike and Mamie held a televised chat with seven "ladies," the preferred usage then. Because the program was aimed at boosting the President's share of female votes, air time was bought for the afternoon. The women asked about the draft, the economy, nuclear weapons, the farmers' plight, and Ike's childhood. The result was an informal picture of the President and his wife, chatting easily with ordinary people.

Birth of the Negative

The Republicans had the money and the air time, but the Democrats, for all their professions of distaste for Madison Avenue, proved to be more innovative in their advertising. They introduced the negative commercial as a form, creating styles that would be repeated in years to come. One innovation, a standard in subsequent campaigns, used film of the opponent to attack the opponent; the particular film footage employed was a further innovation, also one copied subsequently: a clip from the opponent's political advertising.

VIDEO	AUDIO
Camera up on slide: white letters against gray background, "HOW'S THAT AGAIN, GENERAL?"	Announcer [VO]: "How's that again, General?
Cut to freeze frame of TV screen showing Ike; "1952" superimposed in white letters.	During the 1952 campaign, General Eisenhower promised a great crusade—"
Camera moves in until Ike fills screen; action begins, excerpt from 1952 "Eisenhower Answers America" spot on corruption.	Eisenhower [SOF]: "Too many politicians have sold their ideals of honesty down the Potomac. We must bring back integrity and thrift to Washington."
Freeze frame.	Announcer [VO]: "How's that again, General?"
Clip repeats.	Eisenhower [SOF]: 'Too many politicians have sold their ideals of honesty down the Potomac. We must bring back integrity and thrift to Washington."
Fade to CU of Estes Kefauver, the Democratic candidate for vice-president. Camera	Kefauver [SOF]: "This is Estes Kefauver. Let's see what happened to that promise.

pulls back to show that he's standing beside a curtain on which is hung a series of nameplates: "ROBERTS," "TALBOTT," "STROBEL," "MANSURE," and "WEN-ZELL." Kefauver points to the name of the man he is talking about.

"Wesley Roberts, a Republican National Chairman, sold Kansas a building it already owned for eleven thousand dollars. He got a silver tree from Mr. Eisenhower.

"Hal Talbott pressured defense plants to employ a firm which paid him a hundred and thirty thousand dollars while he was Air Force Secretary. He received the General's warm wishes and an official welcome.

"And then there are many others, like Strobel, the Public Buildings Administrator; Mansure, the General Services Administrator. Let's think it through on November 6."

Cut to slide: white letters against gray background, "Vote for ADLAI STEVEN-SON and ESTES KEFAUVER."

Announcer [VO]: "Vote for Stevenson and Kefauver—vote Democratic."

Another negative spot also featured Kefauver—Stevenson by and large stayed above the battle, as presidential candidates often do, leaving the fighting to their running mates. In it Kefauver compares the robust economy of 1956 with that of 1929, arguing that they share a weakness that could cause disaster: the recession in farming. Over film footage of breadlines, Kefauver says, "Are we going to learn the painful lesson of 1929 all over again?" Finally, a series of Democratic negative spots took on Richard

Nixon. At that point in the campaign, no one would say too loudly that the President would die; it would be poor taste. The anti-Nixon spots made the point implicitly:

VIDEO	AUDIO
Still photo of Nixon in pro-file, shifty-looking, narrowed eyes; small on screen. Super over photo in large white letters, filling screen: "NIXON?"	Announcer [VO]: "Nervous about Nixon? *"President* Nixon?*
Cut to lettering against black background: "VOTE DEMOCRATIC."	"Vote Democratic. The party for you—not just the few."

The other two spots in the series used the same script and close but different opening graphics. One begins with an imposing photo of the U.S Capitol. The other opens with a caricature of a tiny Nixon sitting in a huge chair labeled "THE PRESIDENT." The tactic of attacking a vice-presidential candidate's fitness for the presidency has similarly become a standard in the years since.

The Democrats also traveled the positive road, with Stevenson appearing one-on-one with the home viewer:

VIDEO	AUDIO
Camera up on Adlai Stevenson standing before curtain, medium shot.	Stevenson [SOF]: "I'm Adlai Stevenson, and this is what I believe—that there is only one sound formula for peace: a sturdy defense, cooperation with our friends, and intelli-

1956: EISENHOWER VS. STEVENSON

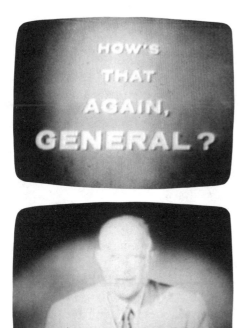

Stevenson Negative Commercial

"General Eisenhower promised a great crusade"

"We must bring back integrity and thrift to Washington"

"Let's see what happened to that promise"

**Stevenson "Man From
Libertyville"
Commercial**

"Oh, I forgot to deliver
the groceries"

gent action to win the hearts and minds of the uncommitted peoples. To achieve this peace, we need new leadership."

Cut to still photos of Stevenson and Kefauver.

Announcer [VO]: "Vote Democratic."

Similar spots, in a series entitled "Adlai Speaks for a New America," showed the candidate discussing science, fair employment, small business, and education.

The Democrats, like the Republicans, invested heavily in five-minute hitchhikes. These featured Stevenson, usually talking with someone else. In "Vice-Presidency" Stevenson, Kefauver, and Stevenson's son and daughter-in-law discuss the importance of the second-highest office. "Farming" shows Stevenson and Kefauver, agreeing that something must be done. "Cost of Living" features Stevenson and his son and daughter-in-law. "Education" has Stevenson talking with the Dean of Northwestern's School of Education. Finally, "Television Campaigning" stars a solitary Stevenson addressing the camera in his library. He talks about the limitations of television and promises that it won't prevent him from getting out and meeting voters. Another, "The Man from Libertyville," shows Stevenson, his son, and his daughter-in-law, carrying groceries into the house. Stevenson pauses outside the door and, grocery sack in arms, soberly discusses the cost of living and other problems, talking directly to the camera. The spot concludes with Stevenson's daughter-in-law coming out the door, taking the sack from him, and chiding, "You're a *big* help." "Oh, I forgot to deliver the groceries," Stevenson chuckles, and, turning to the camera, adds, "and made a speech instead."

The Democrats even produced a few cartoons. In one an animated ballot announces, "I am your ballot. Don't treat me lightly." The talking ballot then summarizes the issues and urges a Stevenson vote. Finally the Stevenson campaign commissioned some longer films. At an early stage of the Democratic effort a young filmmaker named Charles Guggenheim became involved in some primary advertising. Later his political media work would span the presidential campaigns of Robert and Edward Kennedy and George McGovern. Of the Stevenson effort, Guggenheim now recalls, "The candidate had absolutely no interest in that side of the campaign; he left it all to others." And as for those others, Guggenheim says, "No one was particularly knowledge-able about paid spots."

In a way Stevenson was right to focus his attention elsewhere. The ad campaigns became moot when real world events suddenly began to dominate the news in the last days of the campaign. Soviet tanks rolled into Hungary; Israel invaded Egypt; England and France intervened at the Suez Canal. On October 31 Eisen-hower took to the airwaves to reassure the nation—a presidential speech carried free by the networks. The TV appearance boosted Ike's already high popularity, a demonstration of how inter-national crises tend to produce "rally-'round-the-flag" effects.

On election eve both sides bought air time for televised rallies. In a speech from Boston Stevenson made the attack on Nixon explicit: "Distasteful as this matter is, I must say bluntly that every piece of scientific evidence we have, every lesson of history and experience, indicates that a Republican victory tomorrow would mean that Richard M. Nixon probably would be president of this country within the next four years." The Republicans had planned another production like that of 1952, with music and children and fast cuts. But Ike opted to remain in Washington, addressing the rally (also in Boston) by closed-circuit TV—to show that he was too busy being president to engage in politics. Later that night Eisenhower appeared again on TV, to give a quiet, contemplative election-eve talk. "You have done me a very great courtesy in allowing me to come into your living rooms this evening," he said at the end. "I thank you sincerely." Ike had more to thank voters for the next day, when he won in a landslide surpassed to that point only by the Roosevelt victory of 1936. The Republicans again outspent the Democrats on broadcasting, $2.9 million to $1.8 million. Both parties spent more on advertising than they had in 1952; but as we've seen, more can be less when a presidential campaign produces nothing more memorable than a talking ballot.

KENNEDY, KENNEDY, KEN-NE-DY

CHAPTER 6

In 1960 the television advertising arts should have been decisive. Nine out of ten American homes had television sets. Eisenhower couldn't run again, and Stevenson wouldn't; so the faces would be less familiar, more in need of advertising's cosmetic touches. In fact the prevailing wisdom held that Madison Avenue, through television, would elect the next president. Vance Packard's 1957 exposé, *The Hidden Persuaders*, had included a chapter on the selling of the president, and a *Saturday Evening Post* editorial in 1959 declared that the "sinister sorcerers" of Madison Avenue had replaced the financiers of Wall Street as the villains of politics. As it turned out, however, the polispots and admen were overshadowed in 1960 by another form of political television, the Kennedy-Nixon debates.

The debates came about through an odd conjunction of circumstances. First of all, the Congress, alarmed by the rising costs of TV advertising campaigns, held hearings about the issue in the mid and late 1950s. One idea, advanced to contain costs, involved the provision of free broadcast time to candidates. If the equal-time rules—the infamous Section 315 of the Federal Communications Act—could be suspended, the networks would be able to give air time to serious (that is, major) presidential candidates without having to provide equal air time to the Communist and vegetarian candidates. Section 315 had been aimed at preventing discrimination of long-shot candidates and minor parties. In practice, it has enabled broadcasters to avoid "spoiling" their regular schedules, and upsetting their audiences, by providing free blocks of air time to any candidates. But in 1960 it was the broadcasters who wanted Congress to free them from the "restrictions" of 315—a turnaround of position caused in part by industry embarrassment at its scandals of the late 1950s, involving fixed quiz shows and payola. Suspension of 315 meant the networks could appear to the world in 1960 as dignified sponsors of political discourse. In their newfound role of public benefactors, ABC, CBS, and NBC in 1960 donated an estimated $4 to $5 million in air time to political candidates. Of that, the best-used time, worth some $2 million, went for the series of debates between the Democratic and Republican presidential candidates.

The Democratic nominee, John F. Kennedy, the forty-two-year-old junior senator from Massachusetts, had been a contender for the vice-presidential nomination in 1956. He was youthful, bright, handsome, wealthy, and relatively unknown; in short, a perfect candidate to use television to get the presidential nomination. In the Democratic primaries only Minnesota Senator Hubert H. Humphrey actively opposed Kennedy. Their first confrontation, in the Wisconsin primary, offered mixed results—the Roman Catholic Kennedy won but did poorly in Protestant areas. West Virginia was next. A poll four months earlier, taken by Lou Harris, had found Kennedy leading Humphrey seventy to thirty in West Virginia. Arriving in the state, Kennedy strategists found the situation was in fact much less optimistic: West Virginia voters hadn't previously realized Kennedy was Catholic. His religion was the issue, but it was a whispered issue; neither candidate mentioned it publicly. Kennedy decided to confront it on television. His staff tried to talk him out of it, arguing that a candidate ought not mention his own negatives, and in West Virginia Kennedy's Catholicism was certainly a negative. Kennedy couldn't be dissuaded, and on May 8, 1960, he made a statewide paid television appearance, a conversation rather than a formal address. He answered questions put to him by Franklin Roosevelt, Jr., explaining that his Catholicism would not affect his handling of the presidency, and that all Americans, Catholics included, had the right to be president. According to Theodore White, Kennedy had no script; yet White remembers it as "the finest TV broadcast I have ever heard any political candidate make." The program is, as far as we can determine, lost to history; no transcript was kept and no film exists in the Kennedy Library in Boston.

Fortunately for the record, Kennedy used the same arguments in TV spots, written by his staff, subsequently aired in West Virginia, and now preserved in the library collection:

VIDEO	AUDIO
Camera up on Kennedy holding microphone in the midst of large crowd.	Kennedy [SOF]: "The question is whether I think that if I were elected president, I would be divided between two loyalties, my church and my state. There is no article of my faith that would in any way inhibit—I think it encourages—the meeting of my oath of office. And whether you vote for me or not because of my competence to

> be president, I am sure that
> in this state of West Virginia,
> that no one believes I'd be a
> candidate for the presidency
> if I didn't think I could meet
> my oath of office. Now you
> cannot tell me the day I was
> born it was said I could never
> run for president because I
> wouldn't meet my oath of of-
> fice. I came to the state of
> West Virginia, which has
> fewer numbers of my coreli-
> gionists than any state in the
> nation. I would not have
> come here if I didn't feel I
> was going to get complete
> opportunity to run for office
> as a fellow American in this
> state. I would not run for it
> in any way if I felt that I
> couldn't do the job. So I
> come here today to say that I
> think this is an issue" [voice
> drowned out by applause].

The Kennedy campaign also borrowed a tactic used by the
California political consultants Whitaker & Baxter. In 1946 Whitaker & Baxter had represented Roger Lapham, the San Francisco
mayor then facing a recall vote. Rather than defending Lapham's
record, Whitaker & Baxter created "The Faceless Man"—a mys-
terious-looking, shadowy face shown on billboards and in newspaper ads and presented as someone trying to take over the city.
In 1960 the Kennedy forces tried to pin on Humphrey the ac-
cusation that he was nothing but a front for the faceless bosses

who wanted to pick the next president (later the Kennedy men would say that the bosses' vote had been destined for Lyndon Johnson, the Senate majority leader):

VIDEO	AUDIO
Camera up on quick series of still photos of West Virginians.	Announcer [VO]: "This is you, the people of West Virginia. Are you, you, and you going to let yourself be used by the forces who,
Cut to photo of pols, their backs to camera, waving cigars.	in their smoke-filled rooms in Los Angeles,
Cut to photo of White House.	expect to handpick the next president of the United States?
Cut to photo of pols.	Well, they know they can't do it—unless
Cut to map of West Virginia. Super appears over map: white letters, "STOP KENNEDY."	here, in West Virginia, they stop Kennedy. So what do they do, these scheming politicos?
Cut to quick series of photos of voters.	They ask you, you, and you, the people of West Virginia, to walk into their trap and
Cut to slide: "Hubert" in white letters.	support Humphrey. But will
Cut to photo of pols.	they themselves support

Cut to slide: "HUMPHREY" in white letters.	Humphrey at the convention? Of course not.
Black "X" appears over "HUMPHREY."	They'll drop Humphrey like the hot potato he is,
Cut to newspaper headline: "Hubert Can't Possibly Win Nomination."	because everybody knows Humphrey couldn't possibly win the nomination, much less the election.
Quick cuts to slides of state names, white letters against gray background, as announcer names each state.	In state after state—New Hampshire, Wisconsin, Pennsylvania, Massachusetts, and Indiana—
Cut to different still of pols in smoke-filled room.	the bosses also tried to stop Kennedy.
Cut to various shots of Kennedy with voters. Super in white letters: "KENNEDY WINS IN ALL STATES."	But the people spoke up, and Kennedy overwhelmingly won each primary. Make it an overwhelming people's vote,
Cut to smoke-filled room with super: "STOP KENNEDY."	not a bosses' vote,
Cut to film of Kennedy speaking in front of state capitol building.	here in West Virginia. May 10,
Cut to slide: map of West Virginia, with super in white letters, "VOTE KENNEDY MAY 10."	vote Kennedy!"

Another series of spots showed Kennedy holding a microphone like a news reporter and talking with everyday Americans:

VIDEO	AUDIO
Camera CU on elderly man, in open-neck shirt, glasses, wearing hat, standing in front of brick wall.	Man [SOF]: "I think our problem is today that we can't produce thirty-cent eggs on four and a half and five-dollar feed. That feed is too high for the price that we're getting for our eggs. Do you think there's something that could be done to get it more economical, on a more economical basis?"
Cut to slide showing map of West Virginia, with white block letters overlaid: "YOU AND KENNEDY!"	Announcer [VO]: "John F. Kennedy goes to the people to know their problems. Here, he answers Roy Kaye, farmer of Cabell County."
Cut to medium shot of man, at left, looking up to Kennedy. Kennedy, in coat and tie, holds a microphone in one hand, and gestures with the other hand.	Kennedy [SOF]: "The farmer's income has dropped nearly fifteen percent in the last twelve months, and his cost of doing business has gone up about ten percent, the same thing you have with your feed. That gives him a total loss, in his position, of almost twenty-five percent. Now, if this continues, it's going to affect our entire

economy. I would say that the first and most important task, really, domestically, on the desk of the next president, will be an attempt to arrest the decline."

Cut to slide of map with white block letters overlaid: "VOTE KENNEDY MAY 10."	Announcer [VO]: "It's up to you. Vote Kennedy for president May 10."

Several spots tied Kennedy to coal, vital to the West Virginia economy. In one five-minute hitchhike Kennedy lectures a group of miners about foreign aid and Social Security. Another spot closes with an announcer saying: "Help Kennedy bring prosperity back to coal, and thus to West Virginia. Vote Kennedy May 10." In all, Kennedy, the son of one of America's richest men, outspent Humphrey four to one in the state. Humphrey tried to hold his dwindling support with a thirty-minute phone-in telethon. Unfortunately no one screened the calls; one woman told Humphrey to "git out" of West Virginia. A few minutes later an operator came on and ordered everyone off the telephone line for an emergency. Kennedy later joked that had he known the calls weren't being screened, he would have called himself—or had his brother Bobby call.

It wasn't necessary. Kennedy won West Virginia by twenty points, and Humphrey dropped out. With running mate Lyndon Johnson, Kennedy prepared to face Richard Nixon and his running mate, former Massachusetts Senator Henry Cabot Lodge. Nixon, concerned about the Madison Avenue connection, decided against a direct link with BBD&O. Instead, the Republicans formed their own, in-house ad agency called Campaign Associates. The staff of fifty was headed by Carroll Newton, the BBD&O vice-president who had worked on Eisenhower's 1952 and 1956 campaigns, and also included the producer Ted Rogers, from Checkers days.

An in-house agency, the Nixon people reasoned, would attract good people from other agencies and the networks, rather than having to rely on any one agency. Campaign Associates rented offices on Vanderbilt Avenue; Nixon had explicitly prohibited a Madison Avenue location.

Nixon Answers America

Campaign Associates might just as well have been located in the Aleutian Islands. They were the same talented people who had helped with Ike's effective spots, but, with rare exceptions, Nixon ignored them. His TV advisers, for instance, wanted to make two long-form programs. One would be called "Khrushchev As I Have Seen Him," featuring Nixon talking about the Soviet leader. Khrushchev would be visually characterized "in the melo-dramatic image of an international villain," filmmaker Gene Wyckoff proposed, while "in juxtaposition, Nixon would be char-acterized as the American who best understands what peace demands." The film would emphasize Nixon's experience, underscore his opposition to Communism, and cast in good light his Tricky Dicky image—you've *got* to be a street fighter to deal with the toughs of the world. Campaign Associates also wanted to do a film "You and Your Family," with Nixon talking informally from his home about the circumstances facing everyday families such as his. This would show Nixon's human side. It would remind some viewers of the Checkers speech, and Nixon's strength in facing adversity. And it would implicitly raise the point that Kennedy's privileged background had kept him re-moved from the concerns of the common American. Nixon turned down the Wyckoff proposal, feeling it was more important to continue his personal campaigning, and fulfill his pledge, ill-considered, to visit all fifty states before election day. While Nixon was unwilling to appear in such formats, his running mate Lodge proved difficult to work with and unconvincing on camera.

Out of necessity, Wyckoff turned to existing still photographs of the candidates, and a new style of political advertising was born. An animation camera created a sense of motion by a combination of zooming and panning actions. Within two weeks Wyckoff completed two five-minute hitchhikes, "Meet Richard Nixon" and "Meet Mr. Lodge." The latter had a voice-over by President Eisenhower. The technique, Wyckoff later declared, "was extraordinarily suitable for conveying an impression of heroic image, perhaps because each still photograph in itself is a slightly unreal impression, a moment frozen from life, that makes it easier for viewers to accept and be moved by an illusion of the candidate's heroic dimension." Ruth Jones, a talented time buyer on loan from J. Walter Thompson, convinced Carroll Newton to let the Wyckoff heroic image films run in some already purchased daytime slots. Response was good, and shortly thereafter the hitchhikes began running in prime time as well.

The campaign also ran shorter spots, mostly with Nixon talking straight at the camera. In some he took questions asked by an announcer offscreen, a kind of Nixon Answers America format, but much tougher than the Eisenhower replies:

VIDEO	AUDIO
Camera up on medium shot of Nixon, sitting ramrod straight on edge of a desk, hands folded neatly in lap. Plain background.	Announcer [VO]: "Mr. Nixon, what is the truth about our defenses? How strong should they be?"
Camera moves in slowly as he speaks, to CU.	Nixon [SOF]: "Well, they must be strong enough to keep us out of war, powerful enough to make the Communists in the Soviet Union and Red China understand that America will not tolerate being pushed around, that we

can if necessary retaliate with such speed and devastation to make the risk too great for the Communists to start a war anywhere in the world. We have this kind of strength now, and we are getting stronger every day. We must never let the Communists think we are weak. This is both foolish and dangerous. And so I say, let's not tear America down. Let us speak up for America."

Fade to side-by-side still photos of Nixon and Lodge, underneath black letters on white background: "NIXON AND LODGE." Below pictures: "They understand what peace demands."

Announcer [VO]: "Vote for Nixon and Lodge November 8. They understand what peace demands."

Nixon made no paid TV appearances in the three-month period July 25 to October 25. Then in the final twelve days of the campaign, Campaign Associates saturated the air: a Nixon rally; an Eisenhower speech; a program featuring Nixon, Lodge, and Eisenhower; a Nixon fifteen-minute national "fireside chat" each weeknight of the final week. A heavy spot schedule continued, and local party organizations bought time on their own. On the afternoon before the election a four-hour telethon, "Dial Dick Nixon," was broadcast on ABC, preempting all regular programming. Questions were phoned in from across the country and relayed to the candidate by Hollywood's Ginger Rogers and Lloyd Nolan. The telecast, as Theodore White observed, showed

1960: NIXON VS. KENNEDY

Kennedy Anti-Humphrey Commercial, West Virginia Primary

"Are you, you, and you going to let yourself be used?"

"Everybody knows Humphrey couldn't possibly win"

"Make it an overwhelming people's vote, not a bosses' vote"

Kennedy Religious Issue Commercial

"You cannot tell me the day I was born it was said I could never run for president"

Kennedy as "Interviewer"

"The farmer's income has dropped nearly fifteen percent"

Nixon Answers America

"We must never let the Communists think we are weak"

Nixon "at his best (talking of peace) and at his worst (discussing the high cost of living with Ginger Rogers, who said she too had to live on a salary)." Later that night before the election, speeches by Nixon, Lodge, Ike, and Dewey were aired. All in all, the Republicans spent around half a million dollars on election eve. The final effort, White believes, "contributed mightily to the last Nixon surge."

"Viva Kennedy"

The Democrats aired fewer half-hour speeches than the Republicans, but one Kennedy speech is still remembered for the way the candidate handled the nagging questions about his Catholicism. On September 7 a group of Protestant leaders, headed by Norman Vincent Peale, charged that a Catholic president would be under "extreme pressure" from the Vatican in making policy decisions. Once again Kennedy met the Catholic issue head-on—and also once again contrary to the wishes of some advisers—in an address to Protestant ministers in Houston. Evenly, he said: "I do not speak for my church on public matters—and the church does not speak for me."

One sixty-second Kennedy spot got less favorable press notices. "Senator John F. Kennedy visits Mr. and Mrs. McNamara," the voice-over begins. Kennedy is sitting on a porch with an elderly couple. Mrs. McNamara, wearing a hat and broach, is smiling; her husband scowls. Kennedy says, "What I think is the serious problem for Mr. McNamara and Mrs. McNamara, he's retired, he's living on Social Security, then because he had an accident he incurred a debt of over six hundred dollars to pay for his medical bills. The average Social Security check is only around seventy-eight dollars a month, and whatever savings they had would have to be spent to pay for his bills." Kennedy says he supports Social Security assistance for medical bills, to help unfortunates like the McNamaras. The wife continues to smile, the husband scowls, and the spot ends; the McNamaras haven't said a word. Later the reason for the husband's scowl came out: he had told Kennedy that they didn't need any federal program—the couple had gotten Blue Cross coverage. Kennedy, according to subsequent press accounts, had told the McNamaras to keep that fact to themselves.

Several positive Kennedy spots feature the candidate addressing the camera directly. He deals with medical care, automation, and full employment. But when the tougher spots get going, the candidate gets out of the picture, and surrogates take over:

VIDEO	AUDIO
Camera up on news footage of foreign demonstrators throwing rocks at cars, waving banners, shouting angrily at camera.	Announcer [VO]: "Do you believe that America's world prestige is at an all-time high? Then vote Nixon. But if you believe that America's
Cut to medium shot of Kennedy shaking hands with crowd of supporters; camera pans down to outstretched hands; then cut to CU of Kennedy.	world prestige has gone downhill in these eight Republican years, that new leadership is needed to make America first again, then vote for the man who faces up to these facts and will do something to correct them. Vote Kennedy for president."

In another spot the Democrats turned to film footage to make a point, as had the Stevenson campaign four years earlier. This time the target was Nixon's self-proclaimed strong suit, his experience:

VIDEO	AUDIO
Camera up on still of Nixon.	Announcer [VO]: "Every Republican politician wants you to believe that Richard Nixon is, quote, experienced. They even want you to believe that he has actually been making decisions in the White House—but listen to the man who should know best, the President of the United States. A reporter recently asked President Eisenhower this question about Mr. Nixon's experience."
Cut to press conference film: Eisenhower, standing, arms folded, listening to question.	Reporter [SOF]: "I just wondered if you could give us an example of a major idea of his that you had adopted in that role, as the, as the decider and final—" Eisenhower [SOF, after long pause]: "If you give me a week, I might think of one. I don't remember." [Laughter]
Cut to different footage of Eisenhower.	Announcer [VO]: "At the same press conference, President Eisenhower said:" Eisenhower [SOF]: "No one can make a decision except me."

Cut to first footage of
Eisenhower.

Announcer [VO]: "And as for
any major ideas from Mr.
Nixon—"

Eisenhower [SOF]: "If you
give me a week, I might
think of one. I don't
remember."

Cut to film of Kennedy smil-
ing, in midst of large crowd.
Then cut to slide: photo of
Kennedy, with white letters
on black background: "VOTE
for JOHN F. KENNEDY for
President."

Announcer [VO]: "President
Eisenhower could not re-
member. But the voters *will*
remember. For real leadership in the sixties, help elect
Senator John F. Kennedy
president."

The Democrats also used Eleanor Roosevelt comparing Kennedy favorably to Franklin Roosevelt. "He is a man with a sense
of history. That I am well familiar with, because my husband
had a sense of history. He wanted to leave a good record for
the future. I think John F. Kennedy wants to leave a good record."
Adlai Stevenson does his Kennedy endorsement sitting at a desk:
"Under his leadership, we will win the fight for human rights."
Finally, Jacqueline Kennedy praises her husband in slow, meticulous Spanish in a spot used in cities with large Hispanic pop-
ulations. The production is minimal; the sixty-second spot shows
Mrs. Kennedy standing in a nondescript room, wearing a short-
sleeved dress, unchanging half smile on her lips while the camera
keeps her framed in a simple head-and-shoulders shot. The lack
of artifice enhances the message; the viewer's eyes stay on the
speaker as she builds to her punch line, "Viva Kennedy."

The Great Debates

The 1960 election turned out to be so close that spots, in English
or Spanish, may have made the difference; with so narrow a

margin—a swing of a few thousand votes in Illinois and Texas—
nearly anything that reached large groups of people could have
been decisive. An individual man's or woman's voting choices,
we understand, result from a whole range of interior forces: race,
class, religion, images of the past, visions of the future, hopes,
fears, information, ignorance. In any other election spots might
have been critical. But in 1960 only one set of television images
really mattered. The Kennedy-Nixon debates were the main
media force in the campaign, providing a common gauge against
which voters could measure their inner feelings. The gauge wasn't
as "objective" as it seemed. But the candidates sensed its importance. At first, the Nixon staff quietly opposed the various
proposals to open the way to debates by repealing Section 315,
in the belief that the lesser-known Kennedy would have more
to gain from such side-by-side appearances. Candidate Nixon
himself said privately he would never debate Kennedy. Then, at
a news conference after the Republican convention, Nixon suddenly announced he would accept an invitation to debate. The
reversal amazed his senior staff; press aide Herbert Klein later
speculated that Nixon "did not want his manhood sullied by
appearing as if he were afraid to debate his opponent face-to-
face, and he was confident that he could win such an encounter."
Nixon's self-proclaimed strength was foreign policy—he had
traveled widely in the Eisenhower administration—and so he felt
that that would be his best debate topic. Nixon also believed that
the TV audience would increase as the debates went on. So his
side pushed for foreign policy to be the fin 1 of the four scheduled
debates.

Nixon miscalculated. The first debate, held in Chicago on the
evening of September 26 at the WBBM TV studios, had the
largest audience by a slight margin, and the largest impact on
the audience by far. Nixon came off poorly in how he looked,
the result of a combination of loss of weight, exhaustion, an
infected knee, unflattering lighting, and badly applied Lazy Shave
makeup. But as far as what he said was concerned, Nixon came

out ahead. People who heard the debates on radio generally told opinion surveyors that they felt Nixon had won, whereas those who had seen them on TV said that Kennedy was the winner. Nixon did better visually in subsequent debates. He drank milk shakes to gain weight, so that his shirt collars no longer hung loose about his neck; he tried to go after Kennedy more sharply. But the impression made in the first debate of the cool, elegant Kennedy and the hot, ill-at-ease Nixon remained strong. Marshall McLuhan, the communications theorist, suggested the encounter had been a kind of television Western: Nixon looked like the slick, shady railway lawyer about to bilk the townspeople, while Kennedy was the shy young sheriff ready to thwart the scheme. Nothing in the 1960 state of the art of political jingles, still photos, and sixty-second spots could match that encounter for pure theater. Just so voters didn't forget, the Kennedy campaign produced a spot from the debate footage, called "Historic Moment." It features a calm, confident Kennedy framing the election in Cold War terms: "The question before us all—it faces all Republicans and all Democrats—is, Can freedom in the next generation conquer, or are the Communists going to be successful? That's the great issue."

Nixon would later complain that, in the campaign as a whole, he wasn't as rested as Kennedy, or as suntanned, or as well served by courtiers. In his memoirs Nixon also went so far as to make the un-Republican claim that money kept him from using more TV in 1960: "television time costs money," he wrote, "and our campaign had run short. We could afford only one telethon, which we scheduled for the day before the election." He also complained (in *Six Crises*) that he had been too conscientious in 1960, spending "too much time . . . on substance and too little time on appearance: I paid too much attention to what I was going to say and too little to how I would look." He seemed to be saying, I only looked like the crooked railroad lawyer. This is revisionist history. Nixon's problems were broader than money, TV images, even Chicago Mayor Richard J. Daley's legion of phantom voters on election day. Nixon tried to manage his own campaign, and he did it poorly. He rarely consulted, and often overruled, his staff. Even on minor advice—not to face the camera so intently—he ignored his media advisers. "He reduced us all to clerks," one adviser complained when it was over.

In victory Kennedy took a long view, offering a courtier of the press, Rowland Evans, a lofty paean to the new communications arts: "Television gives people a chance to look at their candidate close up and close to the bone," Kennedy told Evans. "For the first time since the Greek city-states practiced their form of democracy, it brings us within reach of that ideal where every voter has a chance to measure the candidate himself." Perhaps, but it is an ideal that often remains just beyond our grasp. Unquestionably, though, the 1960 campaign demonstrated that television had arrived as a significant force in American political life. It was not just the near total penetration of TV sets or the new campaign techniques of visual and aural presentation practiced by skilled hands like the filmmaker Gene Wyckoff. More important were the qualitative changes in social routines brought about by the presence of television; almost all American households not only had television but Americans—young and old, rich and poor, urban, suburban, and rural, black and white—were watching on the average more than two hours each day. These watchers were coming to depend on TV for much of their information about national affairs, as well as for their entertainment. Communications theorists such as McLuhan began speculating, sometimes overimaginatively, about how television was changing not just leisure time or news-consuming habits but the broader society and culture. Kennedy was hailed as the "first television president," a title he himself thought was appropriate. Political advertising, it also became fashionable to say, was now too important to be left to the politicians, or for that matter, to the advertising agencies. In 1964 a cadre of new communications specialists began to arrive in force to take over a significant part of the work of the political campaign. Accompanying some of them was a new style of advertising.

THE NEW ADVERTISING: SOFT SELL ARRIVES

CHAPTER 7

During the Eisenhower fifties the nation had slumbered, basking in the radiant warmth of the genial President. For the voting classes it was a time of getting and getting on. Manufacturers bent to the task of satisfying pent-up consumer demands of the World War II and Korean War years. People married, moved into homes with washers and dryers, backyards and barbecues, and had children, several of them. Just about everyone bought a television set, and by the early 1960s there were homes with two TVs, and sometimes a third for the children of the baby boom. Advertising and communications arts prospered along with corporate America. And Rosser Reeves reached for fame by publishing his USP ideas in a book with the no-nonsense title *Reality in Advertising*. It eventually sold 800,000 copies and was translated into over a dozen languages. But Reeves and Madison Avenue also paid some dues for their successes—they were targets of criticism for the loud, hammering huckster spots, and their "manipulative methods" were exposed by Vance Packard and others. But the critics were years behind the newest development. The latest "reality in advertising" was emotion, which when employed in the political messages of the 1964 campaign—and in all subsequent campaigns—struck many people as much more manipulative than the transparent artifices of "Eisenhower Answers America."

Hard-sell advertising had used brain-pounding repetition to make its unique selling proposition. Soft-sell, emotional advertising, also known as the new advertising, depended on affect, on how the viewer felt about what he or she was seeing and hearing. Emotion, obviously, was hardly new to advertising. Decades before TV, for example, the 1848 Rogers Brothers Silverplate Company had appealed to the fear of being unpopular; in one of its 1910 print ads the Foster family—Dad, Mom, and daughters Mildred and Joan—were seen hanging around the house and moping because they didn't get invitations to parties. Why weren't the Fosters asked out? Because, the ad explained in its hard-edged way, they didn't have a complete silver set, and couldn't give parties themselves. In the years that followed, makers of toothpastes, mouthwashes, deodorants, soaps, shampoos, facial cleaners, and other personal products appealed to similar fears and hopes using gentler techniques. Later emotion-based advertising extended to the act of buying a soft drink—McCann-Erickson's Mean Joe Greene spot—and to the use of long-distance telephone services when in the late 1970s the N W Ayer agency created the AT&T "Reach Out and Touch Someone" campaign. It told people that they didn't need a "real reason" to call long distance, that wanting to say "I love you" or "I'm thinking of you" was enough. Another series of AT&T television commercials used a pop standard called "Feelings" as the spots showed family members and good friends calling one another on the telephone. Nobody was told to call, call, call, on the phone, phone, phone, now, now, now! The commercials were intended to make people feel like calling. One of the premier admen of the new era, William Bernbach, a founder of Doyle Dane Bernbach, explained the basis for the emotional appeals of the new advertising shortly before he died in 1983: "It is fashionable to talk about *changing* man," Bernbach said. "A communicator must be concerned with *unchanging* man—what compulsions drive him, what instincts dominate his every action, even though his language too often camouflages what *really* motivates him. For if you know these things about a man, you can touch him at the core of his being."

Appeals to "the core of being" are now so smooth and familiar in spot advertising that we seldom consciously remark on them. Bill Bernbach, Ned Doyle, and Maxwell Dane, who helped engineer that change, had formed DDB in 1949 with an investment of $1,200. By 1983 DDB had become the tenth largest advertising agency in the world, with annual billings of more than a billion dollars. As much as any single agency DDB helped bring about the new advertising of the late 1950s and 1960s. DDB's trademarks were bold headlines, short copy, and taut layouts, all with a message of humor and humanity. The agency's greatest creative hits came within a few years of one another. For Levy's Jewish-style rye bread, DDB ads showed a big picture of, among others, a young black boy and an older Chinese man, each holding a slice of the product. "You don't have to be Jewish to love Levy's," read the prominent headline. For Avis rental cars, perennially number two to the bigger Hertz company, DDB's ad pledged: "We Try Harder." For the Volkswagen automobile, a direct descendant of the Nazi army vehicle, DDB had to go against history—the year was 1959, and many people still vividly remembered Hitler and the war—and the tradition of the then-dominant Detroit models which stressed size, power, and ornamentation. "Think Small," proclaimed the headline of the DDB ads, with a photo of the little beetle-shaped car centered on white space. The trade paper *Advertising Age* designated the Volkswagen ads the best campaign of the half-century.

While emotion-based ads were challengers of hard sell, the advertising agencies were themselves changing rapidly, not only in the styles of advertising but also in the kinds of people engaged in agency work. Advertising's old-line, Republican, WASP image began to fade, geographically, socially, and ethnically. Men of Irish, Jewish, Italian, and Greek ancestry rose to prominence. Women advanced to executive jobs. Agencies in Chicago, Los Angeles, Dallas, and San Francisco flourished. Many newcomers, particularly in the creative ranks of writers and art directors, were Democrats, liberal Democrats at that. One measure of how much the advertising business had changed was a 1971 memo written by Nixon campaign aide—and later memorable actor in Watergate—Jeb Stuart Magruder, complaining about how hard it was to find "conservative copywriters." The older stereotype was partly fiction; advertising in practice was never as homogeneous as the stories portrayed it. But social changes took place at the same time that new blood came into advertising during the 1960s, in newer agencies such as Doyle Dane Bernbach, as well as Papert, Koenig, Lois, and Della Femina, Travisano & Partners. Indeed, it was no accident that the USP hard-sell doctrines were being challenged by soft-sell and no-sell ads; the new breed of advertising men and women nurtured the new advertising.

The ads of the hammer away school of persuasion did not fade away in the 1960s; too many people were convinced of their usefulness if not their aesthetic qualities. But they did modulate a bit, and because political candidates were always somewhat uncomfortable with hard-sell commercials, the subtler emotion-based styles of the new advertising were soon being adapted to the strategies of electoral campaigns. Among the earliest, and most electric, examples of emotion-based advertising in politics appeared in 1964, when Doyle Dane Bernbach recruited a New York recording specialist named Tony Schwartz to work on media for the Lyndon Johnson reelection campaign.

The Wizard of West 56th Street

In the ranks of the new media specialists, Schwartz stands apart. Schwartz has never worked a day of his life on the staff of an ad agency, has never rung a single doorbell on behalf of a candidate for public office. Yet in 1964 he created, together with Doyle Dane Bernbach, what most people consider the single most memorable political commercial ever seen on television, the Daisy spot.

Schwartz has lived, worked, and made radio-television commercials since 1961 in his studio-home in a brownstone on West 56th Street near 10th Avenue, in a neighborhood of bars and bodegas well off Madison Avenue. Hundreds of seekers of public office—presidential candidates, senators, congressmen, and governors, who regard Schwartz as a modern magician of the media— have visited him there over the last two decades. Schwartz says he suffers from agoraphobia and has great difficulty in traveling; only rarely does he leave his high-ceilinged studio, with its cork lining for soundproofing and its broadcast-quality TV cameras, editing tables, and wall shelves holding thousands of tapes. The setting makes the magician image apt. Like some sorcerer of sound and sight, Schwartz sits in his cavelike quarters, surrounded by the instruments of his craft.

Schwartz was among the first of a new group of media specialists who became involved in political advertising in the years after Eisenhower. These men (few women have been centrally engaged as yet) either had no experience in advertising agencies or else had served short apprenticeships before breaking away from the business. Schwartz's training and ideas reflect that nontraditional background of the new breed. He had been an artist/draftsman working for the Navy Department during World War II and then found work after the war as an art director at the Graphics Institute in midtown New York. A self-described gadget nut since birth, Schwartz walked into a record store off Fifth Avenue one day in the early 1950s and bought a Webcor wire recorder selling for the then-princely sum of $139.95. (The Webcor still sits in his studio today, along with what seems like every Ampex, Magnacorder, and other audio machine built since.) Immediately, Schwartz says, he got hooked on sound. New York in the early

1950s was the place where many folksingers performed, relatively well-known singers like Burl Ives, Josh White, and Pete Seeger, as well as struggling newcomers. Schwartz began by recording songs off the radio, and then called up the singers—many of them too poor to afford air check disks—and offered to play back their recordings for study. Then Schwartz began wandering around his neighborhood and recording the sounds of Midtown West and of children playing street games. These sounds became part of his first two records, *New York 19* (his 1950s, pre-zip-code postal zone) and *One, Two, Three, Zing, Zing, Zing*, a record of children's games. An art director at the Wexton agency, co-owned by a cousin of Schwartz's, heard the latter. The director asked Schwartz if he would be interested in doing free-lance commercials with children in them for Wexton. "He told me that they had never used children before in commercials, but only women imitating children," Schwartz recalls. Schwartz agreed. "The first commercial I did was for Johnson's Baby Powder. It was a huge success and that put me in a new business. Instantly I got orders for commercials from Ivory Snow, Ivory Flakes, Hoffmann's soda. I became a specialist in children's recordings; I was typecast. But I kept recording in terms of my own interests."

One of those interests was in what Schwartz calls "the world of numbers." This led, circuitously, with false starts and lurching progress—as frequently happens in imaginative endeavors—to the one simple, direct execution of the Daisy spot for Lyndon Johnson. As Schwartz remembers: "I wanted to do a record essay on numbers without any narration, just the world of numbers. I saw a book that IBM put out, called *The World of Numbers*, and I thought, I would love to do a record to go with that. . . . The most complex use of numbers was the countdown on the atom bomb or a rocket blast-off. The simplest use of numbers was a child counting from one to ten. I had previously done a free-lance commercial with a child, my nephew, who was four years old, for Doyle Dane Bernbach and Polaroid. They had a Polaroid

camera where it was, 'One, two, three, four, count to ten and
open the door,' the procedure for taking a picture. I used that
counting from that commercial with my nephew, and I started
fooling around with the atomic bomb countdown." Schwartz took
the result, a short radio essay cross dissolving from the countdown
to the child, to IBM's ad agency, Ogilvy, Benson & Mather (now
Ogilvy & Mather). They paid him a standard fee of $500 for his
submission but rejected the idea. Eventually, in mid-1962, he
played the essay on a radio program he did for WNYC, the city-
owned, commercial-free station, to show "the need for a real
United Nations and peace."

Meanwhile, on his WNYC program, Schwartz was developing
his ideas of broadcasting as a medium of feelings, ideas later
published in his two books, *The Responsive Chord* (1973) and *Media:
The Second God* (1981). Advertising has power, Schwartz concluded,
when people feel that the ad "is putting them in touch with
reality," when they feel the ad "strikes a responsive chord with
the reality the listener or viewer experienced." A startling demonstration of these responsive chord feelings—and of the ways
Schwartz used media to evoke them—occurred in 1962 when
Schwartz made a series of radio spots for American Airlines.
Schwartz's idea was that each city has not only its visual signature—for example, New York's Empire State Building or San
Francisco's Golden Gate Bridge or Washington's Capitol dome—
but also its sound signature. Doyle Dane Bernbach, American
Airlines' agency, was sold on the idea that these sounds would
make listeners want to get up and go to the city, traveling of
course by American Airlines. For the American Airlines city of
San Francisco, the signature sound was obviously trolley cars and
foghorns off the Bay. Schwartz, with his agoraphobia, had never
been to San Francisco. He did, however, know a New York street
person named Moondog, a shambling, grimy character with long
hair, sandals, and a sackcloth robe, who carried bells, drums,
cooking utensils, and his other life's possessions on his back as
he wandered down Sixth Avenue. One foggy spring day Schwartz

heard the sounds of the Hudson River foghorns, got in touch with Moondog, and invited him to the studio. Moondog played his bells, while Schwartz mixed their tinkle with the bellow of the foghorns recorded by a rooftop microphone. The result was a San Francisco sound—trolley bells against foghorns—that conformed to what listeners already expected and felt about San Francisco. "It was a beautiful series," Schwartz recalls with genuine fondness. Both the agency and the client were also pleased, as the airline's business boomed. Later Schwartz received calls from Young & Rubicam and Benton & Bowles, with each agency asking him to submit work for airline clients.

Reaching the responsive chord in people, Schwartz argued, meant that hard-sell advertising was obsolete. Schwartz dismissed Rosser Reeves and USP as "a kind of gentleman's agreement preventing any two companies from making the same product claim in an advertisement"—that is, the boys in the locker room of the right club getting together and dividing up the market. Reeves, the hard-sell man, had argued that television with its great reach was enhancing the power of USP. Schwartz, the soft-sell man, was now arguing that with television, USP was no longer needed. Specific product claims, he maintained, couldn't match the quality of feelings that spots can produce when emotions are addressed. The Lyndon Johnson advertising campaign of 1964 became a practical demonstration of Schwartz's ideas of persuasion.

DAISY AND THE DIRTY PICTURES IN THE PUBLIC MIND

CHAPTER 8

From the start in the 1964 presidential campaign, the Democrats had the power of incumbency, and a unity achieved following the assassination of the youthful, attractive Kennedy, plus the issues of prosperity and peace (although 16,000 U.S. advisers had taken the first few steps into the Big Muddy of Vietnam). From the start, too, the Democrats made certain they would keep their advantages. Congress debated suspending the FCC's equal-time provisions again, to permit televised debates, but the administration managed to stop the effort. Lyndon Baines Johnson looked unbeatable, though perhaps a well-run GOP advertising strategy might have made inroads into Johnson's strength, while a poorly run Democratic ad campaign—comparable, say, to those used on behalf of the uninterested Adlai Stevenson—might have dissipated Johnson's support. In 1964 it proved to be the other way around; the Republican ad campaign was in disarray, while Lyndon Johnson and his key aides took a very close interest in television advertising. "We were all new at this in 1964," Bill

Moyers, Johnson's press secretary, recalled for us, "and we were willing to experiment to get our messages across."

Rockefeller's Ways

Senator Barry Goldwater of Arizona and Governor Nelson Rockefeller of New York were the leading contenders for the Republican nomination. Each seemingly tried to hand the nomination to the other. Goldwater tended to make outrageous Wild West statements. Rockefeller, for his part, had divorced his wife in 1961 and married a worker in his campaign, and the new wife, in order to marry Rockefeller, had divorced her husband and given up custody of her four children—near-scandalous behavior for a woman in that era. Among the other possibilities, Richard Nixon seemed out of it. He had run for governor of California in 1962, lost, and then shot himself in the foot with a morning-after news conference in which he bitterly told reporters, "You won't have Nixon to kick around anymore because, gentlemen, this is my last press conference." And then there was Henry Cabot Lodge, Nixon's running mate in 1960, who as the year began was ambassador to South Vietnam. Some party leaders felt that Lodge might be able to bring peace, or something like it, to Vietnam and then descend heroically, Ike-like, to accept his party's nomination. A draft Lodge movement began, led by Paul Grindle, a Boston-based direct-mail specialist. From Gene Wyckoff, the filmmaker who had worked for Nixon in 1960, Grindle got a copy of a campaign film narrated in part by Eisenhower. Grindle hired a film editor to recut and "update" the 1960 film, and some skillful editing made it sound as if Ike liked Lodge for 1964. Goldwater later would protest that "a blast of trumpets" at just the right moment drowned out a key word— "vice" in vice-president—in Eisenhower's 1960 remarks. As a result, Goldwater said, most viewers "believed Ike was advocating the nomination and election of Henry Cabot Lodge in 1964." The edited film was used thirty-nine times on New Hampshire's one commercial TV station during the state's first-in-the-nation primary. On March 10 in New Hampshire, Lodge received 33,007 votes, to Goldwater's 20,692 and Rockefeller's 19,504.

Wyckoff recalls how he sat by the phone, waiting for the Lodge campaign to call for his services. "If you keep Lodge out of the country, it would be worth a try," he planned to advise. "As long as television viewers only see him as we want them to see him, he might appear to be much more preferable to Rockefeller or Goldwater." The Lodge campaign never called, but the Rockefeller campaign did. Wyckoff shrugged, signed on, and set to work in time for the Oregon primary. Seeing Rockefeller on TV, Wyckoff reasoned, voters were reminded of the divorce, so he conceived an alternative strategy to keep the candidate off the screen and artfully create "a fresh Rockefeller image via impressionistic television material." The new image would push out "the prevailing moral-libertine impression" through a film called "Rockefeller's Way." Like those Wyckoff created for Nixon and Lodge four years earlier, it was made up of still photos. One series of stills showed the governor playing with children; the background music, a patriotic cornet arrangement, slips into the nursery tune "This Old Man" as Rockefeller hugs a blonde youngster.

At the same time, another Rockefeller media worker, Dennis Kane, filmed short takes showing everyday Oregonians talking freely, without scripts, about their faith in Rockefeller. Wyckoff combined the best of these into a five-minute hitchhike, "The People Speak." It was in some respects intentionally unpolished. One woman, filmed pushing a shopping cart in a grocery store, said supportive things about Rockefeller, then got impatient. "I'm not going to talk any longer," she said, and laughed. "I need a Coca-Cola." Wyckoff left that in. For the last two weeks before the primary, "The People Speak" played daily on every TV station in Oregon. Rockefeller surged in Oregon as Lodge slipped, though as much because of the ambassador's continued absence as anything else. As the Rockefeller slogan put it, "He Cared Enough to Come." Meanwhile Lodge's spot, with its tricky, implied Eisenhower endorsement, was killed after Ike protested. On May 15 Oregonians gave Rockefeller 94,190 votes, Lodge 79,169, and Goldwater 50,105, and Rockefeller and Goldwater moved on to California to face off. (California primary rules prohibited write-ins; that, plus the Oregon result, ended the Lodge campaign.)

The Rockefeller forces hired Spencer-Roberts, a newly formed Republican political consulting firm in California. The Spencer in the title is Stuart Spencer, an Arizonan who came to Southern California as a small child in the late 1920s, which makes him practically an original settler in on-the-move Los Angeles. Like Tony Schwartz, Spencer never set foot in an advertising agency before he became a media specialist. His training was in politics, first as a Young Republican at junior college in Los Angeles and later as a volunteer worker for the Los Angeles County Republican Committee. He found he liked politics so much he quit his job as director of Parks and Recreation for the town of Alhambra to work full time with the county committee, and he hasn't looked back since. Among the clients he has worked for in twenty years as a media manager are Ronald Reagan, Gerald Ford, and—perhaps his favorite—Nelson Rockefeller, whose portrait hung next to the desk when Spencer, now fifty, was interviewed for this book in the summer of 1983. The Rockefeller strategy, Spencer recalls, was not just to ignore Rockefeller's messy divorce but to concentrate on making Goldwater the issue: "Instead of defending Rockefeller's right to a love life, we just attacked Barry Goldwater. 'He's crazy, you can't trust him. What's he gonna do with the hydrogen bomb?' We got everybody thinking about all those scary things instead of the divorce." Spencer-Roberts spent $120,000—money, for Rockefeller, was no problem—on a mailing to all two million registered Republicans in the state. Entitled "Who Do You Want in the Room with the H Bomb?" it was a collection of Goldwater's more incendiary quotations.

The Rockefeller advertising campaign also ran against Goldwater's supporters, on the principle that, as Wyckoff put it, the campaign needed "a first-class villain to make a first-class hero in image-candidate terms." The villain he had in mind was the extremist—John Birchers and other reactionaries who were then a vocal force in California politics. Wyckoff knew that those Republicans would vote for Goldwater regardless of what Rockefeller did. Many Republican moderates, he felt, wouldn't vote at all—unless they were scared into it. The result was a half-hour program characterizing the extremists as the villains against whom Nelson Rockefeller was crusading in California. Wyckoff found several people who'd been threatened by the extremists. Some had received late-night phone calls and anonymous hate mail; one had seen his house firebombed. They were the film's "witnesses," interviewed by Dave Garroway, a popular TV personality and the first host of the *Today* show. Rockefeller filmed a three-minute opening, explaining that he felt it his duty to reveal the goals and tactics of this "incredible fringe on the American political scene." Nowhere in the film is Barry Goldwater mentioned. Instead, it builds on the feelings thought to exist in the audience—that Goldwater, the "ultra conservative" candidate, was supported by the extremists. "Extremists" was shown privately, for state leaders and Rockefeller advisers, and that was as far as it got. Some advisers believed Rockefeller, still leading in the polls, had the primary in his pocket, so why risk anything; some were embarrassed by the film, not wanting the Eastern Establishment–western conservative split aired so publicly. Others opposed the film because they had not been consulted on its production—the typical sort of organizational posturing seen over and over in campaigns. The film was shelved.

As it turned out, the election wasn't in Rockefeller's pocket. On the Saturday before the primary, as Stu Spencer puts it, "nature did us in": the new Mrs. Rockefeller gave birth to a baby boy. "It reopened the wounds of being a woman-chaser, of adultery, all the goddamn questions we had fuzzed over by accusing Goldwater of being a madman," says Spencer. At the same time that the reopened morality issue pushed voters away from Rockefeller, Goldwater tried to pull them to himself with a heavy, last-minute advertising schedule (which in part showed the happy, and intact, Goldwater family). On June 2 Goldwater won California with 1.12 million votes, to Rockefeller's 1.05 million. Wyckoff blamed the shelving of "Extremists" which, he believed, might have increased the turnout of moderate voters. Not so, insists Spencer; the film was "too raunchy—it would have backfired." Spencer blames the loss on the baby, and says he had urged the campaign to keep the birth secret. "My attitude was, if a Rockefeller can't hide a kid for three days, then he ain't a Rockefeller." Spencer admits that Rockefeller could not have won the nomination even with a California victory. "We knew that at the time, sure," says Spencer. "Maybe it's my athletic background. If I'm going through football season and we're zero and six with two games left, I still want to win those two."

In fact, though, California gave Goldwater victory. During the time he had been compiling a mixed record in the high-visibility primaries, he had been methodically gathering delegates in the less-publicized conventions and caucuses. But the primary fights succeeded only in making the convention, held in San Francisco, more bitter than it would otherwise have been. When Rockefeller rose to speak, the boos from the Goldwater forces practically drowned him out. Rockefeller returned the compliment by attacking extremism in politics and comparing extremists' tactics to those of the Communists and the Nazis. "Is it any wonder," Goldwater later wrote, "the voters were learning to fear a Goldwater presidency?" A vigorous campaign might have helped, but Goldwater continued to stumble. The campaign briefly hired Leo Burnett Co. of Chicago, then dumped the agency in favor of Erwin, Wasey, Ruthrauff & Ryan, of New York, whose past clients included Gulf, Tuborg beer, and Carnation milk (and, before the firm's merger, Adlai Stevenson).

"Peace, Little Girl"

Johnson, to no one's surprise, was renominated, and named Hubert Humphrey to be his running mate. The Democrats began and ended the campaign with the advertising help of Bill Bernbach of Doyle Dane Bernbach, the agency identified with the new advertising campaigns of Volkswagen and Avis. Johnson's White House assistants, Walter Jenkins, Jack Valenti, and Richard Goodwin, as well as Bill Moyers, all worked with the ad agency. Borrowing from Rockefeller, Spencer, and Wyckoff, their strategy was to attack Goldwater and put him on the defensive from the start. Then the campaign would switch to more positive advertising, praising Johnson's program. Positive ads were ultimately done—though they were few and, generally, forgettable. 1964 was the year of Daisy.

John Kennedy once said that victory has a hundred fathers, while defeat is an orphan. Bill Bernbach and DDB, the White House, and the Democratic National Committee have at times claimed the paternity of Daisy. They all deserve some credit (or blame), though the one individual most responsible creatively is Tony Schwartz. As Schwartz recalls it, in the summer of 1964 he got a call from Aaron Ehrlich, a DDB producer with whom Schwartz had collaborated for the American Airlines' "sounds of the cities" series. "We have a special product here we'd like you to work on," the executive said. "But we can't tell you what it is." He asked Schwartz to come over to DDB's offices in Midtown Manhattan. The agoraphobic Schwartz asked what floor they would be meeting on. "I have difficulty going to high floors," he said when he heard the answer. "But if you have a place on a lower floor, I'll come see you." Ehrlich said they could use a room on the seventh floor.

At the meeting Ehrlich held up a picture of Lyndon Johnson. "Would you work for this product?" he asked Schwartz. "Sure," Schwartz said. The agency men gave Schwartz some ideas to think about, among them an outline of a five-minute spot, beginning with voice-overs of an American missile countdown—

ten, nine, eight—and a nuclear bomb going off; then a Russian countdown—desyat, devyat, vosem—and a nuclear explosion; then, quick switches back and forth between the English and Russian language countdowns and explosions. DDB asked Schwartz to do a one-minute version of the spot. "I have the perfect thing for you," Schwartz replied, and pulled out the *World of Numbers* tape he had done for IBM, the one that the company and its agency had rejected. "I showed it to Ehrlich and the DDB people and said, 'You have a little child pulling the petals off a daisy. The camera goes in on the center of the daisy, and that becomes the explosion when it detonates.' They thought it was fantastic, and I went and listened to all the recent tapes of Johnson's Rose Garden speeches to find the right sound symbol. I found a quote that didn't make much sense on paper, but that worked emotionally on the listener when cut to the right length." Schwartz added Johnson's quote to his script and, he says, "They flipped for it." DDB chose a little girl and filmed her picking petals off the daisy and counting while walking along the Henry Hudson Parkway north of New York City (the camera, in DDB's execution of Schwartz's idea, moved in on the pupil of her eye rather than the center of the flower). Thus was born Daisy, or, to give the spot the title DDB used, "Peace, Little Girl":

VIDEO	AUDIO
Camera up on little girl in field, picking petals off a daisy.	Little girl [SOF]: "One, two, three, four, five, seven, six, six, eight, nine, nine—"
Girl looks up, startled; freeze frame on girl; move into ECU of her eye, until screen is black.	Man's voice, very loud as if heard over a loudspeaker at a test site: "Ten, nine, eight, seven, six, five, four, three, two, one—"

Cut to atom bomb exploding. Move into CU of explosion.	Sound of explosion.
	Johnson [VO]: "These are the stakes—to make a world in which all of God's children can live, or to go into the dark. We must either love each other, or we must die."
Cut to white letters on black background: "Vote for President Johnson on November 3."	Announcer [VO]: "Vote for President Johnson on November 3. The stakes are too high for you to stay home."

The Daisy spot ran only once, on CBS's *Monday Night at the Movies* on the night of September 7. According to Bill Moyers, the White House switchboard "lit up with calls protesting it, and Johnson called me and said, 'Jesus Christ, what in the world happened?' and I said, 'You got your point across, that's what.' He thought a minute and said, 'Well, I guess we did.' So Johnson was very pleased with it." Lyndon Johnson pronounced himself satisfied with Daisy because it had accomplished the purpose he had in mind. As Moyers remembers, Johnson worried that "Goldwater the radical was becoming Goldwater the respectable as the campaign progressed, and Johnson wanted to remind people of the earlier Goldwater, the man who talked about lobbing nuclear bombs in the men's room of the Kremlin." Moyers said he transmitted those instructions to Bill Bernbach. As for using the spot on Goldwater and the bomb only once, Moyers says that was the plan all along. "We had a variety of other messages we wanted to get out, about other Goldwater radical stands—for example, Social Security." Also, says Moyers, "given the White House's inexperience in this brand new game," the thinking was that ads shouldn't be repeated too often for the sake of the viewer.

1964: JOHNSON VS. GOLDWATER

Johnson "Daisy" Commercial

"One, two, three, four"

"Seven, six, six, eight, nine, nine"

Sound of explosion

"These are the stakes—to make a world in which all God's children can live"

"Ten, nine, eight, seven"

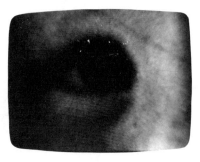

"Three, two, one"

"Or to go into the dark.
We must love each other,
or we must die"

"Vote for President John-
son on November 3. The
stakes are too high for
you to stay home"

If the thought that some people, upon second or third viewing, might regard Daisy as a low blow never occurred to the White House innocents, it did enter the minds of the angered Goldwater campaign staff. Perhaps 50 million people were watching NBC; those who hadn't seen Daisy quickly heard about it because of outraged Republican protests. Senator Everett Dirksen complained to the National Association of Broadcasters that Daisy violated "your widely heralded code of ethics." Republican National Committee chairman Dean Burch filed a formal complaint with the Fair Campaign Practices Committee, charging that Daisy constituted "libel against the Republican nominee." Burch said the GOP had received 1,300 calls of protest, including one from a Virginia woman who said her four-year-old daughter went to bed in tears after seeing it. Burch added: "This horror-type commercial is designed to arouse basic emotions and has no place in this campaign." Goldwater himself called Daisy "weird television advertising." Later, in his memoirs, he wrote: "Every time I saw that hideous Johnson TV commercial with the little girl, it saddened me to realize that all involved—the reporter, the spot writer, the producers, the advertising agency, and the candidate who was then incumbent President of the United States— valued political victory more than personal honesty." Moyers, now a correspondent with CBS News, acknowledges: "It was good advertising and bad politics."

More than a decade later Schwartz met and talked to F. Clifton White, Barry Goldwater's campaign aide, about the Daisy spot. White recalled how "very intelligent people would say to me: 'We just cannot use atomic weapons.' And I would then say to them, 'Well, now, do you know what the Senator said?' 'Yeah, he said he would use atomic weapons.' And I'd say, 'No, he didn't say he was going to use an atomic bomb. He did say that one of the weapons we *could* use in Vietnam was a tactical nuclear weapon for defoliating the forests. A tactical nuclear weapon is like a small bomb, not a big one. . . . Its purpose is to defoliate, to take the leaves off, so that we could see them down there.'

But all the time I'm going through this explanation, the person is standing there, nodding his head, and saying, 'Yeah, but we can't drop the bomb, Clif.' It was so totally emotional. . . ."

Schwartz values White's assessment because it matches so closely his own ideas about inner feelings in advertising messages. As he observes in *The Responsive Chord*, "the best political commercials are similar to Rorschach patterns. They do not tell the viewer anything. They surface his feelings and provide a context for him to express those feelings." Daisy is the prime example, playing "on the underlying public feeling that Goldwater spoke for the use of tactical atomic weapons, whereas Johnson was against the use of any nuclear weapons. When people hear 'atomic weapons,' they don't hear the word 'tactical.' " Goldwater's name was never mentioned, but the spot made people think, "Whose finger do I want on the trigger?" Interestingly, Daisy still confuses people. Talking to us, Rosser Reeves misremembered it as showing a mushroom cloud coming from behind Goldwater's head. One reason for the confusion may be that a few days later a second Democratic spot ran, almost as harsh and naming Goldwater specifically:

VIDEO	AUDIO
Camera up on CU of little girl, blond, oblivious to camera, licking ice cream cone.	Woman announcer [VO]: "Do you know what people used to do? They used to explode atomic bombs in the air. Now, children should have lots of vitamin A and calcium, but they shouldn't have any strontium 90 or cesium 137. These things come from atomic bombs, and they're radioactive. They can make

you die. Do you know what people finally did? They got together and signed a nuclear test ban treaty, and then the radioactive poisons started to go away. But now, there is a man who wants to be president of the United States, and he doesn't like this treaty. He's fought against it. He even voted against it. He wants to go on testing more bombs. His name is Barry Goldwater, and if he's elected, they might start testing all over again.

Cut to slide: white letters against black background, "VOTE FOR PRESIDENT JOHNSON ON NOVEMBER 3."

Vote for President Johnson on November 3. The stakes are too high for you to stay home."

Like Daisy, the spot was shown just once; unlike Daisy, Doyle Dane Bernbach was completely responsible for the idea. It too was criticized. Another spot, based on the crosscut idea Ehrlich showed Schwartz, eventually was broadcast as well. After the countdowns and explosions the scene switches to shafts of sunlight shining through cumulous clouds; John F. Kennedy's voice, as if from beyond the grave, explains the need for a test ban treaty. Finally, it cuts to Johnson, discussing "the stark reality of nuclear power." It too never mentions Goldwater by name, though Johnson refers to "those who" oppose the test ban treaty. A similar DDB spot takes on Goldwater explicitly:

VIDEO	AUDIO
Black screen, then atomic blast. Cut to second blast. Cut to third blast.	Announcer [VO]: "On October 24, 1963, Barry Goldwater said of the nuclear bomb, 'merely another weapon.'
Blast fills screen.	*Merely another weapon?*
Fade to slide: white letters against black background, "Vote for President Johnson on Nov. 3."	Vote for President Johnson. The stakes are too high for you to stay home."

In case this spot didn't make the point clear, DDB also did "Hot Line":

VIDEO	AUDIO
Camera up on ECU of telephone. Like a motel room phone, it has no dial, and it has a red light (which is flashing) on the lower right-hand corner. In the center is a round white card—where the room number would normally be—labeled "WHITE HOUSE."	Sound of phone buzzing. Announcer [VO, over buzzing]: "This particular phone only rings in a serious crisis. Leave it in the hands of a man who has proven himself responsible.
Cut to slide: white letters against black background, "VOTE FOR PRESIDENT JOHNSON ON NOVEMBER 3."	Vote for President Johnson on November 3. The stakes are too high for you to stay home."

In its simple construction "Hot Line" belongs to the same minimalist style of DDB's "Think Small" campaign for Volkswagen.

The Democrats also produced a thirty-minute program on nuclear weapons policies, independent of the DDB emotion-based campaign. Aired on election eve on ABC, the program was sponsored by Scientists, Engineers, and Physicians for Johnson-Humphrey, and produced by David Garth—a young New Yorker who had been involved in the Draft Stevenson movement in 1960. The title, remembers Garth, was "Sorry, Senator Goldwater, We Just Can't Risk It," and its overall intellectual tone was set by the appearance of such academics as Jerome Wiesner of MIT and Herbert York of the University of California at Santa Barbara.

Looking back on the DDB advertising effort, it seems that the overkill in 1964 was Johnson's, not Goldwater's. One spot quoted Goldwater as wishing the country could "saw off the Eastern Seaboard and let it float out into the Atlantic," followed by sounds of a saw on wood, and then a heavy object floating out to sea. Just as DDB's advertising sought to portray Goldwater as separating an alien East from the rest of America, so too did it try to separate Goldwater from his own party. Johnson himself declares that "the opposition" represents "not a conservative philosophy, not a Republican philosophy; it is a radically different philosophy." Another spot shows posters of the other GOP candidates earlier in the year, with the voice-over quoting their remarks against Goldwater. "If you're a Republican with serious doubts about Barry Goldwater," the voice-over concludes, "you're in good company." Still another, "Confessions of a Republican," shows an earnest, well-dressed man sitting in a chair, talking to the camera—seemingly spontaneously, stopping and starting, gesturing, stuttering. He is, he says, a Republican, but he has his doubts. "Men with strange ideas" are working for Goldwater; "weird groups" are supporting him. During the three-minute spot the man is seen struggling toward his decision, which he reaches at the end: "I think my party made a bad mistake in

San Francisco—and I'm going to have to vote against that mistake." One of the harshest spots focused on one "weird group" behind Goldwater. To film of white-sheeted Klansmen and burning crosses, the spot quotes Robert Cleal of the Alabama Ku Klux Klan as saying, "The majority of people in Alabama hate niggerism, Catholicism, Judaism. . . ." The announcer goes on to quote another Cleal remark: "I like Barry Goldwater. He needs our help." The most heavily aired DDB spot was tame by comparison, but it focused on an issue of specific importance to millions of voters:

VIDEO	AUDIO
Camera up on two hands and open wallet. Hands take from wallet a stack of photos, IDs, and credit cards. On top is a photo of a young boy. Hands go through cards until Social Security card; they put the others down and quickly rip the Social Security card in two, and drop it on the table. Hands disappear. Camera moves in to CU of torn card.	Announcer [VO]: "On at least seven occasions, Senator Barry Goldwater said that he would change the present Social Security system. But even his running mate William Miller admits that Senator Goldwater's voluntary plan would destroy your Social Security. President Johnson
Fade to slide: white letters against black background, "Vote for President Johnson on Nov. 3."	is working to strengthen Social Security. Vote for him on November 3."

With all this advertising the early White House fear of the rehabilitation of Goldwater was replaced with a new worry. Johnson's lead in the polls became so commanding that the Democrats feared many Johnson voters would complacently stay home on

1964: JOHNSON VS. GOLDWATER

Johnson "Ice Cream" Commercial

"Now, children . . . shouldn't have any strontium 90"

Johnson "KKK" Spot

"I like Barry Goldwater. He needs our help"

Goldwater "Conversation at Gettysburg" Spot

"Well, Barry, in my mind, this is actual tommyrot"

Goldwater Talking Head Commercial

"We need a clear and resolute policy, one which is based on peace through strength"

election day. The paid media began to urge people to vote. One fifteen-second spot consisted of footage of lightning, rain pouring down on streets, and people bending to keep hold of wind-whipped umbrellas. "If it should rain on November 3," says the announcer, "please get wet—go to the polls and vote for President Johnson."

A deluge did come on election day, sweeping the Republican ticket away. The name of Goldwater's running mate became a trivia question in the years to come. The Democrats had done many things right in their campaign, and right things broke for them. But Goldwater also shared blame for his debacle. Over the years he had made a series of unwise statements; some were ambiguous, lending themselves to chilling interpretations. For example, he did remark that American missiles were so accurate that it would be possible to "lob one into the men's room of the Kremlin"; but he did not actually propose to do so. His campaign slogan, "In Your Heart, You Know He's Right, " was turned on him: "In Your Heart, You Know He Might." By October polls found that voters, by a five to one margin, felt Goldwater was likelier than Johnson to start a nuclear war. "My candidate had been branded a bomb-dropper—and I couldn't figure out how to lick it," said Denison Kitchel, Goldwater's personal aide. "And the advertising people, people who could sell anything, toothpaste or soap or automobiles—when it came to a political question like this, they couldn't offer anything either."

Enter Ronald Reagan

They did try. On September 22, for instance, the campaign aired a half-hour program called "Conversation at Gettysburg" (a sixty-second excerpt was also run as a spot). The program was a chat between Ike and Goldwater. The candidate says, "Our opponents are referring to us as warmongers," and he asks Eisenhower his opinion. "Well, Barry, in my mind, this is actual tommyrot." Goldwater had hoped, by confronting the nuclear bomber image head-on, to minimize it—much as Kennedy had done with his

Catholicism in 1960. But the Goldwater-Eisenhower show lacked the confrontational nature of Kennedy facing the ministers; it came off instead as a tedious conversation between two men who agreed with each other. Johnson, who liked to carry opinion poll results in his pocket to show reporters, began carrying TV ratings that showed the Ike-Goldwater conversation attracted far fewer viewers than the competing programs, *Petticoat Junction* and *Peyton Place*.

In a spot called "Imprudent" Goldwater also tried to draw the Ike mantle about himself:

VIDEO

Camera up on medium shot of Goldwater sitting at edge of desk, reminiscent of Nixon's 1960 ads. He chuckles while the announcer speaks.

Cut to CU.

Cut to original medium shot. Goldwater stands and walks behind desk, sits in chair, and

AUDIO

Announcer [VO]: "Mr. Goldwater, what's this about your being called imprudent and impulsive?"

Goldwater [SOF]: "Well, you know, it seems to me that the really impulsive and imprudent president is the one who is so indecisive that he has no policy at all—

with the result that potential aggressors are tempted to move because they think that we lack the will to defend freedom.

"Now there was nothing impulsive or imprudent about Dwight Eisenhower when he

puts on glasses while continuing to talk.	moved with firmness and clear purpose in Lebanon and the Formosa Straits. Compare these Eisenhower policies with the appalling actions of this administration—in Laos and the Bay of Pigs, in Berlin and the Congo.
Cut to CU.	"We need a clear and resolute policy, one which is based on peace through strength. Only when we have such a policy will we reclaim our rightful role as the leader of the free world."
Freeze frame. Letters appear, superimposed across bottom of screen: "In Your Heart . . . You Know He's Right."	Announcer [VO]: "In your heart, you know he's right.
Then cut to white letters against gray background: "VOTE FOR BARRY GOLDWATER."	Vote for Barry Goldwater."

Misjudgments proliferated in the Goldwater campaign. When the former actor and GE spokesman Ronald Reagan came forward, offering to make a nationwide TV speech for Goldwater, the campaign strategists turned him down cold. They said they didn't like what Reagan proposed to say. Several of Reagan's wealthy California friends, however, footed the bill for Reagan to give the speech in a statewide hookup with a fund-raising trailer at the end. That raised enough money to televise the speech nationally, without any help from the Goldwater campaign. Still Goldwater's advisers objected. Finally, Reagan called Goldwater and asked him to look at the speech before making a final decision. Goldwater didn't call back, which the Californians took to indicate assent. The speech, called "A Time for Choosing," was aired October 27 on NBC, and those Republican loyalists who heard its surefire applause lines found themselves wishing Reagan were their presidential nominee. It included touches of the later Reagan style, such as anecdotes about the Great Society gone awry—it seems a woman with six children planned to divorce her husband, a laborer who earned $250 a month, because she would be eligible for $350 per month on welfare. The speech closes with a peroration that borrowed cadences from Thomas Jefferson, Franklin Roosevelt, and John F. Kennedy:

VIDEO	AUDIO
Reagan, addressing camera.	Reagan [SOF]: "You and I have a rendezvous with destiny. We can preserve for our children this, the last best hope of man on earth, or we can sentence them to take the first step into a thousand years of darkness. If we fail, at least let our children, and our children's children, say of us we justified our brief moment here. We did all that could be done."

The Goldwater campaign preempted the comedy review *That Was The Week That Was* five times in the six weeks before the elections, to air "Conversation at Gettysburg" and other half-hour GOP productions. (The Republicans wanted the sixth week too, but the Democrats had bought a one-minute spot during the program and refused to relinquish it.) Goldwater's appearances

probably hurt *That Was The Week That Was* more than they hurt
Johnson; during that preemption period the competing *Peyton
Place* pulled ahead in the Tuesday night ratings, where it remained
after the election.

To be sure, the Republican campaigners tried their own televised rough stuff. In a memo to the candidate, Clifton White
proposed a half-hour film that would depict the nation's moral
decay under Johnson. Goldwater gave him the go-ahead, and
$45,000 was spent compiling the film. Its stark footage included
news coverage of urban riots, a woman in a topless swimsuit,
and a Lincoln Continental speeding down a dirt road with beer
cans flying from the windows. (This last was a visual reference
to stories about how Johnson drove his big limo down on his
Pedernales ranch.) The film, called "Choice," was sent to NBC
for prescreening. Robert Kintner, the network president, demanded that certain shots, including the topless woman, be de-
leted. Kintner called "Choice" an "appallingly tasteless
production," and other previewers considered it racist. But some
members of the Republican National Committee praised it highly;
one Republican leader said it was "the greatest political film"
he had ever seen. Goldwater himself finally viewed "Choice"
and told White, "I'm not going to be made out as a racist. You
can't show it." From this, campaign strategist White concluded
that his candidate had in effect given up, with the election still
a month away. Still, the Goldwater campaign managed to produce
a spot to make the point "Choice" had been intended to make:

VIDEO	AUDIO
Camera up on series of shots of city park, bustling, well kept. Children playing ball; people walking; picnic tables.	Announcer [VO]: "What has happened to America? We have had the good sense to create lovely parks—
Cut to park at night, empty.	but we're afraid to use them after dark.

Cut to exterior, large museum. People walk by.

We build libraries and galleries to hold the world's greatest treasury of art—

Cut to seedy newsstand.

and we permit the world's greatest collection of smut to be freely available everywhere.

Cut to U.S. Capitol; cut to cartoon of man, labeled "Bobby Baker," reaching through open top of Capitol.

The highest echelons of government are embroiled in scandals—

Cut to medium shot of heavyset, shifty man, chewing gum and looking away from camera, identified in super as "Billie Sol Estes."

that are cynically swept under the rug."

Cut to medium shot of Goldwater, standing, hands clasped. He addresses the camera.

Goldwater [SOF]: "The national morality, by example and by persuasion, should begin at the White House, and have the good influence to reach out to every corner of the land. Now this is not the case today because our country has lacked leadership that treats public office as a public trust. I pledge that Bill Miller and I will restore to America a dedication to principle and to conscience among its public servants."

Frame freezes. Super appears
in white letters: "IN YOUR
HEART . . . YOU KNOW
HE'S RIGHT." Then cut to
slide: white letters against
gray background, "VOTE
FOR BARRY GOLDWATER."

Announcer [VO]: "In your
heart, you know he's right.
Vote for Barry Goldwater."

In its production values the morality spot was unusual, for
Goldwater's campaign ran relatively few spots, and nearly all of
them consisted solely of Goldwater's talking head. Most of the
money went into longer speeches. Goldwater spent a million
dollars on network time in the campaign's final month. The
Democrats, however, also staged a similar final-month drive—
and theirs, consisting largely of spots, reached a greater audience.
In all, the two campaigns spent $11.1 million on broadcast ad-
vertising: the Democrats $4.7 million; the Republicans $6.4 million. Yet the largest audience for any political broadcast of 1964
was less than a quarter the size of that for the first Nixon-
Kennedy debate.

Perhaps because the race seemed over from the start, the level
of interest had sagged early. Just as Stevenson had used a radio-
age technique at the beginning of the television era, Goldwater
had followed outmoded advertising tactics at the moment the
art was changing. Schwartz suggests that Goldwater should have
switched to the new styles rather than fought them. He says,
"Goldwater could have defused Daisy by saying, 'I think that
the danger of total nuclear war should be the theme of the
campaign this year, and I'd like to pay half the cost of running
this commercial.' If he had, the commercial would not have been
perceived as being against him. He would have changed the
feelings and assumptions stored within us. Instead, it was like
the woman who goes to the psychiatrist and is shown a Rorschach

pattern and says, 'Doctor, I didn't come here to be shown dirty pictures!' The Daisy commercial evoked Mr. Goldwater's pro-bomb statements. They were the dirty pictures in the public's mind."

HIGH-TECH POLITICS

CHAPTER 9

Toward the end of the 1960s when American servicemen died by the hundreds each week in Vietnam, when inner cities burned and elite campuses rioted, politics seemed too important to be left to politicians, and movements for reform and change—outsiders pushing to get inside—took hold within the two-party system. The Democrats in recent decades had proclaimed themselves the party of the people, and "the people" tried to make real the rhetoric. Reformers—younger, more female and more black and brown than traditional party workers—were able to capture the Democratic party apparatus temporarily in 1972. Even the Republican party, bastion of conservative ways, was shaken by upheavals between East and West, the Yankee and Cowboy wings. These struggles for control within each party played out in the presidential primaries and general elections of 1968, 1972, 1976, and 1980; they help explain a good part of the dynamics of national electoral politics over the past sixteen years, and no discussion of media campaigning can be complete without them.

The reformers' efforts intended to open up the parties' presidential nominating process, for example, have led to a straight-line increase in the number of important primary contests from three in 1964 to twelve in 1972 to thirty-five in 1980. These primaries replaced the "bad" state party conventions and caucuses—a move widely hailed as bringing more democracy to the process. It also brought more paid advertising and more television marketing of candidates. When there were six or eight primaries, Raymond Price, a veteran of two Nixon presidential campaigns, explained to us, it was possible for the candidate to spend two or three weeks campaigning in each state, meeting voters and exploring issues. Now, with thirty or forty primaries, candidates can spend at most a few days in each state and must rely on heavy TV advertising to make their points. The retail personal politicking of the past has more and more been pushed aside by wholesale television marketing.

In the 1960s few of the reformers envisioned making campaigns more dependent on advertising and marketing. Communications technology was rapidly growing more complex and more pervasive while promising more flexibility. Color television became standard in the 1960s, increasing the appeal of television's entertainments. The old style recording system of sound on film (sound narration put down on the same piece of film that was recording the picture) was replaced by the more flexible double-chain method (sound and sight recorded separately and then mixed and synchronized). Cheaper, easier-to-edit videotape and lighter, more portable video cameras began displacing film stock and cumbersome film cameras. Zoom lenses increased the range of shots available to camera people. Electronic equipment opened up new possibilities for generating words and graphics on the screen. Directors could electronically split screens; frames could be squeezed, zoomed, rotated, and exploded on and off the picture tube. While several of these developments grew out of work in television news organizations, all were soon adapted to the needs of making TV commercials. This technology became an important part of the new advertising.

The arrival of this sophisticated new technology helped change communications messages, just as the influx of new people and the arrival of more clever selling styles were making major contributions. But perhaps the most critical shift in the communications arts came in the way that advertisers began to regard the audience for their products and services. In the first five decades of the century, advertising tended to treat the market as a mass—Bruce Barton's undifferentiated Americans. Albert Lasker of Lord & Thomas, one of the few Jews to make it to the top of the agency business in the old days, suggested to his staff in the 1920s that advertising was a part of an acculturation process that was "making a homogeneous people" out of a nation of immigrants. By the end of the 1960s, however, advertisers began to prize people for their special characteristics, and Bruce Barton's despised special interest groups began to be courted. Thanks to computers and survey research, the ratings services like Nielsen and Arbitron no longer just informed advertisers how many people were watching their programs; now they told viewership by age, sex, region (and eventually, zip code and neighborhood—which revealed clues to income and education). The buying of advertising spot time came to resemble a political transaction—we offer a romantic movie, we get younger women who purchase cosmetics; we offer the network news, we get older homeowners who vote.

Among the chief tools of demographics marketing was the public opinion poll. Gallup, Roper, and others had scientifically charted the electoral races of major candidates since 1936. The candidates themselves started investing time and money in their own private polling operations in the 1960s, another development that nudged the old-line party leaders farther from the center of campaign management. Polling became a big business, using elaborate attitudinal surveys, pretesting of campaign themes and commercials, and focus groups. In the 1968 Hubert Humphrey campaign the development of an advertising strategy was hampered when Humphrey couldn't find $10,000 to pay for a public opinion survey already taken (the pollster refused to turn over his data without getting his money). Today surveys can cost up to $30,000 for one national sampling, and no respectable campaign organization would proceed without having assured itself of regular—and in the case of Ronald Reagan in the 1980 campaign, daily—samplings of public opinion.

These developments in television production, in marketing methods, and in survey polls created the high-technology political communications of today. High-tech politics has had two profound consequences for electoral campaigns. First, high tech makes politics more expensive. By the time the democratic reforms of the 1960s had taken hold in the 1970s and 1980s, campaign dollars had to be ample enough to stretch across dozens of primaries while paying for the expensive new tools of the trade. The price of reaching a thousand people by television, known as the CPM, or cost per thousand, became a standard measurement of television expenditures. For example, during the Nelson Rockefeller years as "permanent" governor of New York—he served four terms between 1958 and 1974—the CPM figure for reaching a thousand New Yorkers with television messages was estimated by his staff to be $100, or about ten cents a household. This CPM could be counted, from one point of view, as a bargain—how else could the candidate visit so many people? But given the vast number of TV households in a megastate, perhaps 10 million in New York during the 1960s, this meant that at least $1 million (in 1960s dollars) had to be allocated to achieve just one hit, or time that each voter theoretically sees one commercial, and most candidates want five or six or more hits. By the 1970s, with candidates using television as if they were Rockefellers, no one could afford *not* to do it, and the CPM became an onerous, if common, burden—because everyone isn't a Rockefeller.

The second consequence of high-tech politics was to ensure the dominant position within campaigns of the new media specialists. Old-line political operatives and advisers had jealously, and by and large successfully, protected their authority when the first wave of advertising agency people came in during the 1950s. The struggles between the political people and the agency people were often bitter. Their differences extended beyond the normal grabbing for power present in every campaign; there was a kind of clash of different cultures and styles of work. Ad people complained that the political people were disorganized: "Fifteen people in a room shouting thirty different things," a Doyle Dane Bernbach account man would characterize the campaign strategy meetings for Hubert Humphrey in 1968. The political people in turn complained that the admen were at once arrogant and ignorant: "They didn't know the issues, and they didn't want to get too involved," a Humphrey man said of DDB. By the end of the 1960s the struggle was for practical purposes resolved when the new media specialists came to power, the ad agencies all but dropped out, and the political people reconciled themselves to sharing authority in the campaign.

THE NEW NIXON AND THE OLD HUMPHREY

CHAPTER 10

Early in 1968 Lyndon Johnson decided he wouldn't run again, Richard Nixon decided he would, and the first high-tech presidential race was on. The men who would make that race go, however, were still in the stands, at that time not much more than spectators. Roger Ailes, then twenty-seven, was the executive producer of the *Mike Douglas Show*. Joseph Napolitan, a Democrat from Massachusetts, had worked with Larry O'Brien for John Kennedy; later, by Napolitan's own account, he had played "a late and insignificant role" in Robert Kennedy's 1964 senate race in New York. Robert Squier, born in 1934, a graduate of the University of Minnesota, was working as an assistant to the president of National Educational Television in New York. By November each of these men would be in the middle of the presidential race.

Nixon, after his "last press conference" performance in 1962, moved to the enemy East and went into law to make some money. He got a new tailor, taught himself the social graces of a downtown New York lawyer, earned big dollars—and missed the old days. Soon Nixon began laying the groundwork for a second try at the White House. He hired two speechwriters: in 1966 Patrick Buchanan, a conservative writer for the *St. Louis Globe-Democrat*, and in 1967 Raymond K. Price, Jr., a Yale graduate and former editorial page editor of the *New York Herald Tribune*. And Nixon tried to generate loyalty from Republican office-holders, by campaigning hard for them in the 1966 midterm elections. His potential competitors for party leader were out of commission; Ike was too sick and Goldwater too unpopular. But there was a possible new challenger arising in, of all places, Nixon's home state.

Ronald Reagan had moved from B movies to PR in the late 1950s, delivering free-enterprise speeches on General Electric's behalf. His televised speech for Barry Goldwater in 1964 had gotten Reagan started in his political career, and in his first try for public office, Reagan in 1966 did what Nixon had failed to do—he beat Edmund G. "Pat" Brown, the incumbent California governor. Soon Reagan and his advisers were talking about taking a run for the Republican presidential nomination. Greg Snazelle, a TV spot producer, and John Mercer, vice-president of a San Francisco ad agency, Meltzer, Aron & Lemen, had worked for Reagan in 1966. Their spots, appealing to liberals, were run in northern California. In late 1967 their first assignment was to produce a half-hour film biography of Reagan. One sequence showed a series of victorious California gubernatorial candidates: Pat Brown, victorious in 1958 over Bill Knowland; Brown again, victorious in 1962 over Richard Nixon; and, finally, Ronald Reagan, victorious in 1966 over Brown. It was like the children's game, rock-scissors-paper—Brown beats Knowland and Nixon; Reagan beats Brown; clearly, Reagan beats Nixon. The bio, called "Ronald Reagan: Citizen Governor," depicted Reagan as a public speaker, labor organizer, hard-working governor, successful candidate (but not as a Hollywood actor).

The Man in the Arena

From the outset it was clear that Nixon's would be a TV campaign. In June of 1967 he received a memo from H. R. "Bob" Haldeman, a former executive of the J. Walter Thompson agency in Los Angeles, who was chief advance man in Nixon's 1960 presidential campaign and manager of his 1962 California campaign. "The time has come for political campaigning—its techniques and strategies—to move out of the dark ages and into the brave new world of the omnipresent eye," Haldeman declared. A candidate could personally be seen by perhaps a few hundred thousand voters, Haldeman argued, while on TV he could reach millions. Furthermore the nonstop pace of personal campaigning leaves the candidate "punchy. . . . He has no time to think, to study his opponent's strategy and statements, to develop his own strategy and statements. No wonder the almost inevitable campaign dialogue borders so near the idiot level." Television could help the candidate avoid that; it could also help the candidate minimize contact with the snapping news hounds of the press. Haldeman urged Nixon to move into the "brave new world" and make strong use of more effective television formats.

Other voices offered similar counsel. In the fall of 1967 Nixon appeared on the *Mike Douglas Show*, a then-popular celebrity interview program originating at KYW-TV, the Westinghouse station in Philadelphia. The executive producer of the show, brash and all of twenty-seven years old, was Roger Ailes. Ailes had reason to be confident; in the three years he worked for Douglas, he helped lead the show to its highest ratings and highest number of outlets. But he was growing tired of doing live TV day after day and was thinking of a change. Private citizen Richard Nixon, Ailes recalled during an interview with us, "appeared as a guest on the show, and he was put in my office to avoid waiting with the other guests—I think we had a stripper, or snake charmer, or somebody else on that day, and everybody said, gee, you can't put Nixon in there." Nixon was accompanied by his aide, and later White House assistant, Dwight

Chapin. The men talked about TV: "Nixon said it's too bad a
guy has to rely on a gimmick to get elected, meaning TV. I got
into an argument with him. I told him TV wasn't a gimmick,
that it's the most powerful means of communication ever devised
by man, that nobody would ever be elected to major office again
without presenting himself reasonably well on TV, that as in
anything else success requires a working knowledge of the media
and a specialist to help get the candidates through—because
otherwise they just are not aware. This got his attention more
than anything else." Ailes says he is quite sure he wasn't looking
for a job and wasn't looking to go into politics; mostly he felt
cocky enough to argue with the former vice-president. Later
Chapin would tell Ailes that was one of the things that Nixon
really liked about him. A few days later Ailes got a call from
Nixon's New York office suggesting he come to New York and
meet with the media group that was being formed for the Nixon
campaign.

In September Nixon's law partner Leonard Garment arranged
for Harry Treleaven to do the campaign spot advertisements. A
former vice-president of J. Walter Thompson in New York, Treleaven had run the 1966 congressional campaign of George Bush
in Texas. Bush had spent 80 percent of his Texas-sized budget
on advertising and won, becoming the first Republican to represent Houston. With Ailes and Treleaven in place, the fall was
a time of memos and meetings. In one memo Treleaven recorded
his thoughts on Nixon's primary campaign ad strategy: "Cuteness,
obliqueness, way-outness, slickness—any obvious gimmicks that
say 'Madison Avenue at work here' should be avoided. They
could, indeed, result in a public backlash that would hurt our
candidate. Imaginative approaches, contemporary techniques—
yes. But we must beware of 'overactivity,' and make sure that
the basic seriousness of our purpose shows plainly in everything
we do." Pat Buchanan, whose background was in newspapers,
worried about the prying nature of television cameras, particularly
in the hands of TV reporters, and responded by memo: "We

don't need TV to prove we are the most experienced, most qualified and most able; we don't need TV to get ourselves known; we don't need it to demonstrate we have the looks and the glibness. Do we need the damn thing at all and do we want it? Yes. But only to do the job we want it to do. We want it controlled."

The divergent voices were pulled together after a meeting arranged by Frank Shakespeare, a smooth, self-assured broadcast executive on leave from the business and sales side of the CBS television network. Shakespeare had a group of Nixon advisers visit the CBS library to look at whatever film of Nixon existed in its archives. Ray Price recalls, "We wanted to see how he came across on TV. After several hours of viewing we found the more spontaneous he was, the better." This translated into television encounters between Nixon and citizen questioners — a kind of press conference, without the hostile press. Nixon, writing about his Checkers speech, had used the Theodore Roosevelt "man in the arena" quote about the doughty, bloodied figure. Nixon saw himself as that fighter; so did his media advisers. That was the real Nixon — why not accept it and build positively on it? The "Man in the Arena" tag stuck for the new format, and Roger Ailes was put in charge of producing and directing the programs.

Nixon wasn't the only man in the arena. California Governor Reagan tentatively pecked away at Nixon from the Republican right, while New York Governor Nelson Rockefeller bore in stealthily from the left. Rockefeller tried to earn his party's presidential nomination without entering any primaries. The strategy required moving the national poll figures and convincing the party that Nixon's nomination would be disastrous. The campaign brought together the ad team that had won Rockefeller's reelection in 1966 in New York, some fifty people including Myron McDonald, a marketing man, and Dr. Herta Herzog, a sociologist. To influence the national public-opinion polls, Rockefeller planned a series of sixty-second spots in thirty key markets. It would begin in mid-June and reach its peak ten days before the convention opened—when the last poll interviews by the Gallup organization would be taking place. Never one to think small, Rockefeller set aside $4.5 million: $2 million for TV spots, $1 million for network TV, and $1.5 million for newspaper inserts. That left only the question of what to say. The Rockefeller group had in hand research from a February poll, listing twenty-one problems from most to least important in the eyes of the voters. It was, by and large, a conservative list, with "Vietnam" first and "Rebuilding the cities" last. Rockefeller's ad people, however, confounded the conservative political strategy implicit in this research by doing a spot about racial justice:

VIDEO

AUDIO

Camera up on slum street, night.

Rockefeller [VO]: "Three thousand black men are among those brave Americans who have died so far in Vietnam. One hundred thousand black men will come home from Vietnam. What will they make of America, these men who risk their lives for the American dream, and come home to find the American slumber? What will they make of the slums where, too often, jobs are as rare as hope? This is Nelson Rockefeller, and I say they deserve more than this. I say they deserve an equal chance. They deserve decent housing, decent jobs, and the schooling and training to fill these jobs. To those who cry, 'We can't afford it,' I say, 'We can't afford *not* to do it.' To those who cry, 'Law and order,' I say, 'To keep law and order, there must be—

Black man suddenly appears from shadows and approaches camera.

justice and opportunity.' "

The ad created consternation among some Republicans. Viewers couldn't really tell who was coming toward them, went one complaint, or what his intentions were. But the ad people justified their liberal efforts as designed to move nationwide public opinion polls, regardless of their impact on Republican sensibilities. The result of the campaign, in any event, was ambiguous. The Harris poll showed Rockefeller gaining; Gallup didn't. One or the other poll was simply wrong. At the convention the delegates voted Gallup, and Nixon.

Television Joins the Party

On the Democratic side, first Eugene McCarthy of Minnesota and then Robert Kennedy, the junior senator from New York and brother of the fallen John Kennedy, challenged the sitting president. Johnson then amazed everyone by deciding not to run for reelection. In retrospect Johnson's decision shouldn't have been as surprising as it was: for months the President couldn't move around the country without attracting crowds of anti-Vietnam War demonstrators; how was he to campaign beyond friendly Air Force bases and the Rose Garden? McCarthy's effort was more moral quest than political campaign. He relied on volunteers, including ad agency people who refunded the usual commission on media buying, making more time buys possible.

Kennedy chose the "new wave" agency of Papert, Koenig, Lois, and PKL in turn engaged the filmmaker Charles Guggenheim to produce spots. Guggenheim, an intense, private man, began his media career as a messenger at CBS Radio in New York in 1948, and then got into television working for the packager of *$64,000 Question*. Over the next ten years he established himself as a distinguished documentary maker. His work *Nine from Little Rock*, about a group of black students who integrated Central High School of Little Rock, Arkansas, with the help of Army troops, won an Academy Award in 1964.

The leading Democratic candidate, Vice-President Humphrey, signed on Doyle Dane Bernbach, Johnson's agency in 1964. Bill Bernbach put twenty-nine-year-old Arie L. Kopelman in charge of the Humphrey account. Kopelman had come to DDB in 1964, after working for the package goods giant, Procter & Gamble. He had never been involved in a political campaign before. "The whole thing was very exciting," Kopelman told us. "I was single, could put in the hours, didn't mind doing any travel necessary. The only problem was, I really didn't know a lot about Humphrey." Kopelman from the start was less excited by the political men around Humphrey, particularly Fred Harris, the forceful Oklahoma senator, who, Kopelman recalls, "just overwhelmed everyone. He was the only person I'd ever met, to that point, who wore a belt and suspenders at the same time." The political people, for their part, didn't like the fact that several DDB people were volunteering for McCarthy on the side. Kopelman tried to minimize the situation, arguing that it wasn't as if employees were "working on Volkswagen here during the day and working for Renault at home at night." Humphrey's strategy was to bypass the primaries, leaving Kennedy and McCarthy to battle it out state by state. The impoverished McCarthy campaign did little TV advertising, but money was no problem for Kennedy. Guggenheim made one spot that virtually gave Kennedy credit for averting nuclear disaster. In it Roger Hilsman, one of President Kennedy's advisers, recalls the Cuban Missile Crisis. Robert Kennedy, Hilsman says, "brought more wisdom to that table than any other. . . . I think that Robert Kennedy deserves more credit than any other of President Kennedy's advisers for the fact that we're here, alive, today." With Guggenheim's spots running heavily, Kennedy won the Nebraska primary but lost in Oregon. In the final match in California, Kennedy took forty-six percent of the vote to McCarthy's forty-two percent. Leaving the Los Angeles ballroom where he had made his victory speech, Kennedy was fatally shot.

All of Guggenheim's work, his spots and his documentaries, were as if preparation for *Robert Kennedy Remembered*, his tribute shown at the 1968 Democratic party convention just a few weeks after the assassination. The Chicago convention was chaotic: city police clubbing longhairs; protesters on Michigan Avenue, chanting "Ho—Ho—Ho/Ho Chi Minh's/Going to win," demonstrations and bitterness on the floor (including Chicago Mayor Richard J. Daley yelling "Fuck you!" at Connecticut Senator Abe Ribicoff on national television)—Theodore White as retold by Nelson Algren. Guggenheim made the documentary in less than a month, working twelve to fourteen hours a day, six days a week, in order, he once said, "to put the importance of Robert Kennedy's life upon the conscience of the convention." He did the film in black and white, using techniques that would become standard in the life-style commercials of the next decade: Kennedy campaigning, Kennedy playing with his children, Kennedy confronting critics in Japan, Kennedy walking on the beach, with brother Edward Kennedy's eulogy as the closing voice-over. On the convention floor when it was over, some people cried, others applauded the empty screen, and still others waved signs ("We miss you, Bobby") and chanted ("We want Bobby"). "Even dead and on film," Norman Mailer would write, "he was better and more moving than anything which has happened in their convention." (The film later earned Guggenheim his second Oscar.)

When Humphrey won the nomination, the *Chicago Daily News* ran a banner on page one: "HUMPHREY IN A SHAMBLES."

With George Wallace of Alabama running as third-party candidate, threatening to splinter the Democrats' "Solid South," Nixon's election appeared certain. Nixon certainly had the better-run, better-financed campaign. When his nomination seemed assured, campaign manager John Mitchell instructed the admen to get to work on the general election strategy. They planned to spend over $11 million—this at a time when the Democrats weren't sure they'd be able to spend more than $2 million. Nixon's advisers were supremely confident, so much so that when a Philadelphia newspaper writer named Joe McGinniss presented himself to Harry Treleaven and the others as someone who wanted to listen in on the media campaign and write about it, McGinniss got permission. "He represented himself as wanting to do a scholarly work," Ray Price says now. "He was actually viciously anti-Nixon." Roger Ailes, for his part, thought it was "queer" that the Nixon people agreed to let McGinniss listen in, but he also thought, "Hell, that's their problem." McGinniss played fly on the wall in the Nixon camp, his seemingly unaided total recall—"I never saw him with a tape recorder," Ailes says—later resulting in *The Selling of the President 1968*. The book makes the case that an amoral band of media men repackaged the mean, gutter-fighter Nixon into the admirable, principled New Nixon and cynically sold him, like cigarettes or soap, to the public. It proved to be convincing to late 1960s readers, who made it a best-seller.

The book's quotes were lively. "Let's face it, a lot of people think Nixon is dull," Ailes was quoted as saying. "Think he's a bore, a pain in the ass. They look at him as the kind of kid who always carried a book bag. Who was forty-two years old the day he was born. They figure other kids got footballs for Christmas, Nixon got a briefcase and he loved it. He'd always have his homework done and he'd never let you copy. Now you put him on television, you've got a problem right away. He's a funny-looking guy. He looks like somebody hung him in a closet overnight and he jumps out in the morning with his suit all bunched up and starts running around saying, 'I want to be President.' I mean this is how he strikes some people." Treleaven was reported to say about the candidate: "There were certain things people just would not buy about the guy. For instance, he loves to walk on the beach, but we couldn't send a camera out to film him picking up seashells. That would not have been credible." Nixon himself is heard, sappily saying: "We're going to build this whole campaign around television. You fellows just tell me what you want me to do and I'll do it."

Later the Nixon people would say that McGinniss had not misquoted but had selectively quoted to reinforce the McGinniss point of view. Ailes says now: "My mother didn't even know I swore until she read McGinniss. She was furious. I asked McGinniss whether I actually swore that much. He said, 'Well, you swore some,' but he admitted to me that he cleaned up other people's language around me because he needed a character who stood out more by being this loud, foulmouthed hot dog. So everybody else said 'gee whiz'; I said 'goddamn' and 'fuck.' Of course that freaked a lot of people, including the Nixon White House."

Organizations of all sorts take care not to admit flies on the wall to their meetings, the more so since *The Selling of the President.* Nixon felt that the press had persecuted him because of Alger Hiss, that the press had nearly gotten him kicked off Ike's ticket in 1952, that the press had been taken in by the Kennedy aura in 1960, and that the press had treated him unfairly in 1962 — yet Nixon, the great press antagonist, had allowed an agent of the enemy inside his command post. It was the only big mistake he made in handling the press, for mainly reporters were excluded. The Nixon campaign in fact broke with almost all past campaign practices to become a paid-media campaign, conducted largely over television. When Nixon did his "Man in the Arena" program before live audiences, not even a press pool was permitted to enter the studio. Reporters were held in a separate room, watching TV monitors just like the folks at home. A Nixon speechwriter, Richard Whalen, later explained that "what was traditionally the main business of campaigning, the speeches and public appearances that the writing press covered, steadily became less important than the unseen media enterprise. Edited film clips and commercials showing [Nixon] at his best were beamed to the audience that mattered—the millions of television viewers who ignored the dull political news in the papers." It was inevitable, then, that as the media campaign became the entire campaign, the key advisers would take it over. Nixon's nominal ad agency, Fuller & Smith & Ross, never played a major role; it implemented decisions made by the Nixon organization. FSR executives became errand boys; their advice, when they offered it, was frequently rejected, sometimes condescendingly.

Treleaven meanwhile planned to construct spots with still photos rather than film. He had used stills in ads for Pan Am during his days at J. Walter Thompson, and he believed that they could evoke reactions in part independent of the accompanying voice-over. Nixon was well enough known that there was no reason to show film footage of him—film anyway might remind people of the kid with the book bag. Treleaven wanted to hire the photographer David Douglas Duncan to shoot the stills. Duncan, busy, suggested Eugene Jones, a documentary maker who had also spent eight years as a producer on NBC's *Today* show. He had not done commercials before, but he impressed Treleaven and was hired. The Jones spots, like Gene Wyckoff's work in 1960 and 1964, employ juxtaposed still photos and an announcer's voice to make their points. Dramatic music, seldom used in political spots before 1968, becomes a major part of the production:

VIDEO   AUDIO

Camera up on white letters
against black background: "A
POLITICAL BROADCAST."

Cut to photo of large crowd, facing camera. Camera pulls back.

Music up: first drum, then trumpet, and other instruments. Quick, busy sound.

Cut to different view of crowd. Camera pulls back.

Announcer [VO]: "The man who is president speaks for America.

Cut to crowd seen from above. Camera pulls back.

What kind of a man do you want speaking for you?

Cut to quick montage of faces, in CU, different nationalities; then different, recognizable world cities (London, Paris, Moscow, etc.).

The peoples of the world will be listening.

[Music changes to soft vibraphone notes; French horn, mournful, comes in.]

Cut to montage of different world leaders (Brezhnev, Mao, Castro, de Gaulle, etc.).

[Music takes on martial sound.]

The man who speaks for us must have the respect of all the world.

Cut to ECU of black telephone, shot from behind and below; then camera moves quickly to ECU of white telephone, next to it.

[Music quicker, softer; strings.]

Think about it.

Cut to medium shot of reporters holding notebooks, looking up expectantly; then

Who's the one man who can speak for America—

1968: NIXON VS. HUMPHREY

Nixon Still Photos Commercial

"The man who speaks for us must have the respect of all the world"

"Who's the one man who can speak for America—"

"Anytime, anywhere? Nixon's the one"

to a dozen microphones,
sticking up into the air.

Cut to ECU, presidential seal.
Fade to White House, with
Washington Monument in
background. Camera pulls
back.

anywhere, anytime?
[Music becomes discordant.]
Nixon's the one."
[Music stops.]

Cut to white letters against
black background: "THIS
TIME VOTE LIKE YOUR
WHOLE WORLD DE-
PENDED ON IT."

Cut to small white letters
against black background:
"NIXON." Letters come to-
ward camera fast, until they
fill the screen.

Jones also produced one spot with film rather than stills, though
it too lacks any footage of Nixon:

VIDEO   AUDIO

White letters over black
background:
"A Political Broadcast."

Fade to city street, night. Re-   Sound of footsteps.
flection of shoes appears on
the pavement, pan up to reveal middle-aged woman
walking along empty street.

She has red hair, white gloves, and a blue collar beneath her coat. She holds her hands together, apparently clasping her purse.

Camera follows her as she passes several barred storefronts. Then she passes the camera; it follows her from the rear. She is completely alone throughout sequence. No other pedestrians or vehicles.
Fade to blue background, with white letters: "THIS TIME VOTE LIKE YOUR WHOLE WORLD DE-PENDED ON IT." Cut to second super: "NIXON."
Camera zooms in until it fills the screen.

Announcer [VO]: "Crimes of violence in the United States have almost doubled in recent years. Today a violent crime is committed almost every sixty seconds. A robbery every two and a half minutes. A mugging every six minutes. A murder every forty-three minutes.
And it will get worse unless we take the offensive. Freedom from fear is a basic right of every American. We must restore it."

Ailes's energies meanwhile were going into the "Man in the Arena" programs. Reporters had criticized the first programs because they were edited before they were shown—which naturally made the arena seem a bit less threatening to Nixon. Sensitive to charges of manipulation, the campaign was being pushed to go live, and Ailes, passionately committed to live television, was pleased. He had, by his count, produced some 2,000 ninety-minute *Mike Douglas Shows* since the early 1960s. Live TV

was Ailes's life, and the "Man in the Arena" idea strongly appealed
to him—"Nixon performing without a net," he termed it when
we interviewed him in his company's offices just off the Broadway
theater district in New York City. The "Man in the Arena" format
was also something Ailes believed Hubert Humphrey couldn't
do: "Having studied tapes of Humphrey I knew that as soon as
the first person asked a question, Humphrey would talk for seventeen minutes. He was totally unable to edit his time."

Like Tony Schwartz, Ailes had concluded that "people watch
TV emotionally," and that view shaped his work. The camera
should come in close on the candidate, the candidate should be
strongly lighted; picture selection should stand in for the human
eye—a rear camera, placed behind the man in the arena, could
show how the arena looked to the man. It sounds elementary
now, but no one had done political advertising in exactly that
way until Ailes. Before the Nixon campaign, Ailes explained,
candidates were filmed in their commercials three-quarters front,
from chest to a point twenty or thirty inches above their heads,
"Eisenhower Answers America" fashion. "I changed this style.
I insisted on close-ups. I felt that's what TV did better than
anything else because people want to feel something from TV."
Ailes, as he tells it, belonged then to the golden gut school of
TV. He possessed, he said, an invaluable working knowledge of
television gained through all those live shows molding the common clay of Mike Douglas, "a sense of what will work and won't
work, of what's good and what's bad, a kind of sixth sense of
what the audience perceives as real and what they perceive as
phony." (The instincts he employed on behalf of Nixon haven't
left him; on his office wall at Ailes Communications is a plaque
noting that *Hot L Baltimore*, the Lanford Wilson play that Ailes
coproduced with Kermit Bloomgarden, won the New York Drama
Critics Circle Award for Best American Play of 1972–73. On
another corridor wall are memorabilia from recent political campaigns managed by Ailes, including a poster for Lew Lehrman,

the millionaire businessman who almost won the New York governorship in 1982 in his first political campaign.)

The brass guts of some other Nixon advisers, however, were telling them to protect Nixon from live TV—and from himself. They remembered the first Nixon-Kennedy debate in 1960 and the "last press conference" of 1962, and they wanted a controlled format. Harry Treleaven took a middle ground: Nixon, he advised, "should be presented in some kind of 'situation' rather than cold in a studio. The situation should look unstaged, even if it's not." At first, then, the "Man in the Arena" programs were done on film and the citizen questioners prescreened—just how rigorously is still a matter of sharp disagreement between Nixon's men and his critics. When the Nixon programs went live, each ran an hour long and was shown by region, rather than nationally. By creating regional groupings of stations, the campaign could tailor its approach more specifically—another Nixon media innovation. A successful football coach of the time, Bud Wilkinson of Oklahoma, served as the host, assuring the audiences that "the gloves are really coming off this time." Generally, though, the questions were soft. Questioners could not follow up, if dissatisfied with Nixon's answer, and that usually let the candidate escape the rare tough question. Because the programs were shown regionally, Nixon could hone his answers to the most-asked questions, and use them over and over, word for word.

Dead End for Madison Avenue

The major issues of the 1968 campaign were Vietnam and law and order. Humphrey was tied to the LBJ record on both counts; nevertheless, in the Gallup and Harris polls taken in June and July, Humphrey was beating Nixon by five to seven points. By September, though, Nixon was leading by as much as fifteen points. Joe Napolitan of the Humphrey campaign later explained this swing by pointing out that Nixon was nominated at an orderly convention in Miami, that Nixon went on the air with well-produced advertising, and that Humphrey was nominated at the riotous Chicago convention (which cost the Democrats at least the law and order vote). Napolitan acknowledged to us that the Humphrey organization perpetuated the Chicago shambles: while Nixon had media professionals running his ad campaign, the Humphrey campaign, six weeks before the election, changed agencies and strategies entirely. Finally, Nixon had money; Humphrey didn't. Of the contrasts the last was to have the greatest impact. The Humphrey organization entered the general election in the red. In the preconvention days, Humphrey had to spend some $700,000 on TV spots to hold his delegates to him; the Democratic National Committee was another $400,000 in debt.

Doyle Dane Bernbach had the Humphrey advertising account initially, with Arie L. Kopelman in charge. Kopelman had a fifty-seven-person staff on the account at the time of the convention. He and fifteen members of the staff flew to Chicago to work out ad strategy with Humphrey and his managers. Kopelman had already drawn up a production timetable for spots with shooting to start no later than August 30. He had also worked on a computer simulation program to discover the value of repeating a specific commercial in a specific market after a certain number of days. He presented a four-page memo to the Humphrey people on August 22, and followed that with a fourteen-page "Media Recommendation: 1968 Presidential Election" two weeks later. There were also sixteen pages of "Media Data Supplements," breaking down state by state totals of TV homes and the cost of reaching them over a seven-week period. Some twenty states with large electoral votes were to be singled out for heavy spot coverage, and this group was further divided into three subgroups. The key concept was "weighting"—giving extra attention to critical markets; the key phrases were "GRP level" (for gross rating points, or the number of people watching network spots or local spots per week), "seven-week reach," and "seven-week frequency." "If Humphrey had followed this plan, he would have been president," Kopelman, now executive vice-president of DDB, flatly declared as he placed the bundle of memoranda in our hands. "No one before had ever done such a full-scale analysis of political advertising. It was a plan for winning the share-of-mind competition."

Clever and innovative as DDB may have been in the business of consumer persuasion, it made a major error in selling its plan to the Democratic leadership. Kopelman put the figure $7 million, the cost of the ad campaign, in the second paragraph of his covering memo. "They saw that number and didn't even read the rest," he says. "They said that they could not afford it, and that was it. They had no understanding of how a weighted advertising campaign works." To Kopelman, it was a simple matter of logic. In 1964 Johnson had spent $4.7 million on broadcast advertising when he was the incumbent president against weak opposition. Obviously Humphrey had to do more. Also, Kopelman's memo predicted, Nixon would spend upwards of $10 million (the Nixon campaign actually spent $12.6 million).

The Humphrey people, as might be expected, have a different version of what happened. To them, it was DDB that didn't understand political campaigns. Joe Napolitan had come to work two weeks before the convention for Larry O'Brien, the Kennedy man who first had worked for Johnson's presumed reelection campaign, then for Robert Kennedy's, and finally for Humphrey's as campaign manager. Napolitan's assignment was to supervise media; however, a media plan written by Orville Freeman, the Secretary of Agriculture (and alarm clock candidate of 1954) who was angling to replace O'Brien, already existed. Like the DDB plans, Freeman's called for a big-budget ad campaign. Protecting their turf, the O'Brien forces drew up their own plan, and in a preemptive strike, got Humphrey to approve it prior to his acceptance speech. When Bill Bernbach presented his storyboards at the meeting in Chicago, the O'Brien missiles turned on him. The first storyboard showed an elephant's head, labeled "GOP." The elephant walks backward and finally disappears. The voice-over delivers a litany of statistics on the GOP's failures; the spot closes with the initials "HHH" filling the screen. The O'Brien-led Democrats let DDB know they didn't like it. It was a "terrible use of television," Napolitan says, shaking his head at the memory. Humphrey's spots needed to be more emotional; statistics presented without any supporting visuals, Napolitan argued, are usually incomprehensible to the average viewer. Worst of all, says Napolitan, DDB had budgeted the cost of the elephant ad alone at $57,000. Another DDB storyboard showed Humphey's picture on a dart board. The voice-over listed Humphrey's firsts— "first to come out for open housing, first for disarmament, first for aid to education"—while a dart flew into Humphrey's face with each item. The intended point was that Humphrey had been criticized for his noble positions, but the Humphrey people wondered if the proposed spot was a kind of subliminal sabotage perpetrated by closet anti-Humphrey dart-throwers at DDB.

"It was a disappointing showing," Napolitan noted in a memo to O'Brien. Of the thirteen storyboards presented, he said, only two or three were worth producing as they stood. "The agency had made no provision for any anti-Wallace material and conceded they were not aware of the political nuances of the campaign. Two of their spots, for example, had Negroes as narrators— an insane thing to do." Napolitan also said that the DDB spots "lacked warmth, conviction and emotional appeal and were slick, maybe too slick." Napolitan's memo added: "My experience working with other producers and agencies has made me extremely cynical and distrustful of advertising agencies per se, and there was little in what we saw today to cause me to change my opinion. I think it would be a grave mistake to let this agency continue unfettered." Napolitan instead urged that "a very small group, and perhaps a single person with authority" be put in charge of supervising the DDB people, and that outsiders be hired to produce documentary films and some spots. He concluded, "Supervising media is a hell of a tough and important job, and it takes a tough and blunt person to do it. This assignment should be filled as quickly as possible with the best man around." The DDB people think they know whom Joe Napolitan had in mind—Joe Napolitan. Says Kopelman: "Here was an opportunity to run something big, with national attention. It was instant credentials. Later, Napolitan went into the political consulting business full time on the strength of this." Whatever the case, O'Brien gave Napolitan full control of advertising, expenses (but no salary), and the title of director of advertising.

Napolitan drafted a memo saying he wanted the filmmakers Charles Guggenheim and Shelby Storck, as well as Tony Schwartz ("a true genius in his field"), to work on media. DDB slipped off the board altogether a few days later when Napolitan went to the agency to look at the first completed spot, made from one of the storyboards he had approved in Chicago. The storyboard called for an elderly woman to talk about why she supported Humphrey. Napolitan complained that DDB had hired a model: "We were shown an elegantly coiffed, beautifully gowned woman wearing a string of pearls that looked as though it had just come out of Harry Winston's window, filmed against a brocaded chair in a lavishly appointed setting, acting for all the world as though she had to get through the spot quickly because she was keeping her chauffeur waiting. And I swear to God she spoke with at least a hint of an English accent." From that disappointing meeting, Napolitan went to another ad agency, Lennen & Newell, which had produced some Humphrey material during the primaries and was interested in continuing to do so on a volunteer basis. A few days later Napolitan dumped DDB and promoted Lennen & Newell; the Kopelman plan was dead. "They didn't want a partner, they wanted a supplier," Kopelman now says.

In truth, beyond the normal ego clashes and power moves, some issues of substance divided the Humphrey people and DDB. Several agency people had volunteered for Eugene McCarthy during the primaries. McCarthy's slogan, "A Breath of Fresh Air," was created by a DDB employee working after-hours. As long as McCarthy and his supporters continued to stand aloof from Humphrey, they were suspect. Further DDB wanted to produce liberal spots, "stressing the dimension of social justice."

But Napolitan had looked at public opinion polls and discovered that the majority of the American people felt that "the Negro has had too many handouts." He advised Humphrey to switch from emphasizing a Marshall Plan for the cities to a law-and-order theme. Also DDB wanted to attack Nixon, according to Kopelman, whereas Humphrey's people insisted on running a positive campaign. "It was clearly necessary to go for the jugular, at least in some of the spots, if Humphrey was to win," says Kopelman. "Particularly after that convention, we felt Humphrey did not look like a strong, tough guy." Later Napolitan would follow some of DDB's killer instincts, using Tony Schwartz's material.

In September, with less than two months to go to the election, Lennen & Newell formed a subsidiary, Campaign Planners, to work for Humphrey. Heading it was Barry Nova, senior vice-president of the agency and an account executive for Muriel cigars. Nova had never done a political campaign before (two years later he would be agonizing over the performance of John Glenn in an Ohio Senate race). The subsidiary also hired Allan Gardner, an account executive at Papert, Koenig, Lois, the agency that had handled Robert Kennedy's campaign. Gardner quickly traced the same path as Kopelman, to Robert Short, the Humphrey campaign treasurer. Gardner presented his plans for a "very conservative" media campaign costing $6.5 million. Short told him he might be able to find $2.5 million, though Short at that moment wasn't sure he would be able to meet that week's payroll.

On September 14 Napolitan wrote another memo to O'Brien, outlining a bold media strategy centered on a sharp break with Lyndon Johnson and an independent Vietnam policy to "win back votes that should be Humphrey's but which now are wavering." He also urged a policy on law and order to separate Humphrey from Nixon and the insurgent candidate George Wallace. Essentially Napolitan wanted a unique selling proposition: Humphrey would be for law and order, like Nixon and Wallace, but he would be for federal aid to communities, which Nixon and Wallace both opposed, in order to preserve law and order. Two weeks later, in his pivotal Salt Lake City speech, Humphrey did move a bit away from Johnson on Vietnam. The campaign recognized the importance of the speech and scraped together $90,000 to televise it nationwide, the first such broadcast by Humphrey since his acceptance speech in Chicago. Short had recommended that a fund-raising appeal come at the end of the speech. Napolitan was skeptical, saying such appeals brought in at most $10,000 to $20,000. "You have any other ways of earning twenty thousand dollars in twenty seconds?" Short said. So an appeal, delivered by Larry O'Brien, was tagged onto Humphrey's speech: "Ladies and gentlemen, you have just heard the vice-president's plan for how he would end the war in Vietnam. If you agree and would like to see him elected president, please send your contributions . . ." Some $320,000 was contributed— and, no less important, Humphrey began to rise in the polls.

Heartbeats and Laughtracks

Tony Schwartz, meanwhile, produced several spots aimed at voter apprehensions about Nixon's running mate, the lackluster Spiro Agnew. One, in the Schwartz signature style of getting down to essential emotions, is called "Heartbeats":

VIDEO	AUDIO
Camera up on screen with names of the two vice-presidential candidates, Edmund Muskie and Spiro Agnew.	Background audio: electronically amplified sound of human heartbeat.
	Announcer [VO]: "Never before in our lives have we been so confronted with this

reality. Who is your choice to be a heartbeat away from the presidency?"

Like Schwartz's Daisy spot that never mentioned Goldwater's name, "Heartbeats" built on attitudes presumed to exist in the subconscious of the viewer.

Another anti-Agnew spot was even simpler in execution:

VIDEO	AUDIO
Camera up on ECU of upper right-hand corner of TV set, showing knobs and a small part of the screen.	Voice-over through entire spot of raucous, uncontrollable laughter.
Camera slowly pulls back to show screen, on which is lettered: "Agnew for Vice-President?"	
Cut to slide: black letters against white background, "This would be funny if it weren't so serious."	

One Nixon staff member, speechwriter William Safire, later a *New York Times* columnist, called it "the most distasteful, unfair, and audience-insulting commercial since LBJ's 'Daisy spot' against Goldwater." "Yes," Schwartz himself says, "that got a lot of attention." Finally, in the same attention-getting style, Schwartz produced a five-minute spot with the actor E. G. Marshall. Written by Tony Schwartz's wife, Reenah, the spot was called "Trust":

VIDEO	AUDIO
Camera up on Marshall on set. Slowly he moves from large mounted photo of Wallace, behind him, to similar mounted photo of Nixon.	Marshall [SOF]: ". . . He has proved that it is the strength of our finest instincts and not our worst that keeps us functioning as the strongest nation in the world. Now he is asking us to trust him and to trust his beliefs that equal justice for every individual is our greatest protection and our greatest strength. He is asking us to trust his belief that the way to bring peace to warring nations and warring groups of people within the nation is to recognize the causes of these wars and to work to get rid of them. This is a time when a good man can become a great man. I believe in Hubert Humphrey and I trust him, and God willing he will be our next president."
Marshall stops in front of similar Humphrey photo.	
Cut to slide: "Citizens for Humphrey-Muskie."	Announcer [VO]: "The preceding announcement was paid for by Citizens for Humphrey-Muskie."

"Trust" is a blind-narrative spot: Marshall's quiet, firm cadences are half over before our eyes and ears, straining to discern whom he is for, realize it is a Humphrey commercial.

1968: NIXON VS. HUMPHREY

Humphrey "Laughter" Spot

Sound of raucous, uncontrollable laughter

Laughter continues

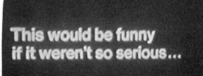

Humphrey "What Has Nixon Done For Me" Commercial

"Medicare? No, that was Humphrey's idea"

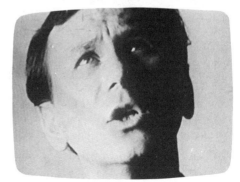

The second free-lance member of the Napolitan team, film-maker Shelby Storck, completed a half-hour telebiography, "What Manner of Man," a look at Humphrey's human side with a review of his record on issues. As Jimmy Durante sings "The Young at Heart," the Humphreys and the Muskies are shown out for a night on the town together, bowling. We see Humphrey at the 1948 Democratic convention, calling on the party to "walk out of the shadow of states' rights and into the sunshine of human rights." Humphrey talks about his retarded granddaughter, and how she "taught me the meaning of true love," while the film shows Humphrey playing with the five-year-old. Napolitan considers the film "a masterpiece" and claims it was the most widely shown political film in American history, carried seven times on network television by an average of 175 stations, and also broadcast about 200 more times on individual stations. "The Salt Lake City speech kicked off Humphrey's climb in the polls, but 'What Manner of Man' accounted for more vote switching than any other single thing we did in the campaign," Napolitan told us. (Storck died a few months after the campaign ended.)

The media managers, tending to view the whole from their special position, often overlook major nonmedia events shaping campaign outcomes. "What Manner of Man" was only one factor in Humphrey's climb in the polls. George Wallace's candidacy, for example, was taking votes away from Nixon on the right. While Nixon's commercials only implied his Hard Right thinking, Wallace's television left little to the imagination about what manner of man the Alabama governor was running as:

VIDEO	AUDIO
Camera up on footage of burning buildings, screaming protesters.	Announcer [VO]: "Look, America. Take a good look. Ask yourself: Why are the anti-American, anti-God

> anarchists also violently anti-
> Wallace? Want to get rid of
> them? Vote for a law-abiding,
> God-fearing America—and
> for Mr. Wallace."

The Wallace spots were done by a Birmingham agency, Luckie & Forney. They seemed, by sophisticated Madison Avenue standards, homemade; that was intentional, a way of demonstrating the candidate's toughness and position apart from the establishment.

In early September the election had seemed over, and the confident Nixon campaign had talked of cutting their budgets in certain states. By October, however, Nixon strategists began to worry about voters' "volatility"—sudden shifts caused in part by a lack of strong commitment to any one candidate. Analyst Walter DeVries warned John Mitchell, the Nixon campaign manager, that Nixon's vote had stayed at about forty percent for five or six months. The other sixty percent, which split between Humphrey, Wallace, and the undecideds, was volatile: "If Wallace and the undecideds start to break for Humphrey a change of strategy will be in order. . . . There should be a plan in the tank in case events or voter movement overtake you the last few weeks." DeVries's memo was ignored.

Many factors were involved in Humphrey's surge: Nixon's complacency; Humphrey's new TV material; his Salt Lake City speech distancing him from Johnson on Vietnam; Johnson's calculated boost in the form of the October 31 bombing halt over North Vietnam. Also contributions had begun to flow in to Humphrey; during the last two weeks of the campaign he was able to spend $2 million on advertising. Blessed with hindsight, some Humphrey advisers later argued that Nixon's TV material was saturating—and boring—voters; within another week, they claimed, Nixon would have driven enough voters to Humphrey for the Democrat to win. On the Nixon side Ray Price remembers that the Nixon media blitz could be explained in the two words, George Wallace: "He took ten votes from us for every five he took from Humphrey." At the end the Humphrey organization decided to turn its lemons into lemonade, emphasizing the "naturalness" of the candidate and the looseness, even the disorganization, of the campaign. Robert Squier, who gave a hand to the film production, deliberately included piles of cable and other stage business in telecasts, as explicit contrast to the slickness of the Nixon programs. By design the Democrats' "Man in the Arena" programs had a slapped-together look. Producers urged the audience to ask harsh questions, frequently angering Humphrey—and making his answers better, even reasonably short. The programs were filmed and edited for later broadcast, so they were actually safer than Nixon's live telecasts. But the footage used often showed Humphrey standing up to a spontaneous attack, something audiences almost never saw during the Nixon programs.

Election-Eve Production Numbers

On election eve, Nixon and Humphrey each did a nationwide telethon, two hours in length. Wallace, unable to compete financially, settled for a half hour. Nixon recalls that some of his advisers urged him not to bother with the telethon; it would be costly, tiring, and unneeded. But, he wrote, "I remembered 1960 and felt I should do everything possible that might make the difference in a close election. It was my best campaign decision. Had we not had that last telethon, I believe Humphrey would have squeaked through. . . ." In his telethon Nixon answered phone-in questions, or at least those approximately matching a series of preplanned answers. Coach Wilkinson again was the host, Jackie Gleason appeared, and Nixon's young son-in-law to be, David Eisenhower, announced that his grandfather, Ike, supported Nixon. But for most of the evening Nixon sat in a swivel chair alone on Ailes's strongly lit stage, his final appearance in the arena.

The Humphrey effort was produced by Bob Squier. Humphrey had a portable microphone and wandered freely over a stage cluttered with equipment. Humphrey also talked directly to callers—again reinforcing the contrast to Nixon's controlled campaign. Humphrey also had the better roster of celebrities, Paul Newman, Buddy Hackett, Danny Thomas, Frank Sinatra, among others. Gene McCarthy called in to repeat his endorsement of Humphrey, first made just a week earlier. In a film segment Edward Kennedy walked along the Hyannisport beach with Larry O'Brien, and talked of his dead brothers, and of waiting for the election results eight years before, when John Kennedy ran against Nixon. The parties bought all three networks' time, leaving the audience little viewing choice—what the TV industry calls road-blocking—and tens of millions of viewers saw the presidential candidates.

The final vote totals gave Nixon a victory of less than one percent, 43.4 percent to Humphrey's 42.7 and Wallace's 13.5. The other important figures appeared in the campaign accountants' books. Nine out of every ten dollars spent on TV went into spots, and the Democrats spent a total of $3.5 million on television, the Republicans $6.3 million, and George Wallace less than $700,000. In total broadcast expenditures, including agency fees, production costs, and radio time, the Democrats spent $6.1 million, to the GOP's $12.6 million.

At Doyle Dane Bernbach, Arie Kopelman took away from his agency's aborted involvement in the 1968 campaign two lessons. He is still convinced that if Humphrey had spent more money within the narrow time period, he would have won, even without the detailed DDB plan. (Perversely, it turned out that the Democrats had more money on hand than their lax bookkeeping showed: $318,000, to be exact, was left in the ad account after the election—enough money to buy ads that, Joe Napolitan believes, could have won Humphrey enough votes to send the election into the House of Representatives.) Second, DDB learned, in Kopelman's words, "never again to take on a political campaign.

That's written, company policy." It was pure grief, he concludes, from getting paid—a four-year wait for the 1964 Johnson work— to getting respect: "They see you as hucksters, one more hand out to take their money." Henceforth DDB would stick to commercial clients, who are "much more organized. They may change opinions as new information comes in, as different players take on different responsibilities. But there is discipline and a knowledge base. In the political world, in those days, the politicians and staff had a million different opinions, and were all squabbling for power anyway. A business has a stepped hierarchy. The troops in the campaign are always in there fighting for position."

But just as surely as DDB butted out of political media work, others butted in. Eugene McCarthy's candidacy had in fact been a breath of fresh air, and one strong enough to rattle traditional party structures. His campaign had moved outside the established parties and achieved some notable successes. The parties were "devastated"—as Arthur Schlesinger, Jr., put it—by the new politics that appealed directly to the voters. McCarthy had ignored the old party bosses and run on new-politics media and ideas. His example was not lost on the generation of media managers coming to prominence.

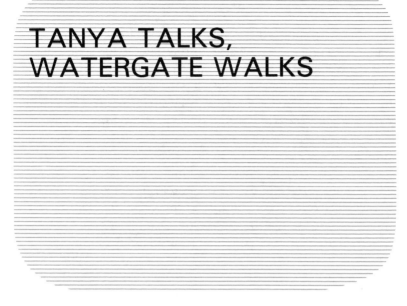

TANYA TALKS, WATERGATE WALKS

CHAPTER 11

If the presidential election of 1972 had been held in 1970, Edmund Muskie would have been the 38th president of the United States. Richard Nixon himself wondered at the time if he would even get the Republican nomination again. During most of 1970 Nixon scored low in public esteem, trailing the tall, imposing-looking senator from Maine by as much as ten points in the popularity ratings. The public also pronounced itself dissatisfied with the economy, with unemployment rising and the dollar falling, and with the war in Vietnam, which still dragged on, killing American servicemen, despite Nixon's pledges to "Vietnamize" the fighting. The public, indeed, seemed to be expressing its dissatisfaction with the whole direction of the country.

Richard Nixon and the people around him knew all about voters' negative feelings because they had established an extensive public opinion polling operation in anticipation of Nixon's uphill reelection campaign against the formidable Muskie. The polls, by Robert Teeter, were designed not to show who was up or who was down but rather to elicit voters' attitudes and opinions. But there were still drawbacks to the new 1970s style polls, as well as to some of the other new strategies of media politics. Despite a sharpening of skills during the campaigns of the 1960s, the marketing of political candidates was still an art. The election of "President" Muskie illustrated some of the limits of the new skills. So did the Nixon strategy for the 1970 congressional campaign.

In 1970 the Republicans ran a confrontational, abrasive campaign, one more reminiscent of the old hot Nixon than of the new cool Nixon. True, there were provocations. During a tumultuous appearance by Nixon on October 29 in California, student demonstrators pelted the presidential motorcade with eggs and stones, creating a scene for the cameras that looked like Chicago 1968. (Some reporters wrote that Nixon had intentionally provoked the attack, to send Middle America pictures of the President attacked by hippies; the White House, predictably, denied the allegations.) Two days later, in a Phoenix speech, Nixon declared: "Some say that the violent dissent is caused by the war in Vietnam. It is about time we branded this line of thinking, this alibi for violence, for what it is—pure nonsense. There is no greater hypocrisy than a man carrying a banner that says 'peace' in one hand while hurling a rock or a bomb with the other hand." The White House decided to use a videotape of the Phoenix speech on election eve, rather than a more traditional, quiet format of the statesman in repose. The only footage of the speech had been shot by a Phoenix TV station; it was black and white, grainy, and nearly inaudible, a low-quality film of a strident President delivering a partisan speech.

The Democrats, in contrast, used Muskie on election eve 1970 in a low-key fifteen-minute televised talk. Robert Squier, the young filmmaker who had directed the Humphrey telethon in 1968, flew to Maine to meet with other Democratic advisers near Muskie's home to plan the program. Squier argued successfully against such formats as phone-ins and town meetings (impractical in fifteen minutes) and for a one-man, one-camera approach. Muskie, he said, should "come in under Nixon" in tone. Squier told us that Muskie did the speech at home in one take, with no one else in the room—even the camera was placed at the doorway, as if looking in on a private scene of Muskie speaking directly to the television viewers, his living room to theirs. With words by expert speechwriter Richard Goodwin and manner by Squier, Muskie's presentation contrasted pointedly with Nixon's harangue. Jeb Stuart Magruder, a cosmetics marketer who had joined the Nixon administration's PR team, later acknowledged: "It was like watching Grandma Moses debate the Boston Strangler." The next day, the Republicans picked up two Senate seats but lost nine House seats and eleven governors' seats. (The Nixon White House put on a cheery public facade but didn't forget; Squier says all of the men who worked with Muskie on that telecast—but, interestingly, none of the women—later found themselves on the White House enemies list.)

But if television gave Muskie a "presidential" aura in 1970, by 1972 real-world events had undone him and the Democrats. By then Nixon's standing had improved. He traveled to China in February 1972, reestablishing Western ties to the world's most populous country, and chipping away considerably at his Cold Warrior image. No longer was he Richard Nixon, street fighter and Republican; for the duration of the thoroughly televised visit, he was World Statesman and The President. Nixon's ratings continued to rise as he traveled to Moscow to initiate a détente with the Russians, implemented wage-price controls, and ended the draft. No artful use of a medium can match the force of such messages. Meanwhile Muskie's own message grew increasingly confused. On the same weekend American television news programs were showing Nixon being toasted in the Great Hall in Peking by China's rulers, Muskie was being televised in dreary Manchester, New Hampshire, standing on a flatbed truck in the snow with tears in his eyes, angrily reacting to a slur printed about his wife in the rabidly conservative *Manchester Union Leader*.

A paper campaign with little organizational substance, the Muskie presidential express shortly thereafter was overrun by George McGovern's candidacy. That campaign would soon go off the tracks too, but the Nixon people continued to prepare for the worst.

Teeter's polls were telling the Nixon men that the President wasn't well liked, but he was respected. According to Magruder, the polls found Nixon's public image to be "experienced, competent, safe, trained and honest. He was not seen, relatively speaking, as warm, open-minded, relaxed, or as having a sense of humor." Consequently the campaign message would be, not "You like Nixon," but "You need Nixon." That meant emphasis on Nixon's incumbency, downplaying party affiliation. Then as now, the GOP was the minority party; Nixon wanted to maintain an arm's-length distance from his party—and from his running mate, Spiro Agnew (Agnew had not yet developed his difficulties with grand juries investigating corruption; his aboveboard conduct of the vice-presidency was embarrassing enough). The Nixon campaign chose a name for itself that made no mention of Republicanism or Agnew: the Committee to Re-Elect the President, soon known as CREEP. And, though the committee's early polls found widespread dissatisfaction about the nation's direction, the researchers found the feeling seemed directed mainly at intangibles of government and bureaucracy, not at Nixon.

Incumbency and poll results were part of the picture, but other factors also pushed the Nixon campaign toward a different advertising strategy from that employed four years earlier. Magruder thought that Treleaven, Ailes, et al., had done "a brilliant series of television commercials" but that the accompanying "confusion, expense, and conflict" had to be avoided this time. Also he wanted no free spirits giving out colorful quotes to interviewers. "I stayed in touch with Nixon," Roger Ailes now recalls. "I sent memos periodically about his TV appearances, but I had the feeling that my notes were not getting through to him. They were being stopped in the White House." The man who ran the

Nixon White House, H. R. "Bob" Haldeman, had told Magruder, in effect, not to repeat 1968. Magruder recommended that CREEP undertake an internal advertising effort, where "we could control hiring, salaries, and loyalties." Also an in-house group could take the fifteen percent commission on air time—normally turned over by TV stations and networks to the purchasing agency— and put it into more advertising, upwards of $1 million more for every $8 million or so spent on advertising time. CREEP approved Magruder's plan and hired Peter H. Dailey of Los Angeles, a highly successful, conservative advertising executive who had built Dailey & Associates into the largest independent ad agency on the West Coast. Dailey established the November Group, a separate company with a separate budget, nominally independent of CREEP but paid by the committee. It would become a fully staffed advertising agency started for the sole purpose of working for Nixon, to be dissolved after the November election. The November Group began operating in February 1972 from spacious Manhattan offices. Dailey hired, at the peak, forty-five people from Madison Avenue firms. Their agencies were reimbursed for any expenses incurred due to the person's absence.

No campaign believes it can be too rich. Without money there can be no polling operations, no canvassing for votes, no telephone banks, no travel to create events for the news, and no advertising, spot or otherwise. To get the money, campaign fund raisers have never been too fastidious, and 1972 was for CREEP the year of living unfastidiously. Two years later, at the Watergate hearings, the TV audience heard eye-popping accounts of how millions of dollars in cash were stockpiled at CREEP's Washington head-quarters. One theory of Watergate in fact holds that with so much cash around, fevered imaginations, like Gordon Liddy's, kept thinking of crazy ways to spend some of it. In all, CREEP may have raised $25 million; no one knows for sure. For Nixon money was no problem. A 1971 federal campaign had limited candidates' advertising expenditures to ten cents per voter (of

which no more than sixty percent could be spent on broadcasting).
Nixon's campaign committee knew the nomination was in hand.
But the Nixon forces started spending anyhow, using the primaries
to test out strategy, tactics, themes for the general election, while
Liddy and others ran around loose on the fringes.

Cinema Verité All the Way

The man who beat out Muskie on the Democratic side, George
McGovern, announced early, in January 1971, his two principal
campaign promises—getting out of Vietnam and shifting budget
priorities from defense to domestic needs. He got little attention,
then and during the next year; in January 1972 a Gallup poll
of Democrats found Muskie with thirty-two percent support,
noncandidate Edward Kennedy with twenty-seven percent, Hubert Humphrey with seventeen percent, and McGovern with
three percent. Too there was Alabama Governor George Wallace,
running this time for the Democratic nomination. Muskie looked
good in the public polls, but the polls were deceptive because
the Democratic party had reformed its delegate-selection rules
since the 1968 shambles. The new rules had made the primaries
more vital than ever. Humphrey had won the 1968 nomination
without contesting a single primary; that wouldn't work again—
and no one realized it better than McGovern, chairman of the
party commission which had drafted the reforms. McGovern not
only knew the new rules; he hired Charles Guggenheim to make
spots for him. The two had first worked together in 1962 in
McGovern's initial run for the Senate from South Dakota and
knew each other well. One of Guggenheim's first and best-
remembered spots was used through the primary season and on
into the fall campaign:

VIDEO

Camera up on group of dis-
abled veterans, many in
wheelchairs. McGovern introduces himself, shakes hands
with them.

AUDIO

Announcer [VO]: "Most of
them were still safe in grade
school when this man first
spoke out against the war,
risking political suicide in the
hope they might be spared.
For them, his early voice has
now been heard too late. If
the shooting stopped tomorrow, they'd still have to face
their long road back, rebuilding shattered lives and broken dreams. And they're
looking for all the help and
understanding they can find."

Pan from McGovern to ECU
of veteran, early twenties,
mustache. Camera pulls back
as he gestures to his
wheelchair.

Veteran [SOF]: "There's a
parking lot down here, that's
especially for wheelchair people. It's got *ice* on the road.
How far do you think you
can get—we can't even put
studded snow tires on these
things! . . ."

Cut to CU, same veteran.

Veteran [SOF]: "There are
people that have disabilities,
stuck in these things. And
they don't want to be here.
Some of them can't use their
arms, their fingers. That
doesn't make them a non-
productive individual!"

Cut to McGovern.

McGovern [SOF]: "You love the country, there's no question about that, and yet you're halfway mad at it too, aren't you?"

Cut to CU of veteran, in profile.

Veteran [SOF]: "Believe me, when you lose the control of your bowels, your bladder, your sterility—you'll never father a child—when the possibility of you ever walking again is cut off for the rest of your life, you're twenty-three years old, you don't want to be a burden on your family—you know where you go from here? To a nursing home. And you stay there till you rot. . . ."

Cut to CU of McGovern. Reaction shots.

McGovern [SOF]: ". . . I love the United States, but I love it enough so I want to see some changes made. The American people want to believe in their government, want to believe in their country. And I'd like to be one of those that provides the kind of leadership that would help restore that kind of faith. I don't say I can do it alone. Of course I can't. But the president can help set a new

	tone in this country. He can help raise the vision and the faith, and the hope of the American people. That's what I'd like to try to do."
Pan to same veteran.	Veteran [SOF]: "I'd like to get a president that we *can* believe in."
	McGovern [SOF]: "Well, I hope I'll be that kind of a president."
Cut to still photo of Mc-Govern with two veterans, "McGovern" in white letters across bottom.	Announcer [VO]: "McGovern. For the people."

When the New Hampshire ballots were counted, Muskie got forty-six percent of the vote to McGovern's thirty-seven percent; in the metacampaign interpretation, this was regarded as a major defeat for Muskie and an incredible victory for McGovern.

Some of the same Guggenheim spots made for New Hampshire were used in the California primary against Humphrey, despite the wintry scenes with bundled-up people. As with the veterans spot, they were generally done in cinema-verité style, camera looking in on unstaged conversation. McGovern talks informally; the viewer participates by natural observation. If McGovern attacks anyone, he attacks Nixon rather than any of the other Democrats in the race. Guggenheim also produced a half-hour film biography of McGovern with footage of the 1968 convention. The voice-over talks of "the long, dark days of 1968," and the "great sadness in Chicago . . . as if the sacrifices of this violent age had been for nothing." Guggenheim, though essentially a filmmaker, took on a wider range of duties than usual for his

1972: NIXON VS. McGOVERN

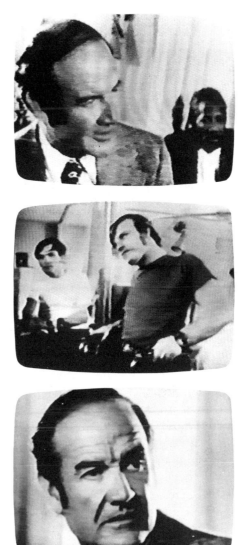

McGovern "Paraplegics" Commercial

"Most of them were still safe in grade school when this man first spoke out against the war"

"You're twenty-three years old, you don't want to be a burden on your family—you know where you go from here? To a nursing home. And you stay there till you rot"

"I love the United States, but I love it enough so I want to see some changes made" friend McGovern. Besides making the film and spots, he helped the campaign select time slots. McGovern's ad agency, Hall & Levine, bought time but did little else. Guggenheim also worked with a twenty-two-year-old Harvard student named Pat Caddell, on leave from school to do the campaign's polling.

In contrast to McGovern, Humphrey went on the attack in spots that showed the Minnesotan talking earnestly to the camera. On May 19, the day after he arrived in California, Humphrey videotaped fourteen spots. D. J. Leary, the campaign's national media director, studied survey research and decided to air just four of the spots, so as "not to dilute the message," Leary said. One spot focused on McGovern's proposals for defense:

VIDEO	AUDIO
Camera up on Humphrey.	Humphrey [SOF]: "Senator McGovern is proposing a forty percent cut in our defense forces—cutting the fleet in half—without any disarmament agreement from the Russians. It shocks me. No responsible president would think of cutting our defenses back to the level of a second-class power in the face of the expanding Russian navy and air force. Negotiated disarmament, yes—weakening our defenses, no."
	Announcer [VO]: "There is a difference. Vote for Humphrey."

McGovern won in California, and went on to win at the Miami Beach convention on the first ballot. Normally, conventions boost support for their nominees; but in 1972, as in 1968, the Democratic convention diminished the nominee's chances. Platform struggles broke out between the regulars and the reformers, and McGovern played a game of pin-the-tail to pick his vice-presidential candidate. McGovern wanted Edward Kennedy, who refused the offer; he then considered Senators Walter Mondale and Gaylord Nelson, and Boston Mayor Kevin White, while Jimmy Carter, the governor of Georgia, put in a bid. Finally McGovern selected Senator Thomas Eagleton of Missouri. The delegates proceeded to cast votes for thirty-nine other candidates, including Roger Mudd, Martha Mitchell, and Archie Bunker. McGovern's televised acceptance speech was delayed until 3 a.m. EST, denying him a substantial audience and showing a party in disarray.

From the start the McGovern campaign magnified its problems. Reporters learned that Eagleton had been treated for severe depression and had received shock therapy at least twice. Though initially McGovern stood firm—his campaign put out a statement saying he backed Eagleton "one thousand percent"—public and press reaction was overwhelmingly negative. Finally, McGovern forced Eagleton off the ticket. Eagleton had been less than honest in covering up his past, but McGovern's handling of the situation could hardly have been more inept. McGovern himself later said the incident "convicted me of incompetence, vacillation, dishonesty, and cold calculation."

The campaign was hardly a day at the beach for Guggenheim either. "We did some good advertising," he now says, "but the campaign was too disorganized, with too many lines of authority." As if the memory still pains him, Guggenheim pauses: "So many unprofessional people . . ." and he lets his voice trail off. Money was a constant problem too. When Guggenheim would call Morris Dees, who ran the campaign's direct-mail effort, to find out how much money was available for production and time buying that day, Dees might put him off, saying, "Well, we haven't opened the mail yet." The dumping of Eagleton made the situation worse: some $3 million in contributions was pledged prior to the convention; afterward, none of it appeared. Consequently fund-raising appeals were tacked onto the end of several of McGovern's longer programs. The most successful was the Guggenheim-produced broadcast of October 10 on CBS, in which McGovern discussed his plans for ending the Vietnam War. The final appeal produced some 15,000 contributions totaling $800,000, at a program cost of $160,000. Filmmaker Guggenheim felt more comfortable with the longer programs, but he also produced some twenty short (thirty- and sixty-second) spots, and another nine five-minute spots. The spots were edited from hours of film footage, recorded by camera crews who spent weeks following McGovern. Some spots combine cinema-verité footage with shots of the candidate addressing the camera, discussing issues in specific terms:

VIDEO	AUDIO
Camera up on black letters against white background: "The following is a paid political announcement on behalf of Senator George McGovern."	Announcer [VO]: "The following is a paid political announcement on behalf of Senator George McGovern, candidate for president of the United States."
Fade to series of shots of McGovern shaking hands, talking, smiling, eating; all outdoors, with friendly voters. Camera wobbles as it moves along with candidate.	McGovern [VO]: "I think the next president of the United States has to be very, very careful to be candid and frank and honest with the American people. The 'credibility gap' is about the saddest phrase that has ever

	crept into the American political vocabulary, because what it means is that millions of people no longer trust even the president of the United States."
Cut to ECU of McGovern, seated.	McGovern [SOF, continued]: "They have seen the country taken into a war that was not in the national interest, and all kinds of explanations made about how it was advancing the cause of freedom and the dignity of man.
Cut to different shot, suggesting new topic.	"I think the real deterrent to a nuclear attack on this country is not some kind of defensive, antiballistic missile system, but the certain knowledge in the mind of any attacker that if they hit the United States, they would be utterly destroyed.
Cut to different shot.	"The most important and most urgent problem right now is to end the war in Southeast Asia, and beyond that, to end the assumptions behind it—the notion that somehow we have to play policeman for the world. Or the notion that you can export freedom to Asia in a B-52."

Cut to McGovern in group of people, outdoors. McGovern nods.

McGovern [SOF]: "Yeah. Yeah. Yeah. Complete withdrawal. We've got to get out. Yeah. I'd set a date and—"

Man [SOF]: "Are you going to do it?"

McGovern [SOF]: "Absolutely. You know, I've been advocating that for years."

Man [SOF, inaudible].

McGovern [SOF]: "I know it. But that's why I'm running against him."

Man [SOF]: "Well, you've got my vote if you can really pull 'em all out."

McGovern [SOF]: "Well, you can count on it. . . ."

"You Need Nixon"

Nixon, for all CREEP's worries, had been smoothly renominated at a convention whose behavior was scripted down to the minute, including the amount of time for "spontaneous" demonstrations, in a schedule crafted by Ray Price. Once the campaign began, little else was left to chance. The November Group believed, unlike Guggenheim, that short spots were desirable as well as necessary; "How long does it take to say to young people, 'Richard Nixon gave you the vote, stopped the draft, and is winding down the war'?" declared creative director Bill Taylor. The principal intent was to depict Nixon capably carrying out the duties of president, in line with the "You need Nixon" approach, and to show him as a man of peace, as in "Tanya":

VIDEO	AUDIO
Camera up on Nixon getting off plane.	Announcer [VO]: "Moscow. May 1972. Richard Nixon becomes the first American president ever to visit the Russian capital. . . ."
Cut to Nixon addressing Soviet people via TV during his visit.	Nixon [VO]: "Yesterday, I laid a wreath at the cemetery
Cut to cemetery scene. Nixon walks forward with wreath.	which commemorates the brave people who died during the siege of Leningrad in World War II. At the cemetery, I saw the picture of a twelve-year-old girl.
Cut to photo of Tanya.	She was a beautiful child. Her name was Tanya.
Cut to cemetery scene.	The pages of her diary tell the terrible story of war. In the simple words of a child, she wrote of the deaths of the members of her family. Zhenya in December. Grannie in January. Leka. Then Uncle Vasya. Then Uncle Lyosha. Then Mama and then the Savichevs. And then, finally, these words, the last words in

her diary: 'All are dead. Only
Tanya is left.'

"As we work toward a
more peaceful world, let us
think of Tanya and of the
other Tanyas and their brothers and sisters
everywhere. . . ."

One subtheme of the spot campaign was to show Tanya's
American admirer as favoring "responsible change." Dailey believed that footage of Nixon's Russia and China trips would help
push that message. Another subtheme was an attempt to combat
images of the Old Nixon. Dailey tried "to create an understanding
of the man as being shy rather than cold." Interwoven into the
documentaries and into some of the commercials were personal
touches to show this humanity. In one ad Tricia Nixon tells a
story: on the night before her wedding the President wrote her
a note and slipped it under her door, an intimate father-to-
daughter note—he just couldn't tell her his thoughts personally.
Dailey also wanted to show Nixon was friendly and warm toward
all citizens in the republic:

VIDEO	AUDIO
Camera up on White House concert featuring Duke Ellington. Nixon, in tuxedo, stands at microphone.	Nixon [SOF, applause]: "Now ladies and gentlemen [laughter]. Please don't go away. [Laughter] Duke was asking earlier if I would play and I said I had never done so yet in the White House. But it did occur to me as I looked at the magnificent program that's prepared for us that

1972: NIXON VS. McGOVERN

Nixon "Tanya" Commercial

"Yesterday I laid a wreath at the cemetery which commemorates the brave people who died during the siege of Leningrad"

"I saw the picture of a twelve-year-old girl. She was a beautiful child. Her name was Tanya"

"And then, finally, these words, the last words in her diary: 'All are dead. Only Tanya is left'"

"As we work toward a more peaceful world, let us think of Tanya and of the other Tanyas and their brothers and sisters everywhere"

one number was missing. You
see this is his birthday.
Now—[Laughter] Now, Duke
Ellington is ageless, but will
you all stand and sing Happy
Birthday to him, and please
in the key of G."

Nixon sits at piano and plays.   Laughter, everyone sings
                                   "Happy Birthday."

The Nixon campaign also went after McGovern in a series of
spots. Dailey and Magruder had proposed that, in Magruder's
words, "the advertising objective should be to persuade traditional
hard-line Democrats to vote for Richard Nixon in November.
No attempt should be made to gain converts to the Republican
party—this is too big a jump to ask most people to make, and
it would take years to accomplish." The instrument of this effort
was John Connally and Democrats for Nixon. Connally, former
Treasury Secretary under Nixon, had been governor of Texas
and a protégé of Lyndon B. Johnson. Tall, silver-haired, and
forceful, he is a model successful Texan—or, if you don't like
him, the consummate wheeler-dealer. Likeable or not, Connally
did effective TV spots:

VIDEO   AUDIO

Camera up on CU of Con-   Connally [SOF]: "Good eve-
nally, addressing camera.   ning. I'm a Democrat, who,
                                   along with many of my fel-
                                   low Democrats, has become
                                   convinced that it is in the
                                   best interest of this country to
                                   reelect President Richard
                                   Nixon. . . . Senator McGovern

has made proposals to cut an unprecedented thirty-two billion dollars' worth of men and weapons out of the United States defense budget. . . . The McGovern defense budget is the most dangerous document ever seriously put forth by a presidential candidate in this century. It would end the United States' military leadership in the world; it would make us inferior in conventional and strategic weapons to the Soviets. The total United States Armed Forces level would be cut to a point lower than at the time of Pearl Harbor. Dean Rusk, Secretary of State in the administration of John F. Kennedy and Lyndon Johnson, has termed the McGovern defense, and I quote him, 'insane.' . . . "

The November Group's three most heavily aired spots, however, didn't show Connally or Nixon at all. The most memorable, called "McGovern Defense Plan," features toys:

VIDEO	AUDIO
Camera up on toy soldiers.	Military drumbeat underneath.

Announcer [VO]: "The Mc-
Govern defense plan.

Hand sweeps several away.

He would cut the Marines by
one-third.

Cut to another group of toy
soldiers; again, hand sweeps
several away.

The Air Force by one-third.

Cut to another group of toy
soldiers; again, hand sweeps
several away.

He would cut the Navy per-
sonnel by one-fourth.

Cut to toy planes; hand re-
moves several.

He would cut interceptor
planes by one-half,

Cut to toy ships; hand re-
moves several.

the Navy fleet by one-half,
and

Cut to toy carriers. Hand re-
moves several.

carriers from sixteen to six.

Cut to toys in jumble. Camera pans across.

"Senator Hubert Hum-
phrey has this to say about
the McGovern proposal: 'It
isn't just cutting into the fat.
It isn't just cutting into manpower. It's cutting into the
very security of this country.'

[Music comes in: "Hail to the
Chief."]

Cut to Nixon aboard naval
ship.

"President Nixon doesn't
believe we should play games
with our national security. He

                                        believes in a strong America
                                        to negotiate for peace from
                                        strength."

Fade to slide, white letters on
black background: "Demo-
crats for Nixon."

The spot borrowed its theme from Humphrey's ad in California
but used toys instead of graphics, Dailey explained, because a
lot of people can't comprehend numbers. The two other spots
getting the most air time took aim at McGovern's domestic policies
and his "vacillating" ways. "Welfare" opens on a shot of a construction worker sitting on a high girder, eating lunch. The voice-
over accuses McGovern of supporting a welfare plan that "would
make forty-seven percent of the people in the United States
eligible for welfare. . . . And who's going to pay for this? Well,
if you're not the one out of two people on welfare, you do."
The spot ends with a tight close-up of the worker, his face grim.
"Weathervane," a standard turn on a now familiar spot style,
shows McGovern's face on a sign. The voice-over accuses
McGovern of changing positions on welfare, amnesty for draft
dodgers, and busing; the McGovern sign spins so that the candidate alternately faces right and then left. Johnson had used
the idea against Goldwater in 1964, and Humphrey had used it
against Nixon in 1968. Dailey's turnabout in 1972 seemed like
fair play.

The Pressure to Go Negative

As the election neared and McGovern remained far behind in
the polls, his advisers urged stronger attacks on Nixon. In speeches
McGovern began to get harsher. Guggenheim was, as the filmmaker recalled, "under great pressure to go negative," despite
his strong views against negative advertising. Guggenheim believed that McGovern's only chance was to make people go to

the polls and say, "You know, I think this man has been so consistently decent and forthright that I'm going to vote for him." But two weeks before the election, Guggenheim got a call from campaign manager Gary Hart. McGovern's advisers were pushing hard for a negative TV campaign, Hart said. Guggenheim acknowledged that "the polls show that I've not been successful, if indeed paid television can be successful." He agreed to drop his opposition and produce a series of tougher spots using crawls — the words of the announcer's script moving electronically across the screen. One focused on inflation:

VIDEO

AUDIO

Camera up on script of words being spoken, moving up on screen.

Announcer [VO]: "Four years ago Richard Nixon said, 'We are on the road to recovery from the disease of runaway prices.' Since Mr. Nixon became president, the cost of whole wheat bread has gone from thirty-one cents to forty-five cents. Since Mr. Nixon became president, the price of hamburger has gone from fifty-eight cents to eighty-nine cents. Since Mr. Nixon became president, the cost of frozen fish has gone from sixty-nine cents to one dollar and twenty-nine cents. Since Mr. Nixon became president, the cost of living has gone up nineteen percent and your wages have been

frozen. So the next time you
are in a supermarket, ask
yourself: Can you afford four
more years of Mr. Nixon?
"McGovern. Democrat. For
the people."

This clean, unemotional, "factual" presentation of materials
quickly became popular and has been widely imitated since.

The Democrats had something else to attack — Nixon and Watergate. In hindsight it looms like a huge, inviting target, as big
as a barn door. The break-in of Democratic headquarters on
June 17, 1972, and the arrests of the CREEP people occurred
five months before the election, but Watergate in those early
months was contained effectively by the White House. Although
the *Washington Post* ran a steady stream of stories tracing the
involvement of higher-ups in Watergate corruption, the *Post*'s
Robert C. Maynard, now editor and publisher (and part owner)
of the *Oakland Tribune*, surveyed some 500 political columns
written between June and November 1972 and found that these
"opinion leaders" had produced fewer than two dozen pieces
about Watergate. The torrent of coverage didn't come until March
of 1973, when James McCord decided to sing; until then the
White House's "deadly daily diet of deceit," as CBS News' Dan
Rather called it, blocked the story from spreading. Still Guggenheim and the Democrats did try, belatedly, to make Watergate
a campaign issue in "Break-In":

VIDEO	AUDIO
Camera up on script crawl across screen.	Announcer [VO]: "Alfred C. Baldwin, a former FBI agent, has stated this. He was hired by James McCord, security

chief for both the Republican National Committee and the Nixon Campaign Committee. Mr. Baldwin was assigned to listen illegally to over two hundred private telephone conversations—calls made by Democratic Chairman Lawrence O'Brien and others from tapped telephones in Democratic headquarters at the Watergate. He sent reports on these conversations to William E. Timmons, assistant to President Nixon for congressional relations, at the White House.

"In 1968 Mr. Nixon said: 'The president's chief function is to lead, not to oversee every detail but to put the right people in charge, provide them with basic guidance, and let them do the job.' This message has been brought to you by the McGovern for President Committee."

Guggenheim became increasingly beleaguered in the backbiting and power plays endemic to the McGovern campaign. Some called his crawl spots newspaper ads on TV. "They gave you too much information," complained John Stewart, communications director of the Democratic National Committee. Finally, Guggenheim stepped aside. Tony Schwartz recalls that he got a call ten days before the election from Larry O'Brien, who said that the campaign had been a disaster and "he just wants to show what could have been done. He came to see me and in three days I did five commercials for him. I have to say that they are masterpieces." The divided McGovern managers didn't agree with Schwartz any more than they had with Guggenheim. Only two Schwartz spots were approved for broadcast. One was called "Voting Booth":

VIDEO	AUDIO
Camera up on CU of voting machine panel in booth, labels "Nixon" and "Mc-Govern" by voting levers. Male voter enters, stands with back to camera. He makes face, fidgets.	Voice-over [obviously thoughts of voter in booth]: "Either way it won't be a disaster. What am I looking for? I mean, so I'll vote for Nixon. Why rock the boat? I'm not crazy about him, never was. I got to decide though, got to make up my mind. I'm not crazy about McGovern. I don't have that much time, I can't keep people waiting. The fellas are voting for Nixon. They expect me to vote for him too. Me vote for Nixon! My father would roll over in his grave. The fellas say they are. Maybe they're not. Crime? I don't feel safe. Prices up. I got a gut feeling: Don't vote for Nixon. Why am I confused? Who am I

	measuring McGovern against? My gut feeling, my gut feeling McGovern.
He looks at hand.	This hand voted for Kennedy. I mean, it's just possible McGovern's straight. Maybe he *can*—
Cut to slide, white letters on black: "Democrats For McGovern."	That's the way!"

The second approved Schwartz spot was called "Deep Feelings":

VIDEO	AUDIO
Camera up on black background, with orange "Nixon" filling screen. Letters change color as the people talk, from orange, to blue, to green, to yellow, to red.	Announcer [VO]: "People have deep feelings about President Nixon."
	First woman [VO]: "He has put a ceiling on wages and has done nothing about controlling prices."
	First man [VO]: "The one thing I knew his last four years was that he knew that in some way he would have to please me come this election. And what frightens me is that if he gets in again he doesn't have to worry about pleasing me any more."

Second woman [VO]: "He was caught in the act of spying and stealing. They used to go to jail for these things. He is the president and should set an example."

Third woman [VO]: "There always seems to be some big deal going on with the Nixon people, some wheat deal or something."

Fourth woman [VO]: "When I think of the White House, I think of it as a syndicate, a crime outfit, as opposed to, you know, a government."

Fifth woman [VO]: "All I know is that the prices keep going up and he is president."

Second man: "I think he's smart. I think he's sly. He wants to be the president of the United States so badly he will do *anything*."

Cut to black, then to slide, white letters on black background: "McGovern."

Announcer [VO]: "That's exactly why this is brought to you by the McGovern for President Committee."

Schwartz recalls that he had scripts prepared for "Deep Feelings" but no one wanted to read the lines he had written; "they all wanted to say their own things. It's interesting how well they characterized him, right to the White House crime outfit."

One of the rejected Schwartz spots was called "Dollar":

VIDEO

AUDIO

Camera up on U.S. dollar bill.

Announcer [VO]: "The dollar? Oh, the dollar was really worth something. It always gave me a kind of comfortable feeling. The dollar, you know, when you earned a dollar, you had a dollar for what the family needed. Then it was looked up to all over the world. It set a standard. You know what they'd say about something strong and solid, they'd say it was 'sound as a dollar.'

Washington's image starts to change.

But it has been changing, hasn't it? I mean, it's just changed. They say it's in trouble internationally. But I don't feel that as much as I feel it's in bad trouble here, right here at home.

Nixon's face replaces Washington's.

I mean, besides that it just isn't worth a dollar anymore, I feel as if something else is gone with it, something really important that used to belong to us, to America. You know what I mean?"

Cut to slide, white letters on
black: "We know what you
mean."

After the campaign rejected "Dollar," Schwartz sent it to a
Nevada TV station late in the campaign, when McGovern had
paid for time and had nothing immediately available to show.
"The sheep saw it," Schwartz says. The final two Schwartz spots
for McGovern have been seen only by those journalists and other
sheep who wander in to Schwartz's studio. One is "Newspaper":

VIDEO

Camera up on fast-changing
montage of newspaper clippings about Watergate.

AUDIO

Sound of teletypes
underneath.

Announcer [VO]: "This is
about the government. This
is about credibility. This is
about electronics. This is
about bugging. This is about
spying. This is about thievery.
This is about espionage. This
is about lying. This is about
payoffs. This is about contra-
diction. This is about special
deals. This is about falsifica-
tion. This is about testimony.
This is about wheat deals.
This is about hiding. This is
about dishonesty. This is
about sabotage. This is about
secrecy. This is about stealing. This is about hidden

1972: NIXON VS. McGOVERN

McGovern "Dollar" Commercial

"You know what they'd say about something strong and solid, they'd say it was 'sound as a dollar' "

"But it has been changing, hasn't it?"

Nixon Anti-McGovern Spot

"The McGovern defense plan. He would cut Marines by one-third. The Air Force by one-third"

"He would cut interceptor planes by one-half, . . . and carriers from sixteen to six"

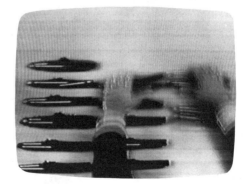

funds. This is about deception. This is about the White
House. And this is how you
stop it with your vote."

Cut to slide, white against
black: "McGovern."

The other is "Vietnam Jet":

VIDEO	AUDIO
Camera up on slow motion news footage, of Vietnamese mother carrying child, running down highway. Child lies limp in her arms, seared and bloody. Camera wobbles as it follows her.	Soundtrack fills with roar of jet engines.
Cut to her seen from behind, running away.	Voice-over [Schwartz's son, Anton, age ten]: "Does a president know that planes bomb children?"

"It was shocking to me that McGovern didn't want to run these," Schwartz says without rancor but feelingly. "They expressed everything he was saying, but he wouldn't stand behind it. He was speaking against the war, and that's probably one of the best antiwar commercials ever done. Simple, simple. But he didn't believe in attacking Nixon. I think McGovern could have gotten more votes by people voting against Nixon than for McGovern."

On the Republican side anti-McGovern spots were run more and more as the Nixon campaign focus came to rest on McGovern's "character." By the end of the campaign virtually all of the Nixon air time went into these spots. Behind this all-out effort were memories of Truman's upset of the overconfident Dewey in 1948 and of Humphrey's strong finish in 1968, and the fear, in Magruder's words, "that some break in the Watergate case—one of the defendants talking, perhaps, or the grand jury reopening its investigation—might blow the campaign sky-high." But the Watergate stonewall held, through election and until the next March.

The magnitude of Nixon's landslide victory, nearly 61 percent of the vote, was perhaps increased by the two candidates' media campaigns, though the result would almost surely have been the same anyway, given McGovern's myriad problems of a warring party, Tom Eagleton, and campaign disorganization. The candidate who really had problems was Nixon, though, and when the elaborate Watergate cover-up burst the next year, he was swept out of office in a torrent of revelations about official high corruption and plain low-down sleaze. When columnist Joseph Alsop, a supporter of the New Nixon, read the transcripts of Nixon's secretly taped White House conversations, he mourned that they sounded like "the back room of a second-rate advertising agency in a suburb of hell." Alsop might have written "law office" because there were more lawyers involved in Watergate (John Mitchell, John Ehrlichman, John Dean, Richard Nixon) than admen (Bob Haldeman, Jeb Magruder). With so much of the conversations about PR, media, and news management, however, Alsop's phrase fits.

After the disgrace of the Nixon crowd in 1974, public and press alike began to reevaluate the way presidential campaigns were being conducted. If there had not been a New Nixon, then maybe it was true that the image men could sell us anything. Given enough money, an effective polling, advertising, and vote-pulling operation could successfully market an idealized candidate, while creating doubts about the less than ideal opposition—so it seemed. The Congress was convinced enough of the power of money that it tightened the federal campaign election laws. But

Congress couldn't figure out what to do about media. There were First Amendment problems, and even those who lost campaigns defended the spot form. Guggenheim acknowledged that campaigns had become "traveling circuses," with a menagerie of facts and fantasies, but also said that "voters in 1972 did get to hear and see and feel most of everything that was going on—certainly more than any other people in the history of man." So Congress left the media alone when it put a cap on money by providing for federal funds to finance presidential campaigns. The candidates in 1976 and in future elections might direct most of their dollars into TV advertising, but at least each would have roughly equal amounts to spend.

BRIGHT SONGS AND BLUE JEANS: THE LIFE-STYLE CAMPAIGN

CHAPTER 12

A few days after the Republican convention in August 1976, Doug Bailey of the political consulting firm of Bailey, Deardourff Associates went to Gerald Ford's vacation home in Vail, Colorado, for a strategy meeting. The 1976 campaign was starting out much like the 1968 and 1972 campaigns—but with the two parties in a startling reversal of roles. This time the Democrats were the united party. On the climactic night of the convention that nominated Jimmy Carter, all the major faces of the party—Carter and Edward Kennedy, Wallace and Humphrey, Muskie and McGovern, Stuart Udall and Mayor Daley—joined together on the platform and smiled for living-room television sets. By contrast, the Republican convention had been divisive, with Ford, the nonelected president, barely beating back a challenge from Ronald Reagan. The public opinion surveys showed how steeply uphill the fight was for Ford. "We were thirty-two points down in the polls, with seventy-five days to go," Bailey's partner, John Deardourff, recalls.

Bailey and Deardourff projected a certain confidence as they undertook the sherpa's task of helping Ford. The men, both in their early forties, were liberal Republicans who had formed their company in 1967. Bailey had earned a Ph.D. from the Fletcher School of Diplomacy at Tufts University and then had worked for Henry Kissinger at Harvard. When Kissinger became an adviser to Nelson Rockefeller in the mid-1960s, Bailey went to work full-time as a foreign policy researcher in the "permanent campaign" staff that Governor (and perennial presidential candidate) Rockefeller maintained in New York City. Deardourff, the son of a small-town Ohio newspaper editor, had become active in campus politics as a Wabash College undergraduate; he also went to the Fletcher School, worked on the Rockefeller campaign during the Oregon primary in 1964, and then became head of the Rockefeller domestic policy research staff. By 1976 their nine-year-old operation was thriving, and they had committed themselves to work on several senatorial and gubernatorial campaigns when Ford's emissaries came to them in early August and asked for their help. Bailey and Deardourff accepted, even though they knew that two previous Ford campaign media teams had been hired and fired in the past few months. Worse, the Ford campaign was without a plan as well as bereft of media staff. No one had looked beyond the convention fight with Reagan; the Ford people had acted as if there was no tomorrow, and now it was here.

Tomorrow dawned so fast that Deardourff had to call on an old friend named Malcolm MacDougall, a compact, energetic advertising man who was vice-president and creative director of the Boston agency of Humphrey Browning MacDougall. One night citizen MacDougall was listening to Jimmy Carter's mother talking endearingly on the phone during a popular Boston radio sports call-in show, and idly thinking, "There goes the sports vote for Carter." The next morning he was being asked to write and produce all the ads for the Ford reelection effort; a few days later Bailey was in Vail with a strategic plan for the campaign, hammered together by the two partners and MacDougall. Their plan became the campaign. Not everything they proposed was accepted at Vail; they wanted Ford to state his "vision of the future"—"New Generation of Freedom" was to be an umbrella slogan over a collection of Ford-backed federal programs, some existing, some new. The Vail meeting backed off on that one. But Vail was still a summit for the media men. Bailey, the hired hand, an employee with no governance responsibilities or elected status, was telling the President and his White House staff what the overarching themes should be. It was a long way from Rosser Reeves tapping out twenty-second spots on his portable typewriter for Eisenhower; it was as if Tony Schwartz had scripted the Great Society as well as Daisy. At Vail the media specialists, the roving consultants, had become insiders, secure enough to suggest national policy. They were being taken more seriously in some areas than Cabinet members.

On the Democratic side the media men had also reached a similar level of influence. Gerald Rafshoon belonged to the small circle of Georgians around Jimmy Carter. Rafshoon had come south to Atlanta in 1963, after working for Twentieth Century-Fox as publicity and advertising director for such films as *The Longest Day* and the Burton-Taylor *Cleopatra*. One day in 1966 he had heard some radio spots for a Georgia agribusinessman named Jimmy Carter who was running for governor. The spots had a country and western jingle about "Jimmy is his name," Rafshoon laughs. "It was a terrible tune. Was it for Jimmy Davis, the country singer? I couldn't figure it out." Rafshoon also heard something more serious: "Here was a Southern politician who was earnest and sincere, who could say Negro without slurring it." Rafshoon picked up the phone, called a mutual friend of his and Carter's, and went to work on advertising and media for the man from Plains. Carter lost in 1966, then in 1970 won the governor's race with the help of Rafshoon, and began planning a run for president immediately after McGovern's nomination in 1972. In their first campaign together, Rafshoon recalls, Carter had said to him about his TV spots, "I don't have to look. You make sure they're good." Rafshoon adds: "That delegation continued all through 1976." The two had one meeting in November 1975, sitting side by side in an airplane and going down a list of topics for commercials. Then, Rafshoon says, he worked on his own for the next six months.

Bailey and Deardourff on the one side, and Rafshoon on the other, had their hands on more than the levers of authority in the 1976 campaign; they also had access to some $22 million each, the federal campaign fund for the presidential nominees mandated by Congress the year before. Of this sum roughly half would go for advertising, and of the ad budget three-fifths would go for TV. In subsequent campaigns the total sum would rise to $29 million each for 1980 and to an estimated $42 million each for 1984, while the proportion for advertising would continue to hold at around half. With the new managers well established at the center of the campaign and ample assured funds secure in place, 1976 became the model of the modern media campaign.

Looking for the Right Style

From the start Gerald Ford knew he would have troubles. His pardon of Nixon in the first days of his presidency had suggested to many a deal had been cut, and that undercut Ford's Mr. Nice Guy image. Ford had never run for national office and was not that well known to Republicans outside Washington. But Ford had certain advantages; he was the President, so he could announce a new VA hospital or $1.2 billion in revenue sharing on the eve of a state primary vote. Ford had brought in Stuart Spencer as his campaign director during the primaries. Spencer had worked for Reagan in the California governor's races, but he had clashed with some of the Reagan staff—the usual power and personality struggles—and had left. Reagan, Spencer told us in talking about 1976, was "a good offensive candidate but a lousy defensive candidate." Quickly, Spencer put Reagan on the defensive in the first primary, in New Hampshire. Reagan had advocated turning $90 billion in federal programs over to the states. Prior to a Reagan visit to New Hampshire, the Ford campaign publicized that stand and the fact that, if implemented, it would mean income and sales taxes for New Hampshire's flinty citizens. "We had him wobbling on that one for two weeks," Spencer recalls. The wobble, and some unseasonable weather for New Hampshire on primary day, helped Ford. February 24 was bright and warm, bringing out more voters than expected (moderates are more likely to stay home in cold or inclement weather than believers). Ford won a narrow victory, 49 to 48 percent of the vote. Reagan had done better than "winners" Eugene McCarthy in 1968 and George McGovern in 1972—but his managers had spoken confidently of beating the President outright. Soon, however, Ford seemed intent on snatching defeat from the jaws of victory.

Ford's initial media campaign was the product of a November Group-style team of admen on leave from various agencies. The nominal head of the in-house agency, called Campaign '76, was Peter Dailey, head of Nixon's November Group. Dailey remained based in Los Angeles, handling his own work. Bruce Wagner, on leave from Grey Advertising, was the day-to-day boss. Ford's men and the Campaign '76 people clashed almost from the start. The Dailey-Wagner spot strategy was essentially a replay of the November Group strategy. "Our plan," said Wagner, "was to be positive and presidential and to stick with those themes." Campaign '76 spots depict Ford hard at work, serious, wearing coat and vest, pulling on his pipe, conferring with aides, walking through the White House, addressing Congress. Regal blue and rich gold colors predominate. Malcolm MacDougall thought the spots were terrible: "It was cold, gloomy stuff, and I suspected that the editing had been done by some assistant at a local television station." The strategy was to show Ford as leader, but MacDougall says the series of commercials made Ford look "pretty damned scared about the whole thing." At the time, though, Ford was methodically gathering delegates, and his managers began to relax. In North Carolina they canceled a heavy advertising schedule and a presidential visit.

Meanwhile Reagan hit on a TV style that helped turn his campaign around. His staff had been doing battle over how to present the Californian on television. One side argued that Reagan was most effective in straightforward addresses; "The best way is to just let him talk," said campaign press secretary Lyn Nofziger. On the other side, Harry Treleaven argued that "you can't go on television for half an hour and talk to people—they'll all go to sleep, change channels, or get upset because you preempted *SWAT*." He wanted spots showing Reagan out on the stump, with the technical quality intentionally mediocre—in order to head off charges of a slick, Hollywood presentation and to make the spots look like news footage. Treleaven won the early rounds, and his spots showed Reagan answering questions at so-called Citizens' Press Conferences in New Hampshire. The film crew hired to shoot footage for Reagan spots would stand beside network film crews at these gatherings. As earnest voters asked the governor his views on various issues, Treleaven's cameras rolled; the resulting footage might easily be mistaken for a story on the evening news:

VIDEO	AUDIO
Camera up on Reagan at lectern.	Announcer [VO]: "An important part of Ronald Reagan's campaign are the Citizens' Press Conferences, which give the people a chance to ask the questions."
Cut to citizen in audience.	Citizen [SOF]: "As president, how would you deal with the congressional Democrats who

	are calling for still further cutbacks in defense spending?"
Cut to Reagan.	Reagan [SOF]: "Well, here again is where I believe a president must take his case to the people. And the people must be told the facts. The people will not make a mistake if they have the facts. But the one thing we must be sure of is, the United States must never be second to anyone else in the world in military power.
Reaction shots, then cut back to Reagan.	[Applause] But the purpose of weapons is not to go to war; the purpose of weapons is to convince the other fellow that he better not go to war." [Applause builds]
	Announcer [VO]: "Reagan. He'll provide the strong new leadership America needs. Paid for by Citizens for Reagan."

Veteran time buyer Ruth Jones (Nixon 1968) bought Reagan time slots within or adjacent to news programs to complete the maneuver. Such newslike spots had been done occasionally before, beginning when television news became a major source of information for voters; the Reagan series made newslike spots a standard media technique.

Treleaven had another reason for avoiding slick spots of Reagan addressing the camera; "Another actor hawking something," they'd say (some perhaps would remember TV spots from two decades earlier, of a younger Ronald Reagan pushing new Boraxo hand cleaner). So Treleaven liked the modified "Man in the Arena" setup, showing Reagan spontaneously answering questions. Treleaven's choice was based on his instincts—the golden gut approach. But the voters, it turned out, didn't care about Reagan's actor background. "Right from the beginning our surveys indicated that was not a problem," the Reagan poll-taker, Richard Wirthlin, said later. "There were only about three percent who even mentioned he was an actor, and those three percent mentioned it in a positive context."

Treleaven was finally overruled in the North Carolina primary. Unless Reagan could win some primary soon, he'd have to drop out of the race. Desperation helped spawn innovation. North Carolina supporters of Senator Jesse Helms wanted to see Reagan at length, rallying the conservative faithful, and Tom Ellis, a Helms aide who was Reagan's state chairman, gave the Reagan high command an ultimatum. If they didn't send a half-hour Reagan speech for him to air, he would find an old one and fund it himself. Nofziger located a half-hour televised speech the candidate had given on free time over a Florida station. Nofziger excised the local references, spliced a fund-raising appeal at the end, and had it aired on fifteen of North Carolina's seventeen TV stations. The film was a hit, featuring many of Reagan's best, most blustery, cheer lines—"When it comes to the [Panama] Canal, we built it, we paid for it, it's ours and we should tell Torrijos and Company that we are going to keep it." People began talking about Reagan, and on primary day he took fifty-two percent of the North Carolina vote, his first win. North Carolina settled the debate over how to televise Reagan.

Reagan still was having money problems, though; his workers hadn't been paid in nearly a month. He pushed for a nationally televised half-hour fund-raising appeal, like the one he had done

Bright Songs and Blue Jeans

for Goldwater in 1964. Some of his aides countered, "This is
1976." Reagan won the argument, and the show went on the
air. An American flag pin in his lapel, he rambled from one
subject to another—Social Security, energy, the Panama Canal,
Henry Kissinger, the Russian dissident Aleksandr Solzhenitsyn.
Ford would later call it "a clever rehash of what he'd said before."
However repetitive or fuzzy it may have seemed to Ford, the
televised speech raised needed funds, attracting some $1.3 million,
on production costs of under $200,000.

On the Ford side, the President was being hurt by advertising
that continued to be, at the very least, unoriginal. A special five-
minute spot was produced for use in the Texas primary. Malcolm
MacDougall found it "filled with the old Nixon commercial techniques. Young American soldiers in foxholes, with an implicit
warning that if you don't vote for Ford they'll be right back in
those foxholes." MacDougall considered it bad strategy; the
Reagan-as-warmonger idea was not catching on with Republicans.
But what made it worse, as far as MacDougall was concerned,
"it was bad advertising." By mid-May Reagan led in the delegate
count, 528 to 479.

Right before the big (167 delegates) winner-take-all California
primary, the Ford staff dumped Campaign '76. The Dailey-Wagner team remained nominally in place, but, as Wagner put it,
"Suddenly a separate loop developed in our advertising." A bluff,
self-confident ad executive named Jim Jordan, president of
BBD&O, produced several spots that were okayed by Ford and
aired in California. Moving away from the august, regal style of
the Dailey-Wagner material, Jordan tried to address voters' concerns directly. One deals with Ford's efforts to stem inflation:

VIDEO	AUDIO
Camera up on long-haired woman, carrying bundle of papers, exiting Ford head-	Second woman [SOF]: "Ellie! Are you working for Presi-dent Ford?"

1976: FORD VS. CARTER

**Ford Slice of Life
Commercial**

"Ellie! Are you working
for President Ford?"

"President Ford has cut
inflation *in half*!"

"In half? Wow!"

Ford Presidential Aura Commercial

"He saw the nation as a partnership between government and the people, working together"

"President Ford's steady, calm leadership has helped put the nation back on track"

"President Ford has trust in America. America has trust in him. Keep him"

quarters (poster of Ford on door, banners all over windows). She takes one step, then runs into short-haired woman, a bag of groceries under her arm.

Ellie fumbles with papers.

Ellie [SOF]: "Only about twenty-six hours a day!"

The women walk to left quickly, off screen.

Second woman [SOF]: "When did this start?"

Camera moves in briefly for CU of Ford poster on door; then cut to the women, now in front of supermarket.

Ellie [SOF]: "Well, let me ask you something. Notice anything about these food prices lately?"

Ellie points to price signs in window. Other woman looks, thinks for a moment.

Cut to CU of second woman, seen over Ellie's shoulder.

Second woman [SOF]: "Well, they don't seem to be going up the way they used to."

Cut to CU of Ellie, seen over other woman's shoulder.

Ellie [SOF, slowly]: "President Ford has cut inflation *in half*!"

Cut to CU of second woman, seen over Ellie's shoulder.

Second woman [SOF]: "In half? Wow!"

Cut to medium shot of both women.

Ellie [SOF]: "It's just that I hate to think where we'd be without him."

Ellie walks off.

Cut to still photo of Ford. Legend below: "President Ford. He knows the way."	Announcer [VO]: "President Ford is leading us back to prosperity. Stay with him. He knows the way."

A second Jordan spot features a man and his son—who are obviously actors standing in a well-lighted studio—supposedly watching President Ford walking through a crowd. The Ford footage is lower-quality, news film footage:

VIDEO	AUDIO
Camera up on Ford shaking hands in large crowd, standing between two Secret Service men. Cut to man, thirtyish, blond, with blond boy, around eight, on his shoulder.	Applause up and under following. Man [SOF]: "He is a good man." Kid [SOF]: "Does he ever tell lies?"
Cut to Ford in crowd.	Man [SOF]: "I don't know for sure, Billy, but I don't think so. He's not the kind."
Cut to man and kid.	Kid [SOF]: "You like him, huh, Dad?" Man [SOF]: "Hate to think of where we'd be without him. Besides—if you grow up to be president, that's the kind I want you to be."
Man turns to look at kid.	
Cut to Ford at dais, holding microphone, smiling.	Announcer [VO]: "President Ford is leading us back to

Scene freezes; legend appears   prosperity. Stay with him. He
at bottom: "President Ford.   knows the way."
He knows the way."

The Jordan work was criticized as "unpresidential" by a Ford
campaign aide, who stayed anonymous. Wagner said, "You can't
try to jerk people around." The ads were aired for only two days
and then pulled. "It looked so 'addy,'" Malcolm MacDougall
told us. "In politics you don't do that. You try to keep the heavy
hand of the advertising copywriter hidden."

Reagan won California, but Ford got 88 of the 97 delegates
at stake in Ohio and all of those in New Jersey. The primaries
were over. Of 1,130 delegates needed to win the nomination,
Ford had 992, Reagan 886. Some delegates already selected were
uncommitted; they would have to be wooed. Additional delegates
would still be selected through conventions. Either way, it was
old politics—promises, threats, and cajolery delivered one on
one. Advertising became irrelevant. Uncommitted delegates were
invited to drop by the Oval Office for informal chats. Not surprisingly, they often walked out of the White House gates with
a new sympathy for Ford, who won the nomination on the first
ballot.

Carter Country

"In 1972, when Jimmy Carter started to run for president,"
recalls Gerald Rafshoon, "we never had a doubt that he would
win." Promoting *Cleopatra*, Sears Roebuck, and Getz Exterminator
("Getz Gets 'Em!") was one thing for Rafshoon; getting Jimmy
Carter elected governor of Georgia was something else; the White
House was another thing entirely. To the media establishment,
Rafshoon was a big fish in Atlanta's small pond. To the political
types, he was an overreacher with the grand total of one successful
campaign behind him. The political folklore holds that the most
dangerous person to have on your side is someone who has run
one winning campaign—he'll do everything exactly the same
way; after all, it worked. But Rafshoon had two particular

strengths. "I may not be the best adman in the country," he once said, "but I am the foremost authority on Jimmy Carter in terms of advertising and how it best suits him." At least as important, he and Carter knew and trusted each other.

Trust in fact would be a major campaign theme in the first post-Watergate presidential election. Carter's inexperience could be portrayed as an asset, and he would run as a decent, moral man. The electorate had heard before of presidential candidates who ran against "the mess in Washington." But now the candidate would run against Washington itself. "Carter just fit the issue of the day," Rafshoon says. "Carter was telling you that, after Watergate, the CIA revelations, Chile, Vietnam, we wanted to get a more open government and a less imperial presidency." As the campaign began, of course, few Americans had even heard of Carter. Rafshoon's first goal was to establish Carter as a person through advertising. In a five-minute campaign biography, he put Carter in blue jeans and work boots, walking through a field, running his hands through fresh-picked peanuts, and joking with his mother. Another primary spot echoed traditional Southern populism:

VIDEO	AUDIO
Camera up on medium shot of Carter, in dark blue suit, with serious expression, standing before pale green curtains.	Carter [SOF]: "I have tried to speak for the vast majority of Americans that for too long have been kept on the outside looking in.
Legend "Jimmy Carter" fades in as large white super.	I have no obligations to those whose only interest in this campaign is to stop the people from getting control of your government.

"I'm running for president
because I have a vision of a
new America. A different
America. A better America. If
you share that vision, help
me fight for it."

| Cut to white letters on blue background: "Jimmy Carter June 8." | Announcer [VO]: "Vote for Jimmy Carter and his delegates, June 8." |

Another Rafshoon spot ends with Carter talking intently from a podium: "Now listen to me carefully. I'll never tell a lie. I'll never make a misleading statement. I'll never avoid a controversial issue. Watch television, listen to the radio. If I ever do any of those things, don't support me." The line encapsulated the Carter candidacy, summing up the candidate's plusses (he really believed in his honesty) and minuses (he really was innocent of the ways of national government). "It was obvious that that theme was very potent. It was something he came up with off the cuff, extemporaneously," Rafshoon recalls, "and I put it into spots." Rafshoon showed the spots to other Carter advisers and finally to the lawyer Charles Kirbo, a principal of Atlanta's most influential law firm. "If you ever get in trouble in Georgia, ever land in a Southern jail, call Kirbo," Rafshoon laughs. After the screening Rafshoon asked, "What do you think, Mr. Kirbo?" Kirbo replied: "Gonna lose the liar vote." Rafshoon said, "What?" "Gonna lose the liar vote." Rafshoon laughed. Kirbo said, "I ain't kidding."

While Carter's message was personal, his strategy was practical. Hamilton Jordan argued that if Carter could win the early contests, he would get the press and party attention he needed—the meta-campaign—and pick up additional support for subsequent primaries. New Hampshire traditionally enjoyed major news coverage as the first primary. This year, though, Iowa would choose delegates several weeks earlier, and in caucuses, not open voting. With so many candidates in the field, the press pack was bound to pay attention there.

The usual approach for winning a caucus state is to identify your voters and get them out to vote quietly; media noise only lets the opposition see what you're doing, and may stir unsympathetic voters. But Carter chose, in Rafshoon's words, "to foster a lot of excitement. We went on television to get new people to come into the caucus." The strategy succeeded. Carter won a two-to-one victory over Birch Bayh, the Indiana senator. Carter also won in New Hampshire and then concentrated on Florida to take on his fellow Southerner, George Wallace. To build a Florida base, the Carter campaign had started running TV spots early, simultaneous with the Iowa caucus. The result was that Floridians began hearing a lot about Carter. Wallace in 1972 had used the slogan "Send Them a Message," which offered Southern defiance; the Carter slogan admonished, "This Time Don't Send Them a Message; Send Them a President," which promised Southern victory. The Wallace campaign used television heavily, in part because Wallace's mobility was limited as a consequence of the 1972 attempt on his life. But his health remained an unspoken negative. Carter won the primary, thirty-four percent to Wallace's thirty-one percent, and a post-election survey found that three-fifths of 1972 Wallace supporters had defected, so they told surveyers, because of the "health issue."

As Carter's freshness faded, voters began to ask what he stood for. Candidates like Wallace were easy to label. Not so Carter: was he a liberal or a conservative? Pat Caddell, who had worked for McGovern in 1972, now was doing polling for Carter. His surveys showed the "fuzziness issue" was on people's minds. In the Pennsylvania primary Rafshoon began running spots with opening lines promising specifics. The rest of each commercial was unchanged:

VIDEO	AUDIO
Camera up on white letters against blue background: "JIMMY CARTER ON JOBS."	Carter [SOF]: "I believe that anybody that's able to work
Fade to Carter in shirt-sleeves, leaning against fence; lettering remains on screen for a few seconds, then fades.	ought to work, and ought to have a chance to work. And I don't think we'll ever have a solution to our present economic woes as long as we've got eight and a half or nine million people out of jobs, that are looking for jobs; another two or three million that have given up hope of getting work, and another million and a half on welfare that never have worked, but are fully able to work full time."
Cut to white letters against blue background: "JIMMY CARTER June 8."	Announcer [VO]: "Vote for Jimmy Carter and his delegates June 8."

Thoughout the spring, Carter withstood pressing challenges from Senators Henry Jackson and Frank Church and Representative Morris Udall. Governor Jerry Brown of California came in late and won two primaries. By then, though, Carter had the delegates he needed. At the convention he won the nomination on the first ballot, chose Minnesota Senator Walter Mondale as his running mate, and prepared to head the ticket of his united, if not overly enthusiastic, party.

"I'm Feelin' Good About America"

The 1976 presidential campaign had everything, on paper: $44 million in federal money to fuel it; the demonstrable skills of media professionals like Rafshoon, Deardourff, Bailey, and MacDougall at the controls; the radar information on the electorate, through the polls of Robert Teeter and Caddell. But the campaign lacked, those polls said, "presidential" candidates. As Teeter later remembered, "Perceptions about both of them were very thin." Voters told the opinion surveyors that they thought Ford was honest, a decent family man, sincere in trying to do what he thought was best. The public's one big question was, simply, was he smart enough to be president? Carter was seen as honest, religious, Christian, a moral man. There were two major questions about him, said Teeter. First, was he qualified to be president, or, as Teeter put it, "was he a quick-packaged commodity that had come on the scene very abruptly?" Second, did his proclaimed religious feelings make him "a little bizarre"?

Of the two camps Ford's had the harder assignment. Ford, in his memoirs, says that when he went out to make a speech, his "approval rating" declined around the country. Stuart Spencer told Ford: "Mr. President, as a campaigner, you're no fucking good." (One measure of the media men's new prominence was that Spencer believed he could talk that way, and Ford believed he had to take it.) Spencer's assessment had accompanied an equally blunt strategy memo making four points: no personal campaigning, "very aggressive media-oriented efforts," careful preparation of "*all* on-camera appearances" (including practice runs on videotape), and the hiring of the best Republican media firm around, Bailey, Deardourff Associates. In August, when the White House called, the partners presented conditions that had to be met, including complete control of the advertising campaign with direct access to the President; freedom to pursue their other commitments—the nine other campaigns they had been working on for months—allowing them only two days a week for Ford;

Ford's support for the Equal Rights Amendment; and the power to hire whomever they wanted, principally Malcolm MacDougall.

MacDougall is a hands-on copywriter. He drove his client's Olds Cutlass, used Titleist golf balls, and drank Salada tea and A&W root beer before extolling them. With Ford he had to begin work without that creative edge. He wasn't even sure he was a Ford supporter. But as he thought about it, he says, he grew more and more interested. "If there ever was a candidate who needed good advertising, it was President Ford. Maybe I didn't know the product too well, I thought. But I could spot a fascinating advertising problem when I saw one." Ford, concluded Mac-Dougall, was "a real professional challenge."

Because the media men had come into the campaign so late, Ford had no advertising ready for the first three weeks in September. Some air time was bought to run excerpts of Ford's acceptance speech, just to maintain some television presence, but the results were hardly encouraging. One excerpt, MacDougall remembers, received the lowest Nielsen rating of any half-hour program of the year. MacDougall knew candidates for lowly offices who had spent months, sometimes years, planning campaign strategy. His commercial clients, like Oldsmobile, might work for years on ad strategy to get consumers to drive their cars. MacDougall had three weeks to prepare for an election less than three months away. "To do what we did in two months for Ford," McDougall told us, "would take the normal agency and client—working diligently together, having their usual meetings—between two and three years, to get even halfway where we were in November."

The media managers held one key meeting. MacDougall spent one hour with Deardourff and Bailey discussing Ford's advertising, then he was on his own to make the plan. Unlike Rosser Reeves, MacDougall argued that a political campaign needs more than one selling proposition. USP might be enough to get people to choose one product over another, "but when you're trying to sell a president, one strategy just won't do. We couldn't elect

Ford by convincing Americans he was a nice guy. Or just by proving he was strong leader (so was Nixon)." MacDougall concluded Ford had to convince Americans that he was a lot of things: "Good guy, strong leader, compassionate, someone who had done a lot and had a good program for the next four years. At the same time we had to try to convince Americans that Jimmy Carter wasn't what he said he was. . . ." Part of the reason the first set of primary ads by Dailey-Wagner had failed, MacDougall told us, was that they used just one strategy. "That whole series of five-minute commercials, Ford wandering around the White House, was aimed at showing him as the President— when everybody in America knew he had only been President for about a week. You had to do a lot of other things too. Who is he? Where did he come from? What kind of guy is he?"

MacDougall moved to Washington to take over Campaign '76, the third change in command. Deardourff and a film crew began interviewing Ford's wife and family, preparing footage for biography spots. Bailey and a second film crew flew to Grand Rapids, Michigan, where they interviewed nearly everyone who had known young Jerry Ford, including Ford's boyhood employer. The man obviously had no memory of Ford, "but that didn't stop him from talking for half an hour about what 'a fine lad' he had been," according to MacDougall. While the grand vision continued to elude them, they did pick up a catchy song.

The background for Ford's advertising, Deardourff has explained, was the Nixon years, and how far the country had come since 1974. When Ford became president, the nation had lived through the spectacle of the beleaguered Nixon fighting off the impeachment process. For almost two years the citizenry had been flooded by the Watergate revelations of corruption and wrongdoing. Ford's presidency might not be "overly impressive," said Deardourff, but there was "a sense that things were in fact substantially better and that people felt better." Ford's spots should "attempt to create a good feeling about the country and to give the president a certain amount of credit for having im-

1976: FORD VS. CARTER

Ford "Feelin' Good"
Images

There's a change that's come
  over America
A change that's great to see
We're livin' here in peace again
We're going back to work again
It's better than it used to be

I'm feelin' good about America
I feel it everywhere I go
I'm feelin' good about America
I thought you ought to know
That I'm feelin' good about
  America
It's something great to see
I'm feelin' good about America
I'm feelin' good about me!

proved the situation." Enter Robert Gardner and "I'm Feelin' Good About America."

One day in early September, Gardner pulled MacDougall and Bailey aside. Gardner, on leave from the J. Walter Thompson agency in San Francisco to work with MacDougall, said he had written a song for Ford. "There is absolutely nothing worse in a political campaign than a bad song," said Bailey. Undeterred, Gardner played a casette tape:

There's a change that's come over America
A change that's great to see
We're livin' here in peace again
We're going back to work again
It's better than it used to be.

I'm feelin' good about America
I feel it everywhere I go
I'm feelin' good about America
I thought you ought to know
That I'm feeling good about America
It's something great to see
I'm feelin' good about America
I'm feelin' good about me!

Bailey listened, stood and said, "There is absolutely nothing better in a political campaign than a good song." MacDougall was also enthusiastic. "It was easy to put pictures to those lyrics; all we had to do was show a lot of people feelin' good." The first commercials were crowded with people feelin' good, "almost every voting group in America," in MacDougall's words.

Next the biographical material was edited into a spot that emphasized Ford's intelligence and energy:

VIDEO	AUDIO
Camera up on still photo, warm brown tones, of three Boy Scouts at flag raising. Camera moves in on one of the scouts, young Jerry Ford.	Announcer [VO]: "He was an Eagle Scout. He was an honor student.
Cut to ECU of hands holding football. Camera pulls back quickly, revealing college-age Ford crouched over the ball.	He was the most valuable player at Michigan.
Cut to large group photo. Camera closes in on Ford.	He was graduated in the top third of Yale Law School, while holding a full-time job.
Cut to still portrait of Ford in military uniform.	He served courageously in World War II.
Cut to Ford on floor of Congress, alongside Speaker John McCormack.	He led his party in the Congress.
Cut to Ford in Oval Office, working at desk near window. Camera moves in for CU.	And in two short years as president, he has brought us peace, helped turn the economy around, and helped make us proud again.
Fade to Ford in profile, looking thoughtful. Camera slowly moves up on photo.	"Gerald Ford has always been best when the going was toughest. Let's keep him in charge."

MacDougall also produced a five-minute spot, featuring Ford's wife and his children talking about Gerald Ford the family man.

"America was desperately wanting to get back to some basic values," MacDougall explained to us. "In the context of that year, the man himself and his family, which is a crucial part of him, *had* to be presented to the people. Carter certainly used his little daughter Amy. Every time there was a flashbulb around, Amy was told she had to kiss her father. We didn't go *that* far." Still, MacDougall allows, "The actual commercial was very cornball." In addition the early presidential theme from the Dailey-Wagner days was repackaged in a typical Rose Garden strategy. For many Americans the White House's aura and physical setting evoke strong associations of country and identity. MacDougall made advertising (as would Rafshoon in his turn in 1980) using this background, which also included such other symbols of national identity as Air Force One and the Oval Office.

While MacDougall labored to get out the Ford spots, the Carter advertising campaign was already on the air, spending over a quarter million dollars before September 21, according to Rafshoon. He had gotten by with two writers and two time buyers, supported by a small office staff, during the primaries. Now he hired thirty new people. His early spots, shown in the South, quoted Reagan's criticisms of Ford—an implicit appeal to conservative Republicans. Other Southern spots spoke to presumed regional pride in having a man from the South as president. The national campaign, however, aimed at more positive, populist appeals. In one such spot Carter declares, "We've seen walls built around Washington, and we feel that we can't quite get through to guarantee the people . . . a government that's sensitive to our needs."

The Ford and Carter ad campaigns resembled each other: they stressed the traditional American virtues of home, family, and country; they were based on survey research and integrated into the wider campaign themes; and they were very well made. Unfortunately for the master builder firms of Rafshoon and Co., and Deardourff, Bailey, MacDougall, there was another campaign underway, one less subject to their control.

In his convention acceptance speech Ford had challenged Carter to debates, and Carter had accepted. They then agreed on three televised meetings; in addition the vice-presidential candidates would hold one debate. Such debates are opposites of advertising spots; they are live, unedited and uncontrolled by the media managers. Though the candidates may have rehearsed many times the "spontaneous" lines written for them by their advisers, they have no chance for a retake if errors are made. When Carter and Ford cleared their throats and began the debates of 1976, the real candidates showed up, and the campaign ghost of Richard Ottinger hovered over the lectern. Ottinger, a pleasant, youngish (and still very much alive) congressman from New York's Westchester County, ran for the U.S. Senate from New York in 1970. His advertising campaign, directed by David Garth, pictured a decisive, vigorous campaigner in shirt-sleeves. But when Democrat Ottinger joined in a live, three-way debate with his Republican (Charles Goodell) and Conservative party (James Buckley) opponents, he appeared to the TV audience slow and unsure of himself. Ottinger lost, in part because of the dissonance between the advertised Ottinger and the real Ottinger. (The Ottinger Effect still thrives, as we saw in the early 1984 campaign of John Glenn, in chapter 1.)

An Ottinger Effect of sorts undid Carter and Ford, though hurting the president much more than his challenger. Carter had chipped away at his carefully created media image with a sappy aside about lust during an interview with *Playboy* magazine. But Ford stumbled live and on camera in front of a wider audience during the second debate, when in a mental lapse he liberated Eastern Europe from Soviet domination. The Ford error got prominent press attention for several days, and Teeter's polls measured its costs. Before the debate Ford had been going up and Carter coming down in the polls. Eastern Europe, says Teeter, "just flattened that right out. . . . We gained nothing for another twelve or thirteen days."

When in Doubt, Attack

Still a sharp chill of panic blew through the Carter camp, and
Rafshoon called in Tony Schwartz. As usual when healthy egos
and big reputations are involved, accounts differ on the motives.
One version suggests last-minute desperation. Rafshoon, em-
phatically, says no. "After the convention I commissioned
Schwartz to do a series of spots to have in abeyance, just in case.
Everybody said you might have to go negative." In any case
Carter appeared at Schwartz's studio for a taping session; the
two men cut twenty-five radio and TV spots in all, many of them
done with Carter closely framed and looking straight at the camera, one-on-one with the viewer. Of these a dozen were never
used, including several slick negative spots. Rafshoon said he
judged them "too rough." One rejected ad shows Soviet tanks
rumbling through Hungary; the narrator incredulously asks (in
tones reminiscent of 1964's "Merely another weapon?"), "Can
the president of the United States be ignorant of this?" Rafshoon
did use one of Schwartz's spots, based on Caddell polls reporting
that half of the voters thought Ford's running mate Robert Dole
was unqualified to be president. The spot was called "MonDole":

VIDEO

AUDIO

Camera up on yellow letters
against black background:
"VICE-PRESIDENT?"

Announcer [VO, very informal and natural]: "Have you
though about the *vice*-presi-
dential candidates?

Fade up on left half of screen
black and white photo of
Mondale, looking at camera.

What do you think of
Mondale?

Fade up on right half of
screen, alongside Mondale
photo, black and white photo
of Dole.

What do you think of Dole?
    "What kind of men are
they? When you know that
four out of the last six vice-

| | presidents wound up being president, who would you like to see a heartbeat away from the presidency? |
| Fade to color photo of Mondale and Carter. | "Well, this is why many people will be voting for Jimmy Carter and Walter Mondale." |

Simultaneously Carter used radio ads to talk to different constituencies, a form of narrowcasting not possible on TV. Black-oriented stations played spots about Carter's civil rights stands; white country and western stations were used, as Caddell put it, "to wave the bloody rebel flag":

AUDIO

Announcer [VO]: "On November 2 the South is being readmitted to the Union. If that sounds strange, maybe a Southerner can understand. Only a Southerner can understand years of coarse, anti-Southern jokes and unfair comparisons. Only a Southerner can understand what it means to be a political whipping boy. But then, only a Southerner can understand what Jimmy Carter as president can mean. It's like this: November 2 is the most important day in our region's

1976: FORD VS. CARTER

Carter Five-Minute Bio

"By any stretch of the imagination, Jimmy Carter has come a long way"

"My children will be the sixth generation on the same land"

"We've always worked for a living. We know what it means to work"

"I'll never tell a lie. I'll never make a misleading statement"

history. Are you going to let
it pass without having your
say? Are you going to let the
Washington politicians keep
one of our own out of the
White House? Not if this man
can help it."

Carter [VO]: "We love our
country. We love our government. We don't want
anything selfish out of government, we just want to be
treated fairly. And we want a
right to make our own
decisions."

Announcer [VO]: "The South
has always been the con-
science of America—maybe
they'll start listening to us
now. Vote for Jimmy Carter
on November 2."

The Ford campaign did its own version of narrowcasting, talking
to its suburban and mid-America constituency with ex-ballplayer
and sportscaster Joe Garagiola and Ford chatting informally—
the Joe and Jerry Show. Ford, who had been visibly awkward
on camera, now looked comfortable with Garagiola. The ex-
catcher played Joe Six-Pack: "Hi, I'm Joe Garagiola, and for the
next half hour you're in for a treat!" one program began. Garagiola asks Ford the difference between a Nixon and a Ford
administration. Says Ford: "Well, there's one fundamental difference. Under President Ford there's not an imperial White
House, which means no pomp. There's no ceremony. There's
no dictatorial authority. We've tried to run the White House as

a people's house, where individuals have an opportunity to come in individually or in groups and express to me their views and recommendations."

The Higher Ground

On election eve both sides attempted to close more positively. Carter's show, produced by Robert Squier, sat the candidate behind a desk in his Plains, Georgia, study:

VIDEO	AUDIO

After introduction, camera cuts to Carter in library of home, in coat and tie. He puts down glasses and addresses camera.	Carter [VO]: "Good evening.
	    "Twenty-two months ago, when I began my campaign, I was a lonely candidate. I walked the streets, went into private homes, saw one person at the time, at most three or four. But when the returns came in from the early primaries, we had won. And the reason was, and it surprised a lot of people, I had a close, personal, individual, direct relationship with the people of this country, in New Hampshire and Florida and North Carolina and Illinois.
	    "And that's the kind of relationship that was disturbed as we *did* win. We had larger crowds, Secret Service, a lot of newspeople between me and the people of this country.

"Tonight is an opportunity,
at the last moment of the
campaign, to let the American people see again, individual Americans, the way I see
them—people, in families,
sometimes unemployed,
sometimes elderly, sometimes
concerned about the image of
our country—just in a direct,
person-to-person relationship
with me, the man who hopes
to be the next president of
our country.

"Hope you enjoy the show.
It's going to be untarnished,
and direct, and unrehearsed,
a good presentation of the
proper relationship between
the future president and the
people he hopes to serve."

During the rest of the half hour people on city streets and
elsewhere ask questions. The style is like Ike's 1952 election-eve
effort, though if anything less slickly produced.

The Ford effort was smoother, complete with Garagiola, shots
of Air Force One ("This might be the first election that was won
by an airplane," the writer Elizabeth Drew said drily), "Feelin'
Good," and an endorsement:

VIDEO	AUDIO
After voice-over introduction, cut to Joe Garagiola, in coat	Roar of plane.

and tie, sitting in plane seat, grinning.

Garagiola [SOF, shouting to be heard]: " . . I believe in this man. You know, I've never done much more before than just vote. But this year the stakes are just too high to sit on the sidelines. So, on this last night before the election, I want you to see a film about Jerry Ford, a documentary about his background, about his family, about the job he's already doing, and about his hopes for America. And then I want you to hear from President Ford himself.

"But before you see this film, or hear from the president, somebody else has something to say about this election and about this man. Now all America knows her, and all America loves her. It's Pearlie! Miss Pearl Bailey."

Cut to medium shot of Pearl Bailey, serious expression, sitting on couch, addressing camera.
Cut to CU.

Bailey [SOF]: "I've never done this before in my life. I'm not here to judge men; the Bible says I am not to judge.

"But I do hope that you think before you vote. Use all the goodness within you. Don't, just because some people will say, well, yeah, but what happened a couple of years ago? Yes, you're right, a couple of years ago our country was truly shaken. And a man was put at the head of it named Gerald Ford.

"And I really believe, in his heart—oh, he's made some mistakes, honey. You better believe he has! I wouldn't sit here, and even try to say he didn't. But I'll tell you what, if a man is trying, and a man has more than dreams; he has something called get up and go, and truth, and most of all he has something I like very much in every human being, simplicity and honesty. 'Cause I really believe he's an honest man.

"That's why I like Gerald Ford. And that's why I hope that—I don't know. Please, think about it. It's so important. It really is."

Cut to Garagiola on plane.

Garagiola [SOF]: "That's a real lady. Gives you a lump in your throat. She's talking about my kind of guy—and I think he's your kind of guy too. . . ."

Ford spent some $6.4 million on TV to Carter's $7.6 million. Like Nixon in 1968, Carter took a commanding lead and saw it shrink to a point where he nearly lost the election. As with Humphrey in 1968, Ford's campaign created original, memorable advertising. Deardourff in fact thinks that Ford "won" the election the Sunday before Tuesday when a published poll showed him ahead. Ford's suddenly improved position, paradoxically, may have done him in. The serious prospect of four more Republican years stirred memories of Nixon, and of the Nixon pardon; some voters switched back to Carter. In the end Ford just couldn't shake Nixon, despite all the advertising that $6.4 million could buy.

TV PITCHMAN TO PRIME-TIME PRESIDENT

CHAPTER 13

The presidential elections of the 1960s and 1970s had brought the media managers to prominence within national campaigns. By 1980 these new insiders were attracting the close attention of journalists and commentators. The addition of the right name expert to a campaign could give a certain credibility in the press's eyes, while movements of key people out of the candidate's organization were often read as signs of trouble or decay. When John Deardourff and Doug Bailey went to work for the candidacy of Tennessee Senator Howard Baker in early 1979, for example, the senator figured to be a serious force in the race for the Republican nomination. Deardourff and Bailey—the men who came in belatedly to help Ford in 1976—had gotten involved early this time, and they had another up-tempo song, "What's Special About America," to lift American spirits, now battered by the seizure of American hostages by Iranian militants.

With his reputation as an effective Republican leader in the Senate, Baker appeared to be a fresh candidate, an early frontrunner; so too did another attractive Republican, George Bush. Bush's résumé was impressive: experience as a congressman, head of the Republican National Committee, envoy to China, ambassador to the United Nations, and director of the CIA; establishment roots in the northeast (his well-to-do father had been a U.S. senator from Connecticut, and Bush had grown up there and gone to Yale), as well as connections with the more freewheeling wing of the party in Texas, where he had moved after college and made his own fortune in the oil business. Bush also had an impressive campaign organization, including Ford's 1976 delegate hunter, James Baker; Reagan's 1976 Southern strategist, David Keene; and a hyperenergetic media man from Baltimore named Robert Goodman, with a solid list of successes behind him and a taste for big production numbers in his spots.

By contrast, another Republican favorite, Ronald Reagan, in his third try for the nomination, gave every sign of struggling: he changed media teams, sacked several key campaign aides on the day of the New Hampshire primary, spent relatively little money on rather indifferent advertising, and in general appeared, to put it charitably, too old and too tired for the race.

It was of course the candidacy of Howard Baker that quickly expired, even more rapidly than "President" Muskie's had in 1972. Bush's soon followed. There was, as Baker's song declared, still something special about America after four years of Jimmy Carter. But neither Baker nor Bush lasted long enough as a presidential candidate to benefit from it. While good media may have become necessary for success, the campaigns for Baker, Bush, and Reagan—and of Jimmy Carter and Edward M. Kennedy on the Democratic side—demonstrated that good media by itself was not sufficient for success.

The first demonstration of this rule came early, on November 3, 1979, a year before the election, three months before the first primary, and two months before the first delegates were selected in Iowa. Baker announced on November 2. His campaign managers had choreographed an elaborate plan to get him off to a good start: the day after the announcement, he and a planeload of national reporters would fly to Portland, Maine, for a day of speeches by presidential candidates, followed by a straw vote. The vote would be meaningless; no delegates were at stake. But it would be the first indication of strength. In 1976 Jimmy Carter had surprised everyone with an Iowa win that opened the way to the nomination; in 1980 reporters vowed not to be surprised. Early tests, pointless though they might be, would receive heavy press attention. Heading for Portland, the Baker campaign staff felt optimistic. Senator William Cohen of Maine was a Baker supporter, and Cohen's forces were running the gathering. They had obligingly given Baker the final speech assignment right before the balloting, and the Maine group was itself weighted in Baker's favor. Baker would arrive, speak, and win; the national reporters would spread the word.

The Bush campaign strategists, David Keene and David Sparks, thought it important that Bush emerge with something. He couldn't win, the way the meeting was stacked. But he could at least elicit an enthusiastic response from the audience. So young Bush supporters, clad in red and blue "George Bush for President" T-shirts, came by bus from Boston. Bush at least would rate a mention in news stories, as the candidate with a crowd of strong-lunged supporters. Bush gave an upbeat talk touching on patriotism, optimism, and his experience. The cheering section made it sound more exciting than it was. Baker, when his turn came, spoke of how politics was an honorable profession. He was thoughtful, low-key, and unexciting. Even his supporters had trouble looking enthusiastic. When the votes were counted, George Bush had narrowly won. The next morning's *New York Times*, the well-circulated Sunday edition, featured a lead story on Bush's surprise win. One day old, the Baker campaign was already dying.

Although Baker the candidate never caught on, Deardourff and Bailey produced the most dramatic spot of the 1980 primaries:

VIDEO	AUDIO
Camera up on Baker at podium, leaning forward, speaking intently.	Baker [SOF]: "America must resolve that she's not going to be pushed around. That doesn't cause a war—that stops a war!"
Baker leans back, scratches nose. White letters superimposed across bottom of screen: "Sen. Howard Baker." Baker points to questioner, nods.	[Applause]
Cut to long-haired, agitated Iranian, waving pamphlet in hand.	Iranian [SOF]: "When the Shah's army killed more than sixty thousand Iranian people with their U.S.-equipped weapons, why weren't you raising your voice of support of international law?
Quick cuts between Baker, tight-lipped, and Iranian.	"And United States government shipped a hundred and fifty thousand barrels of oil for the Shah's army to kill the Iranian people, why weren't you concerned about international law—"
Baker leans forward and points angrily.	Baker [SOF]: "Because, my friend, I'm interested in fifty Americans, that's why! [Applause begins.] And when

	those fifty Americans are re-leased, then I'm perfectly willing to talk about that."
Cut to Iranian, waving arms hopelessly. Camera pans crowd, smiling and applauding.	[Loud cheering]

Cut to crowd rising for stand-ing ovation, then pan stand-ing crowd.
Cut to Baker at podium, smil-ing at applause. Red letters superimposed across picture: "BAKER/REPUBLICAN/ PRESIDENT/NOW."

Jingle begins:
That old pride
That we used to have
I believe it's coming back.
You see—
What's special about America,
Is mighty special to me.

The Bailey-Deardourff camera angles make the diminutive Baker look like a giant; the editing spliced in a standing ovation that actually came later, when Baker had finished his talk.

The Reagan campaign manager, John Sears, a lawyer and political strategist who worked for Nixon in 1968, saw little need for such dramatic action. Reagan was well known and well liked by party conservatives. He barely campaigned at all—sort of a Rose Garden strategy without the Rose Garden. "It wouldn't do any good to have him going to coffees and shaking hands like all the others," Sears said at the time. "People will get the idea he's an ordinary man like the rest of us." The relaxed strategy fit the candidate's no-sweat personality. Reagan took it easy, avoiding joint appearances with his opponents (including a tele-vised Des Moines debate, attended by all the others). His campaign spent just $6,000 on spots in Iowa.

George Bush, however, concentrated on Iowa. He didn't have wide support among Republicans; the Eastern Establishment wing, too tired or too fragmented, didn't rally to him. But Bush had studied the Jimmy Carter example of 1976. The Bush staff felt that Bush could win the nomination by coming in a close second to Reagan in Iowa, and establishing Bush as Reagan's principal competition. Bush spent long days going from one sparsely attended coffee meeting to another, trying to build a base. The Iowa delegates would be selected in caucuses rather than a primary. That demanded organization, and here too Bush was doing well. He also put some $26,000 into TV spots made by Robert Goodman.

Goodman and the Rising Multitudes

The son of a Baltimore surgeon, Goodman had planned to be a doctor. At Haverford College, though, he discovered new interests—philosophy, history, English, and especially music. He became Broadway-struck, and during college he wrote musicals. One was seen by a theatrical producer, who brought Goodman to New York in 1949 after graduation. Goodman worked on a show (never produced), studied music at Peabody Institute, and grew bored and desperate: "What was I going to do with my life? Here I was, a year out of college. So I walked into an ad agency in Baltimore, Joseph Katz agency, and got hired as a copywriter." Goodman, among other assignments, did commercials for Amoco and Ex-Lax. Katz had worked for Stevenson in 1952 and still had the Democratic National Committee as a client. Goodman worked on the account and found himself growing interested in politics. Goodman did his service in the post-Korean army—as a press officer in Japan—and returned to Katz, and then ventured out on his own in 1959. At first he did no political work.

Then one day in 1966, a candidate for governor of Maryland, a Democrat named Tom Finan, came to see him. "He was a nice guy, very appealing but somewhat on the dull side," Goodman recalls. Finan did not interest him, but the campaign did. "I remembered this obscure Baltimore County executive who'd just taken office. I'd met him in the mayor's office, on some

1980 PRIMARIES: THE LOSERS

Bush "Submarine" Commercial

"George Bush: an authentic American hero"

Kennedy Anti-Carter Spot

"When it came to inflation, his attitude was: 'I'll keep my fingers crossed.' Today we have twenty percent inflation"

Baker "Iranian" Commercial

"America must resolve that she's not going to be pushed around. That doesn't cause a war—that stops a war"

"When the Shah's army killed more than sixty thousand Iranian people with their U.S.-equipped weapons, why weren't you raising your voice of support of international law?"

"Because, my friend, I'm interested in fifty Americans, that's why!"

United Way drive or something. So I decided, before doing any-thing, to go see this man." This was how Goodman came to work for Spiro Agnew and helped the county executive rise to national attention. Goodman looks back on that first race with more humor than guilt. "You have to remember that Agnew was, of course, the liberal hope in those days. Honest, straight, didn't have five cents in the bank." Goodman cast Agnew as the white knight of Maryland politics. His Democratic opponent, George Mahoney (who beat Finan in the primary), ran as a conservative with the slogan "A Man's Home Is His Castle"— words that in the 1960s carried a code message about integration, housing, and other social concerns. After that first meeting with Agnew, Goodman says, "I went back to my office and said, 'We are gonna turn down the million-dollar Finan campaign because I like this guy Agnew better.' I thought I was making the biggest sacrifice of my career. As it turned out it was probably the biggest step up." Agnew ran against Mahoney with Goodman spots featuring the jingle, "My Kind of Man/Ted Agnew Is" (to the tune, "My Kind of Town/Chicago Is").

After Agnew became governor, Democrat Goodman changed his party registration and began taking on Republican candidates. But he never forsook his earlier theatrical interests. "I felt in those days—and I still do, to a degree—that elections are pieces of drama, and I was more interested in the dramatics than in the logical common sense of things." Goodman began writing music for his political commercials—uplifting, patriotic themes, scored for seventy-eight-piece orchestra; "epical kinds of things," in his words. "The honest reason I turned to music was that I understood it. It wasn't that I had read books about it, or had a philosophy about it. It was the way I could communicate."

Goodman didn't have original lyrics for his 1980 candidate, as Bailey-Deardourff did for Baker, but he had production. His first spots showed Bush surrounded by throngs of delirious sup-porters. These were aimed at taking care of Bush's "vulnera-bilities." ("To be vulnerable is to be human, which is good,"

Goodman says.) George Bush was vulnerable in Goodman's view
because he was one percent in the polls. His answer to that was
spots featuring big crowds and minuscule information:

VIDEO	AUDIO
Camera up on Bush in happy crowds.	Announcer [VO]: "This time, Americans have seen the opportunities of the 1980s—for the country and for the world. This time, there'll be no replays of the past. This time, there is George Bush.
Cut to audience, standing ovation; cut to Bush and his wife Barbara shaking hands with supporters.	"George Bush has emerged from the field of presidential candidates because of what he is—a man who has proven that he can do the tough jobs and lead this country.
Cut to white letters against blue background: "GEORGE BUSH FOR PRESIDENT."	"George Bush—a president we won't have to train. This time."

Another Goodman spot shows the candidate at an airport rally:

VIDEO	AUDIO
Plane taxies toward camera, nighttime, in driving rain. Cut to Bush walking through rain with Hugh Gregg, manager of his New Hampshire organization. Quick cuts of Bush in midst of adoring crowd.	Loud chanting off-camera: "We Want Bush!"

Announcer [VO, over chant-
ing]: "Not just here, but in
every state that he's been,
the spirit of the Republican
party has soared to meet the
real opportunity of the 1980s.
What has won out is very
simple: great personal energy,
experience, and knowledge at
the highest levels. *Quality*. Ladies and gentlemen, this is
George Bush."

Cut to medium shot of Bush.   Bush [breathlessly, SOF]:
                                     "Thank you. Thank you. I
                                     bring you word from across
                                     America: we're going all the
                                     way!"

Cut to white letters against   Announcer [VO]: "George
blue background: "GEORGE   Bush. A president we won't
BUSH FOR PRESIDENT."   have to train."

Such creative spot making caused a little embarrassment; the
CBS program *60 Minutes* disclosed that Bush had actually arrived
at the airport by bus, boarded a plane, and taxied to the crowd.
But Goodman liked the idea of multitudes greeting the larger-
than-life candidate fresh from his journey. Goodman's candidates
always look physically impressive. "We're always making our
man heroic in some sense," Goodman admits. "But George of
course *was* heroic; you could justify it." Goodman got his chance
to play on Bush's authentic heroism when Bush supplied a de-
caying film of World War II vintage, which Goodman recycled
enterprisingly in a spot introducing the candidate to voters:

1980: CARTER VS. REAGAN

Reagan "Soviet Arms" Spot

"Ronald Reagan spoke out on the danger of the Soviet arms buildup long before it was fashionable"

"He has a comprehensive program to rebuild our military power"

"Well, it's nice to be liked. But it's more important to be respected"

VIDEO	AUDIO
Camera up on submarine, surfaced. Bobbing figure in water is helped on deck, then walks toward camera. Freeze frame on face. (Grainy black-and-white film.)	Announcer [VO]: "This is not a professionally made film. It was made September 22, 1944, by a crew member of the USS *Finback*, a submarine that outraced a Japanese patrol boat to rescue a downed American flyer.
Fade to color still of Bush at desk, smiling.	"For George Bush, the Distinguished Flying Cross was the beginning of a career of outstanding service to our country: ambassador to the world; to China; director of the CIA—a dedication to country and experience that will make him a president we won't have to train.
Cut to white letters against blue background: "GEORGE BUSH FOR PRESIDENT."	"George Bush: an authentic American hero."

Running on the Issues

The Bush campaign's effort and organization paid off—Bush won Iowa. Reagan, badly shaken by the loss, agreed to debate his opponents as the New Hampshire primary approached. A campaign shake-up cost John Sears his job and brought in a new media specialist, Elliott Curson of Philadelphia. Curson went to Stanford to pore through the Reagan archives. He studied Reagan's speeches and positions—much like Rosser Reeves had done with Ike in 1952—and in one day of taping in Los Angeles Reagan cut eleven issue-oriented spots, which then ran through much of the primary season. One was on defense:

VIDEO	AUDIO
Camera up on Soviet military parade, quick cuts: tanks, red flag, Brezhnev, missile carriers, CU on missile.	Announcer [VO]: "Ronald Reagan spoke out on the danger of the Soviet arms buildup long before it was fashionable. He's always advocated a strong national defense and a position of leadership for America. He has a comprehensive program to rebuild our military power."
Cut to Reagan in medium shot, wearing blue suit, red tie, white shirt, against black background.	Reagan [SOF]: "We've learned by now that it isn't weakness that keeps the peace, it's strength. Our foreign policy has been based on the fear of not being liked. Well, it's nice to be liked. But it's more important to be respected."
Cut to slide, white letters on bright blue background: "REAGAN."	

Reagan's issue-oriented commercials represented a change in strategy: Reagan would come out fighting, and voicing the familiar doctrines of the Republican faithful. Bush's commercials show him in friendly meeting with the Chinese leader Mao as ambassador to China; Reagan's commercials show the Russian leader Brezhnev as the menacing opposition. Bush has the cheering crowds, the waving placards, the balloon drops—the momentum—in his advertising. Reagan has the conservative issues—the message—in his. In New Hampshire Reagan routed Bush, taking fifty percent of the vote to Bush's twenty-three percent.

Media attention then shifted to a different fresh face, Congressman John Anderson of Illinois. In the crowded Republican field Anderson stood out with specific liberal positions, strongly articulated. Robert Sann, Anderson's media man, capitalized on the distinction with advertising that boasted of the "Anderson Difference":

VIDEO	AUDIO
Camera up on Reagan speaking, then camera pulls back to reveal that we are actually watching a bank of six TV monitors, each showing a talking head candidate: Reagan, Bush, Crane, Baker, Connally, Dole.	Audio from six candidates is mixed together.
Anderson is standing in front of the monitors.	When Anderson begins speaking, other voices fade quickly.
	Anderson [SOF]: "If the secret to becoming president is telling people only what they want to hear, then we are indeed a nation in trouble."
Cut to large white letters on black background: "Think about the ANDERSON difference."	Announcer [VO]: "Think about the Anderson difference."
Cut back to Anderson.	Anderson [SOF]: "To promise an increased budget on one

	hand, while promising to cut your taxes with the other, is a cruel trick.
Gestures to monitors behind him.	"You know, I know, and even they know this can't be done. A tax cut may be popular, but it is irresponsible.
	"They all love to talk about women's rights. But none of them will support the ERA extension, the *only* hope for the women's movement."
Cut to slide: "Think about the ANDERSON difference."	Announcer [VO]: "Think about the Anderson difference."
Cut back to Anderson.	Anderson [SOF]: "I wish I too could blame our inflation and declining productivity on foreign countries, but I can't. The problem is a lack of self-discipline."
Cut to slide: "Think about the ANDERSON difference."	Announcer [VO]: "Think about the Anderson difference."
Cut back to Anderson.	Anderson [SOF]: "What does leadership really mean, if we can't openly discuss the sacrifices that will be required from all of us in this decade?"

| Cut to white letters on red background: "ANDERSON for President." | Announcer [VO]: "Anderson for President. Think about the Anderson difference." |

Sann professed surprise when reminded that the slogan evoked the "Anacin Difference" work he had done on behalf of the headache relief tablet and declared it was strictly coincidental. Anderson's "Difference" earned him second-place finishes in several early primaries, victories so far as the metacampaign was concerned. In fact the congressman never won a Republican primary, including that of his home state. But he did well enough to decide to run independently for the presidency. Meanwhile Bush began to bounce back, winning the Pennsylvania primary, but by then it was too late in the delegate count. At the convention Reagan was nominated on the first ballot, and after brief negotiations with former President Ford, he turned to Bush as his running mate.

Cultivating the Rose Garden

Bush, Baker, and Reagan each had his troubles during the Republican primaries. Edward M. Kennedy had a share of everybody's troubles during the Democratic primaries. Like Baker, his candidacy peaked before he announced; like Bush, he seemed unable to articulate a clear vision of his candidacy; like Reagan, both his strategists and his advertising changed several times. In mid-1979 the public opinion polls showed Kennedy leading the faltering Jimmy Carter forty-six percent to twenty-nine percent. By December *Time* magazine was reporting Carter leading Kennedy by twenty points.

More than any other factor the seizure of the American embassy in Teheran by followers of the Ayatollah Khomeini contributed to this 180 degree swing. Later the Soviet invasion of Afghanistan helped Carter still more. In each case American public opinion rallied 'round the office of the president (a "genial but dopey instinct," Arthur Schlesinger, Jr., called this traditional habit of support for the president—any president—in times of foreign policy crisis). Kennedy, however, had himself helped make the shift to Carter easier for many. Carter's administration had been judged so inept that Democrats thought the answer to their problems would be as simple as ABC—"Anybody But Carter." But when Kennedy submitted to an interview with Roger Mudd of CBS News, he appeared tongue-tied when asked such simple questions as why he wanted to be president; it was such an embarrassing performance that the derided Carter looked good by contrast. (A film sequence on the program didn't help the senator either: CBS attached a camera to the front end of an automobile to recreate, in police documentary fashion, the route of his car the night of the Chappaquiddick bridge accident that claimed the life of Kennedy's passenger, Mary Jo Kopechne.)

  Kennedy's campaign organization mirrored the candidate's seeming lack of preparation. Brother-in-law Stephen Smith had ultimate authority, though several surviving knights of Camelot days sat at his roundtable. No public opinion sampler was hired until one month after the announcement. Herbert Schmertz, a worker for Robert Kennedy in 1968 who had moved on to head the public affairs division of Mobil Oil, was called in to organize the media effort. Schmertz had provided millions of Mobil's dollars to underwrite such Public Broadcasting fare as *Masterpiece Theater*; he lasted just six weeks in the Kennedy campaign. Next the "media coordination" was taken over by Philip Bakes, former counsel to the Civil Aeronautics Board and a man with no experience in political campaigns. David Garth, an established New York media manager with a string of successes, was approached by the Kennedy people but opted out ("They didn't understand media," he told us). Tony Schwartz arrived and departed early in the campaign ("There was no real direction," he remembered, then added, in a phrase that echoed Arie Kopelman twelve years earlier in the Humphrey campaign: "Twenty different people proposed twenty different things."). David Sawyer, the New York filmmaker and political consultant who did his first political work for Rhode Island Governor Frank Licht in 1970, worked briefly and then quit. Charles Guggenheim stayed longer.

Guggenheim filmed a thirty-minute paid speech in which Kennedy, seated at a desk and looking directly into the camera, addressed Chappaquiddick: "While I know many will never believe the facts of the tragic events at Chappaquiddick, those facts are the only truth I can tell because that is the way it happened, and I ask only that I be judged on the basic American standards of fairness." Guggenheim also produced spots dealing with Chappaquiddick, to be aired in Maine and New Hampshire. The effort was reminiscent of John Kennedy facing the issue of his Catholicism before the Houston ministers. But while John Kennedy had offered a coherent argument, Edward Kennedy was saying he had nothing more to say. In another early spot, Kennedy's wife Joan spoke on camera (wearing a tennis dress) about her role in her husband's decision to run. At the time Kennedy and his wife were living apart; the notion that he had consulted her on his plans quite simply was not credible. Equally harmful, the approach seemed defensive. Instead of making Carter the issue, Kennedy's record became the focus. In the absence of polling, testing, and the other research tools of a high-tech campaign, the Kennedy effort stumbled on. "It was a moment-to-moment nonstrategy," a participant later recalled.

Alerted by its own polls, the Carter campaign offered Kennedy a shoving hand, evoking the ghosts of Chappaquiddick. Early ads, aired in Iowa and New Hampshire, featured the tag line: "President Carter—he tells you the truth." Later spots were stronger (if not excessive): "You may not always agree with President Carter, but you'll never find yourself wondering if he's telling you the truth. It's hard to think of a more useful quality in any person who becomes president, than telling the simple truth. President Carter: he tells you the *truth*."

If one part of the Rafshoon advertising strategy was to run Carter against Kennedy's record, another part was to run Carter more positively as the President facing the Iranians. Howard

Baker had faced down one wild student; Carter could take on a whole nation, and from the White House. Carter followed a rigid Rose Garden strategy, insisting that the tense situation in Iran— and later, in Afghanistan too—kept him in the White House night and day, working to solve the crises. (He did find time to telephone voters and delegates, night after night, in search of convention support.)

Carter's early spots used the White House unabashedly:

VIDEO	AUDIO
Camera up on medium shot of Carter in meeting around long table. He talks slowly and gestures. Cut to CU.	Carter [SOF]: "My own inclination is to get the nose of the federal government out of local affairs and out of state affairs whenever they can be handled in a state or in a community."
Cut to reaction shots of others around the table. Cut to Carter, seen between the backs of two people across the table, listening to someone else make a point. Cut to others around table.	Announcer [VO]: "He used to be a full-time farmer. He does a different kind of work today, but it's still work— long hours of hard work."
Cut to Carter, seen between two others at the table. He looks down and fidgets, preoccupied, and speaks softly.	Carter [SOF]: "I'll make a decision on it today."
Cut to Carter walking down hallway into Oval Office, camera following. He walks	Announcer [VO]: "His decisions reach out to touch the lives of millions. In the course

briskly to desk, lightly touching a world globe beside his
chair in passing. He leans
over desk, reading a paper,
still standing.

Cut to CU of Carter at table
with others. Cut to medium
shot, showing him sitting
next to the HEW Secretary,
Patricia Harris.

Cut to medium shot of Carter
at podium, gesturing. Various
charts on military matters
stand behind him.

Cut to reaction shot of people
in seats, applauding. Then cut
to Carter shaking hands with
members of audience.

Cut to slide: white letters
against green background,
"RE-ELECT PRESIDENT
CARTER in the Democratic
Primary April 22."

of any day, he focuses on
every vital issue facing the
nation."

Carter [SOF]: "Our comprehensive nationwide health
program has been presented
to the Congress. For us to de-
part from those two basic
documents is a serious
mistake."

Carter [SOF]: "My number
one responsibility is to defend
this country, to maintain its
security."

Announcer [VO, comes in
over Carter]: "It's nothing at
all like being alone in a Georgia field driving a tractor for
ten hours in the hot sun. Yet
no other candidate can match
his work experience, or his
life experience.
    "President Carter—a solid
man in a sensitive job."

The camera work in the spot was done by Robert Squier, who
spent several days around the White House filming presidential

scenes. Another spot produced from Squier's footage shows the President as family man. In one scene Carter helps his daughter Amy with her homework, while in the voice-over he links together his family and his government roles: "I don't think there's any way you can separate the responsibilities for a good husband or a father and a basic human being from that of being a good president. What I do is to maintain a good family life, which I consider to be crucial to being a good president." The tag line, in case a viewer missed the point, hammers it home yet again: "Husband, father, president. He's done these three jobs with distinction."

The Full-Service Media Campaign

Each upward move in Carter's public opinion ratings registered as a jolt to the Kennedy campaign. Stephen Smith approached Sawyer again. The first time Sawyer had met with the Kennedy men, he recalled, he had been accompanied by Scott Miller, a new associate who had been the creative writer of the Coca-Cola life-style ads. At that first meeting Sawyer, Miller, and a large group of Kennedy advisers had discussed how to present film of Kennedy's announcement. "Everybody was talking," says Sawyer. "Somebody said, 'We've got to make this spot more oil wells and wheat fields, fields of grain. We've got to make it like a Coke commercial—that's what we've got to do!' Scott and I looked at each other in horror, because that's *not* what it should be." After that meeting Sawyer backed out.

The second time around, Sawyer said he would accept the assignment provided he could run the communications strategy himself, rather than work in some organizational niche taking orders by committee. Smith agreed about two weeks before the New York primary. Up to that point Kennedy's campaign had been organized in what Sawyer considered a 1960s style: one group doing TV, another group radio, a third strategy, a fourth operations—and always, naturally, with the family inner circle in firm control. It truly was a new era now, as well as a sign of desperation, when the closed Kennedy ranks admitted an outside professional.

Sawyer confidently dismissed the old ways. They may have been suitable "for the dark ages of political advertising," but no longer. Modern media campaigns now required modern media organizations, and Sawyer, who had moved from filmmaking to political media, was no longer satisfied with shooting film or making commercials. His became a full-service political agency, adding to his staff political generalists, as well as research and issues specialists. "We stayed in daily contact, sent staff people out to the field on a continuous basis, and tried to integrate the different pieces of the campaign. The TV ads are only one expression. The same message has to be developed and expressed in other ways—by the candidate in speeches, by the press operation, by door-to-door workers, by the surrogates, by the organizations. We found that we had to get involved and stay involved, in basic strategy and in ongoing operations, so that all communications efforts reflected the basic theme of the campaign."

For Kennedy, Sawyer immediately commissioned research; it told him to abandon the defensive strategy. Four spots were rushed onto the air the week before the March 25 primaries in New York and neighboring Connecticut. One was called "Comparison":

VIDEO	AUDIO
Camera up on photo of Carter, silly grin on face.	Announcer [VO]: "This man has misled the American public into the worst economic crisis since the Depression. He's broken promises and cost New York a billion dollars a year. In his latest

	foreign policy blunder he betrayed Israel at the United Nations.
Cut to Kennedy shaking hands with supporters.	"This man has endured personal attacks in order to lead the fight for specific solutions to our problems, like mandatory wage and price controls to stop inflation, and programs to help the poor and elderly on fixed incomes. Let's fight back. Let's join Ted Kennedy in stopping four years of failure."

A second spot featured the actor Carroll O'Connor, television's blue-collar character Archie Bunker, calling Jimmy Carter "the most Republican President since Herbert Hoover" and urging viewers to vote for "my friend Ted Kennedy." Bunker-O'Connor, Sawyer explains, was speaking to working people "who should be Kennedy voters."

In New York Kennedy had been behind nearly thirty points. But outside events this time favored Kennedy. On March 1 the United States had voted in the United Nations Security Council in favor of a resolution calling on Israel to remove civilian settlements from occupied Arab territories, Jerusalem included. When American-Jewish voters expressed outrage, the White House explained the vote as a "communications failure." The blunder also reawakened slumbering perceptions about Carter and his competence. The UN vote and the Bunker ads brightened Sawyer's outlook. "They made Carter the issue of the campaign," he says. The defensive communications strategy had been reversed. But while the Kennedy campaign was spending $175,000 on New York TV time, the Carter campaign put in $750,000.

Rafshoon tried to deal with the Israel issue indirectly, running heavy schedules of spots emphasizing Carter's role in the Camp David accords. "More than most presidents, Jimmy Carter has been a peacemaker," one spot begins. "President Carter is a responsible man," New York Mayor Edward Koch tells voters, "who, when he makes a mistake, admits it rather than covering it up."

Kennedy won New York and Connecticut, a remarkable recovery, but one that made little difference in the final outcome. Even with those big wins, he needed two out of every three of the next delegates selected, which proved impossible. To some his was a gallant race, though too little and too late. A more apt epitaph, however, considering the Roger Mudd interview, might be too much, too soon. Carter then turned back another challenger, Governor Jerry Brown of California, and won the renomination with ease.

Master of the TV Form

After Kennedy's belated run the general election seemed almost anticlimactic. Peter H. Dailey, the Los Angeles ad man who had helped Nixon in 1972 and Ford in 1976, came in to form an in-house Reagan agency called Campaign '80, with offices in New York and Washington and a budget of some $19 million. Both Carter and Reagan struck dignified postures: Reagan's advertising referred to him as Governor constantly, while Carter continued to run from the White House as the President in charge of the hostage crisis. When Pope John Paul II had visited Carter on a tour of North America in late 1979, Rafshoon had had cameras deployed. "I thought it was legitimate to show what a president does," he told us, "the people he has to meet, and that he wouldn't embarrass you with world leaders like the Pope." Public levels of disenchantment with both the "Governor" and the "President" were so high that many voters found themselves being reminded, by the footage of the Pope's visit in Carter's spots, what real leadership looked like. Though voters couldn't pull a lever for John Paul on election day, John Anderson tried to offer a third alternative. Anderson's candidacy got a substantial boost when he announced the hiring of David Garth to do his advertising and television. Garth had never run a presidential campaign in a general election, but he had been enormously successful as the forceful media manager for, among others, mayoral candidates John V. Lindsay in New York and Tom Bradley in Los Angeles. It was another sign of the media manager's new authority that word of Garth's hiring helped legitimize John Anderson in the metacampaign, among big campaign contributors and the press.

Garth has a deserved reputation as the tough-talking, take-charge media man; he was the model for the Alan Garfield character, a consultant to senatorial candidate Robert Redford, in the motion picture *The Candidate*. Garth grew up on Long Island, where his mother was a Democratic party worker for Franklin D. Roosevelt. Garth worked as a television producer in New York and became active himself in the Democratic party in 1960, when he was cochairman of the New York State Draft Stevenson committee. The thirty-year-old Garth's cochair was Eleanor Roosevelt. In 1964 he produced a thirty-minute, paid political show aired on ABC on behalf of Scientists, Engineers, and Physicians for Johnson-Humphrey. In 1968 Garth worked for McCarthy in the Oregon and California Democratic primaries. Anderson did not sign up Garth until May. More important than time, in Garth's view, was money; Anderson had put some $4 million dollars into state organizations before Garth arrived. "I had under $1 million for a total national media campaign, which is a joke," Garth now says, as if talking about small change. (Some of Anderson's staff, especially those displaced when Garth arrived, later publicly complained that Garth had cut himself in for a lucrative share of Anderson's money; Federal Election Commission records indicate that Garth collected $229,000 in the six months he worked for the campaign. Anderson himself has said he has no such complaints.)

For all practical purposes, however, the campaign died when Anderson failed to qualify for the League of Women Voters candidates' debate. The League had set a standard of sixteen percentage points in the polls for Anderson by a certain date before the debates. Anderson fell short of the mark by one point, and it was over for him. It wasn't a question of whether people liked him or didn't—the polls showed that they did. People felt a vote for him would be a wasted one. (Anderson still got six percent of the vote, enough to requalify him for federal funds for the 1984 presidential race.)

While Anderson had a polling problem, Jimmy Carter's polls showed that he had an Anderson problem. A Harris poll taken just before the Democratic convention asked voters whom they would vote for, assuming Anderson had a chance of winning: Anderson edged Carter, twenty-five to twenty-three percent, behind Reagan's forty-nine percent. Carter had never run as an incumbent, and it showed. His strategy in 1976 had been to run as an outsider, to run as much against Washington as against Ford. "It would have been difficult in 1980 for us to run against Washington, as an incumbent president," Rafshoon says, and adds with a laugh, "but I think Reagan's going to do it in 1984." The political scientist Richard E. Neustadt, in his *Presidential Power*, argued that what voters want in a president changes with time and events. Carter, inexperienced but decent, was right for the post-Watergate election of 1976. Reagan in 1980 was an idea whose time had come. "It may have been deceiving to run on the idea that all problems are going to be solved with tax cuts and higher defense budgets and cutting programs and getting government off our back," Rafshoon says, "but that's exactly what the American electorate was looking for."

Rafshoon says his main goal was to communicate what the Carter presidency was. "I don't think we could've done anything else." Thus the first Rafshoon spots were positive. Some showed Carter the President and emphasized the toughness of the job. Others showed Carter meeting with voters. A five-minute spot

1980: CARTER VS. REAGAN

Carter "Decision" Commercial

"I'll make a decision on it today"

Carter "Light" Spot

"In the past four years, working day and night, President Jimmy Carter has hammered out America's first energy program"

sought to strengthen Carter's image, by showing him inspecting carriers and missiles ("When President Carter sits down at the White House with the Secretary of Defense, he brings a hard, military professionalism to the meeting."). The Camp David accords were emphasized frequently, in spots showing Carter with Begin and Sadat. Voter research showed Camp David was regarded as "one of the most legitimate accomplishments of the Carter administration," Rafshoon says. Another Rafshoon spot concentrated on the toughness of the presidency, emphasizing Carter's long hours—and implicitly raising the comparison to Reagan, who, it was said, insisted on afternoon naps. To video of Carter hurrying through rounds of meetings, the voice-over says: "The responsibility never ends. Even at the end of a long working day there is usually another cable addressed to the chief of state from the other side of the world where the sun is shining and somᵕthing is happening." The shot switches to the White House, with a light coming on upstairs. "And he's not finished yet," the voice-over concludes. "We couldn't get out and say you're better off, the economy is good," Rafshoon told us. "We had to say that we are trying very hard, in this complicated world."

One Rafshoon spot made good television but embarrassing politics. It shows an Ohio woman asking Carter about needless regulations and red tape that were hampering her family business. Carter tells her to come to meet with him in Washington and he'll take care of everything. The woman blows Carter a kiss. When the spot began running, the woman appeared on NBC's *Today* show. Carter's aides had put her off, she said; she never got in to see the President; her business was now nearly bankrupt. She planned, she told the eight million *Today* viewers, to vote for Ronald Reagan.

So, it seemed, were a lot of other people. Walter Cronkite was ending his CBS newscasts with the hostage day-count, nearly as devastating as the body counts that had helped drive Lyndon B. Johnson from office—"the hundredth day of captivity for the fifty Americans in Iran." The failed rescue mission in April had temporarily boosted Carter's stock, reinjecting a note of crisis. But that dissipated quickly, and Carter knew he had to campaign, at least selectively. He refused to debate Anderson, who was taking votes from him. The Reagan camp naturally did what it could to keep Anderson going. So Reagan and Anderson debated, one on one, on September 21. Peter Dailey, who had taken over Reagan's advertising during the general election, produced a spot with the camera holding on an empty podium. A woman announcer says: "The League of Women Voters invited President Carter to join in the 1980 debates. He refused the invitation. Maybe it's because during his administration, inflation has gone as high as eighteen percent, the number of Americans out of work has reached eight million, housing starts have hit a new low, while interest rates have hit a new high."

Mostly, however, the Reagan advertising effort remained positive, as befits the front-runner. Various spots praised Reagan's California record, and the governor's boundless energy. The strategy called for peaking in the last ten days of the campaign, and outspending Carter as much as two and a half to one. Carter, as befits the rear runner, had pushed hard for a Reagan-Carter debate. The Reagan campaign kept insisting that Anderson be included. Finally, in mid-October the Reagan campaign suddenly accepted a two-man debate with Carter. Stuart Spencer, who had been brought in to travel with Reagan, wanted the debate because "I felt we were dead in the water, stalled." Other advisers felt it was risky. Reagan listened to Spencer.

Reagan handled Carter easily in the October 28 debate. The telegenic ex-actor understood the value of humor and patience— "There you go again," he said to defuse a Carter point. Carter appeared to be in hot pursuit, attempting to shake Reagan's geniality by picturing him as the candidate whose election would endanger the future of humankind. But Carter trivialized the matter, declaring that his daughter Amy spoke frequently to him of her concern about nuclear proliferation. Later it turned out that Reagan's advisers had obtained copies of Carter's debate briefing book, an access that probably contributed to Reagan's confidence—though the candidate maintained equanimity without briefing books in other circumstances. Because at least part of the damage to Carter was self-inflicted, no one was prepared to say the election outcome would have been different in the absence of the purloined papers.

As also befits the rear runner, Carter went on the attack in his TV advertising. One series, "Empty Oval Office," included a spot about Reagan's economic plan:

VIDEO	AUDIO
Camera up on an empty Oval Office. Camera slowly moves in. Then crawl begins, in small white capital letters superimposed over picture:	Announcer [VO]: "When you come right down to it, what kind of person should occupy the Oval Office?"
"SHOULD IT BE A PERSON WHO, LIKE RONALD REAGAN, HAS PROPOSED THE MAGICAL KEMP/ROTH ECONOMIC PLAN, A PLAN THAT *BUSINESS WEEK* CALLED 'COMPLETELY IRRESPONSIBLE,' A PLAN THAT REAGAN'S OWN RUNNING MATE CALLED 'VOODOO ECONOMICS'?"	Announcer reads copy as it crawls over the screen.
Fade to photo of Carter and Mondale, alongside white letters on black background: "PRESIDENT CARTER."	Announcer [VO]: "Or should there be in the Oval Office an experienced man who is working to solve America's

> economic problems and isn't
> kidding anybody about them?
> Figure it out for yourself."

A majority of the voters wanted to believe in the "good" Reagan. The polling and research done on both the Democratic and the Republican sides pointed to an electorate that was ready to give Reagan his chance "to get government off our backs." The one obstacle to Reagan's victory was the doubt about his hawkishness (his ex-actor's image didn't bother voters appreciably). Once Reagan's paid media, and his manner in free media like the debate, eased fears that he was some kind of "mad bomber," his election was assured.

On election eve both campaigns retreated to safe programming, acceptable to the prime-time television audience. Carter used what federal money he had left for a twenty-minute paid appeal, moderated by the revered Hollywood actor Henry Fonda. Reagan bought half an hour on all three networks for a low-key, earnest speech. Reagan talked of his vision for America and evoked the presence of an even bigger star: "Last year I lost a friend who was more than a symbol of the Hollywood dream industry. To millions he was a symbol of our country itself. Duke Wayne did not believe our country was ready for the dustbin of history. Just before his death he said in his own blunt way, 'Just give the American people a good cause, and there's nothing they can't lick.' "

The speech had been shot that morning in Peoria, near Reagan's birthplace. The candidate was five minutes into the recording when he realized that the taping was flat, and that he felt like he was "putting himself to sleep," in Stuart Spencer's recollection. They fussed a little with the stage business: "It was the way he was sitting in this chair. So Reagan says, 'I'll just move up and sit on the edge.' " Looking and feeling more alert, Reagan started over. The resulting election eve show, says Spencer, is "a classic. No producer should ever mess with that guy."

When that guy, Ronald Reagan, also a product of the Hollywood dream industry, won the presidency the next day, his victory provided one measure of how much candidates' attitudes had changed since 1948. Back then Harry S. Truman had been contemptuous of television. For Reagan, the televised campaign was like coming home. In victory the President was magnanimous to his media man Dailey: Reagan appointed him U.S. ambassador to Ireland, and later, in January 1983, brought him back home to help sell the U.S. Pershing and cruise missile programs to Western Europeans. For Reagan's reelection effort, however, Dailey was dumped. Key Reagan advisers, such as aide Michael Deaver and Nancy Reagan, were said to feel his political advertising approach was "too soft and laid back" for 1984.

STYLES

PART III

THE MAN ON THE WHITE HORSE, AND OTHER TALES OF MEDIA TECHNIQUES

CHAPTER 14

The reasonably attentive viewer watching the 1976 political commercial for Malcolm Wallop, a Republican candidate for the U.S. Senate from Wyoming, might be reminded of the Marlboro Man spots before cigarette advertising was banned from television, or of the similar upbeat action spots for Michelob beer, GM pickup trucks, and other male-oriented consumer products. To anyone who has spent any time looking at political commercials, however, "Ride with Us, Wyoming" has all the hoofprints of the Robert Goodman style:

VIDEO	AUDIO
Camera up on three cowboys saddling up. Quick cuts as they mount horses and ride off; brief CU of one of them, a cigar stub in his mouth,	Upbeat, western music up and under. Announcer [VO]: "The Wallop Senate Drive begins here.

TECHNIQUES: WALLOP SENATE DRIVE, 1976

Come join the Wallop Senate Drive,
The Wallop Senate Drive!
It's alert and it's alive
And it's Wyoming to the spurs,
The Wallop Senate Drive!

pulling his hat brim over his eyes. They ride through a stream and gallop over a hill crest, a dog running behind.

Three riders with a proclamation."

Words begin in jingle, in deep bass voice:

Come join the Wallop Senate
    Drive,
The Wallop Senate Drive!
It's alert and it's alive
And it's Wyoming to the
    spurs,
The Wallop Senate Drive!

Fade to another rider, Malcolm Wallop. He wears a hat (white), like some of the others; unlike the others, he also wears a business suit (blue). The camera is near ground level, making Wallop and his horse look huge. Quick cuts show scores of men on horseback following Wallop. Then quick cuts as they parade through a town. Crowd, with American flags and Wallop pennants, waves and cheers. Wallop smiles down on them.

Announcer [VO]: "Go forth for Wyoming, Malcolm Wallop. Tell them in the United States Senate that the people of Wyoming are proud of their land and life, and that a Wyoming senator will fight every intrusion upon it. That you, Malcolm Wallop, will serve the nation best by serving Wyoming first—the very special needs of this great state. And by so doing share its blessing with America."

Jingle words come in again:

Come join the Wallop Senate
    Drive,
The Wallop Senate Drive!

Super fades in around his face: "Wallop for U.S. Senate."

Announcer [VO]: "Malcolm Wallop for United States Senate. Ride with us, Wyoming!"

Goodman is the political advertising specialist who told Maryland voters in 1966 that Spiro Agnew was their kind of man; in 1980 Goodman's elaborately staged commercials, with bands, balloons, and jump cuts, conferred media momentum on George Bush. Goodman says he prefers music to issues in his advertising, and that he bases his spots on emotions rather than research. He has used seventy-eight-piece orchestras—"always with about twenty violins; I'm nuts on strings"—to produce a moving, epical sound in his spots. "I try to capture the sense of the state, the sense of the candidacy, and interpret that musically. . . . Alaska! My God! When I got there, I could feel the music!" The media mercenary label, frequently used to put down the work of the political consultants, appears not to bother him at all. "The fun is being out in the field like a bunch of Green Berets, six months before the election, in some wild state that you've never seen before," he told us disarmingly.

For his client Malcolm Wallop, Goodman jumped into Wyoming and found the widest vista yet for the excitement he likes to generate in his advertising campaigns. At the outset, he recalls, Wallop was fifty points behind the incumbent, Democrat Gale McGee, a three-term senator. "One of the things we noticed was that people always voted for McGee. He was always right, but he was kind of pontifical," Goodman says. "His personality was that of a Nebraska schoolteacher—which he had been—who would give little speeches on street corners." Goodman's strategy was to go "to the heart of Wyoming, to catch the flavor of the place and the candidate." He wrote and scored the "Senate Drive" music, put Wallop on a horse, and used seventy-five riders to create the implicit drama of rugged Wyoming cattle man against pious, schoolteacherish senator. As it happened, Wallop was a Yale-educated patrician landowner who raised polo ponies—"but not in our films," Goodman says. Still, Wallop was a rancher: "I don't put guys on horses who don't ride, let's put it that way. I dramatize virtue, and one of the virtues was that he really cared about Wyoming. He was really a Wyoming kind of guy."

Goodman claims to spurn dull research in favor of big production operations; but his casting of Wallop as a political Marlboro Man owed as much to Goodman's thorough understanding of public attitudes as to his instinct for the dramatic. Many voters, and especially many voters in the Far West, had come to believe that the heavy hand of big government was meddling in their lives; they would express to public opinion samplers a yearning for the (presumed) good old days of American individualism and initiative (these same feelings, as we've seen, continued to show up in the research undertaken for John Glenn's 1984 presidential campaign). Goodman shrewdly exploited these themes in one of his most memorable spots for Wallop, "Porta-Potty":

VIDEO	AUDIO
Camera up on cowboy in blue workshirt and tattered straw hat, saddling and mounting his horse.	Announcer [VO]: "Everywhere you look these days, the federal government is there. Telling you what they think. Telling you what they think *you* ought to think. Telling you how you ought to do things. Setting up rules you can't follow. I think the federal government is going too far.
Cowboy shakes head in disgust. Then cut back to a donkey, tied behind cowboy's horse; strapped on donkey's back is a portable toilet. Cowboy rides off.	"Now they say, if you don't take the portable facility along with you on a roundup, you can't go!

Cut to slide: "Wallop for U.S. Senate."   "We need someone to tell 'em about Wyoming. Malcolm Wallop will."

The spot is something of a cheap shot. OSHA had proposed a set of "field sanitation rules," mandating that employers provide toilet facilities for agricultural workers. Reaction was strongly negative, and the proposal died quickly (the migrants who do the back-breaking labor don't usually write letters to OSHA). If the precise facts eluded Goodman, the mood didn't. The Wallop ad caught the spirit of what Goodman considered to be government interference in the lives of Wyoming's individualists. Real men don't need portable potties.

Goodman is hardly the first political media manager to cast horses in his productions, nor is the style exclusively Republican. Six years before the Wallop Senate Drive, Charles Guggenheim put a long-shot candidate on horseback and almost rode to victory. Senator Albert Gore of Tennessee, in office since 1952, was an early critic of the Vietnam War, he opposed the Nixon administration's antiballistic missile and supersonic transport programs, and he had taken a strongly pro-civil rights stance—all of which left him vulnerable in his 1970 reelection campaign. Guggenheim produced a spot with Gore, astride a white horse, riding over the Tennessee countryside as the announcer voice-over proclaims, "I may have run ahead of the pack sometimes, he says, but I'm usually headed in the right direction." Gore's opponent in the Democratic primary, Hudley Crockett, predicted that the spot would backfire: "Mark my words. The people of Tennessee know it's packaged by an out-of-state man and paid for by out-of-state funds." Gore won the primary by 32,000 votes. But not even white horses could drag him to victory in the general election—as Vice-President Agnew had said in speeches, Gore was the administration's number-one target. With help from the White House, Republican Bill Brock won the seat, although by a smaller margin than expected. Guggenheim considers the campaign to

be one of his best. "We were thirty points behind; we ended up
losing by one," he told us. "The material was right to the point,
directed toward the problems that we had. It was positive; it was
interesting to watch." As for putting Gore on a white horse,
Guggenheim says there was no master manipulation involved.
"Gore had a farm and rode horses. If he had owned a black
horse, we still would have used it."

So far in this account we have been careful not to credit Goodman, Guggenheim, or any of the other media men with too
great an influence on election outcomes. The conventional wisdom, we know, has endowed the media arts with near-magical
powers, especially after Joe McGinniss's account of the selling
of Richard Nixon in 1968. With the election of Ronald Reagan
in 1980, the dramatic development of media campaigns seemed
to reach its natural resolution: at last the country had sent an
actor to the White House. We also know that political candidates
actually do look for, as one senior congressman told us, media
wizards who possess the "magic bullet" to help them get elected.
Is there, in truth, magic in the spots? How effective are they in
winning elections? These two questions are the subjects of this
and the following chapter.

The galloping horses of Goodman and Guggenheim can lead
us to the answer to the first question. After analyzing some 650
spots produced between 1952 and 1984, studying the techniques
of the political advertising trade, and interviewing nineteen of
the most active media managers, we found not so much magic
as routine. In 1952 adman Rosser Reeves met with candidate
Dwight Eisenhower and together they produced forty spots in
one sitting, a feat that has the quality of wizardry. As late as
1968, Doyle Dane Bernbach could draw up an advertising plan
for Hubert Humphrey using the size of the audience and the
number of times the spot would be aired to create a simple
formula, totemic in its promises. Today Reeves's work would be
classified as prehistoric and the DDB plan as something from
the Dark Ages, for political advertising campaigns have become

a new, much more complex world. With this complexity has come—necessarily—survey research that is standardized, campaign strategies that unfold in predictable stages, political advertising styles that have become repetitive. This happens in every art form after a time. At first there may be wit, originality, freshness, even memorable work. Soon these exemplary models are studied—the videotape technology makes this easy—and imitated. The best media men tend to repeat their own work from year to year, campaign to campaign, and when they don't their opposite numbers will.

This routinization in the styles of political advertising has not escaped notice. Charles Guggenheim told us he was disenchanted with what he termed "cookie cutting" in the business: "They take a technique that works in one state and apply it in another, changing only the name of the candidate." John Deardourff chooses a kinder comparison; after a time, he says, the viewer begins to recognize each media man's works, the way a gallery-goer knows a Kenneth Nolan or a Helen Frankenthaler. We ourselves have come to think of political spots as a creative form somewhere in between the domestic arts of cookie making and an artist's work suitable to be exhibited in museums. They are, to us, video playlets that unfold in four usually distinct acts, each performed in familiar rhetorical styles.

Our use of a theatrical metaphor is not original. Others employ it too, particularly the more forthright media men. "Political ads are really classical drama," Goodman told us. "You try to become the good guy. You dramatize virtue where it exists. You compensate for weakness, real or perceived. You draw a contrast, put the white hat on. You orchestrate it, almost like a production, so that they leave the theater singing your song—or singing your praises." Like much of Goodman's political ad work, Goodman's words have an element of hype. But the idea rings true, as we found.

Phase One: ID Spots

The first act of the advertising strategy ensures that the voters have some sense of the candidate. At its most basic level this means establishing name identification as a foundation on which to build subsequent information. Spots aiming for name ID are easily recognizable; they hammer home the candidate's name repeatedly and often show it on screen as well. The rhetoric is simple. In the early 1950s a California Senate candidate aired twenty-second spots featuring animated letters that danced around to spell his name while the voice-over pronounced it. In 1960 John F. Kennedy used a two-minute jingle that repeated "Kennedy" dozens of times but also managed to address the issue of his religion:

And do you deny to any man
The right he's guaranteed,
To be elected President,
No matter what his creed?
It's promised in the Bill of Rights
To which we must be true.
So, it's up to you.
It's up to you.
It's strictly up to you.
And it's Kennedy, Kennedy,
Kennedy, Kennedy,
Kennedy, Kennedy,
Ken-ne-dy for me! . . .

Now as then name IDs are frequently among the most simplistic of the polispots. Perhaps because of their blunt-instrument purpose the ID spot style often produces a cleverness at the edges, an artifact in which most of the artist's energies go into the details. For example, when Tony Schwartz made spots for Daniel Patrick Moynihan's 1976 Senate race in New York, he showed Moynihan's name across the screen in the same typeface that would appear on the ballot; to enliven the picture, the name shifts from color to color. A now-standard ID style builds on mispronunciation of the candidate's name. Spot makers especially favor this for a first-time candidate with an unusual name. Edward Mezvinsky, running for the U.S. Congress in Iowa in 1972, ran spots showing different people trying, without success, to pronounce his name: "Meza-vin-isky . . . Mens-vinsky . . . I can't say it [laughs]." The campaign thus earns points for gentle self-deprecation while finding an amusing way to hammer the name home to viewers. Paul Tsongas, a successful (as was Mezvinsky) candidate for the U.S. Senate from Massachusetts in 1978, used the same idea, ending with a little girl whose laborious pronunciation comes out closer to "tickets."

Candidates whose names are Smith and Jones—or Carter and Bush—don't need cute kids saying the darnedest things. Then ID spots may attempt to associate the candidate with certain implicit themes framing the candidate and, by extension, the election. In 1972 Peter Dailey showed the 1950s Communist-fighter Nixon in a Leningrad cemetery—a 1970s Man of Peace. Gerald Rafshoon's 1976 ID for the then-unknown Jimmy Carter not only put the candidate in workshirt and boots but had him use such good post-Watergate words as "love," "family," "trust," and "hard work" several times. To frame the candidacy, the Carter campaign also employed a jingle, one that makes Ford's "Feelin' Good" seem packed with information:

I heard a young man speaking out
Just the other day,
So I stopped to take a listen
To what he had to say.
He spoke straight and simple,
But then I was impressed.
He said, "Once and for all,
Why not the best?"

He said his name is Jimmy Carter,
And he was running for President.
And then he laid out a plan of action.
It made a lot of sense.
He talked about the government,
And how good it could be,

For you and me.
That's the way it ought to be,
Right now, once and for all,
Why not the best?

Boston media man Dan Payne employed not music but sports to make a delicate point in an ID spot. Payne's client, Barney Frank, had been elected to Congress from suburban Boston two years earlier; redistricting forced him to run in 1982 against incumbent Republican Margaret Heckler, an eight-term member who had concentrated on constituent service. "It was important that Barney be seen as a guy who, in just one term, had done some fairly important things," Payne told us. The campaign decided to publicize the fact that Frank's fellow members had voted him outstanding freshman—but, Payne says, that raised potential problems in a predominantly blue-collar district: "Here he is, kind of the class president, the wise-guy Jewish kid, the overachiever, who's now coming in and saying, 'I was the smartest kid in Congress last year—vote for me.' We had to find a way to make that argument in a way that blue-collar people would be able to understand." Payne's solution was to put Frank in a softball jersey:

VIDEO	AUDIO
Camera up on Barney Frank, a heavyset, fortyish man with black-rimmed glasses. He is wearing a softball jersey and standing at home plate, swinging the bat to limber up. The pitch is tossed. Frank hits it, throws down the bat, and runs. Quick cuts back and forth between Frank, running the bases, and an	Announcer [VO]: "In 1981 Barney Frank's colleagues named him rookie of the year in Congress. They were impressed with how Barney chopped millions of dollars in wasteful farm subsidies, how he helped stop the Republicans from cutting Social Security, how he opposed the Reagan tax program because

outfielder chasing the softball across the grass.

Frank slides into home plate just as the catcher tries to tag him. Frank stands up quickly and jogs to his teammates, who cheer and clap him on the back.

Cut to white letters on blue background: "Barney Frank. A Congressman you can trust."

it favored the rich over average people, and how he even stood up to a Democratic tax plan that favored big oil.

"Barney Frank: the best new Congressman in Washington—a Congressman you can trust."

Payne, echoing Guggenheim and Goodman defending their equestrian candidates, insists that Frank is a dedicated softball player. "He plays in two leagues in Washington; he takes it very seriously." Payne admits, though, that the Frank team "got clobbered, eighteen to two or something," in the game filmed for the spot. Frank did better in the election, beating Heckler 122,000 to 83,000 votes.

War, like sports, is a popular metaphor in polispots. In 1979 Robert Squier employed it in advertising for William Winter, candidate for governor of Mississippi. Winter's principal opponent in the Democratic primary was Lieutenant Governor Evelyn Gandy. Squier produced a spot showing Winter standing in the midst of Army tanks. "The governor is commander in chief of the National Guard. . . . The Guard is the first line of national defense," the candidate says—framing the election around the nearly irrelevant military aspect of the job, with the implication that a woman couldn't handle the Guard. As Squier proudly notes, no one had ever made an issue of the National Guard before. Winter won.

Within the frame of his spots for George Bush in 1980, Robert Goodman tried to create constant excitement. "Bush's vulnerability was that nobody knew him; he was one percent in the polls," says Goodman. "My answer to that was the spots we called 'Magnitude.' You never were going to see Bush in a spot unless there were thousands of people around him. We went out to an Iowa candidates' convention, and we filmed George. All the candidates were there, but the way you see this film it's just George, and multitudes rising, and all the Bush signs—it almost looks like a real nominating convention." Goodman hired actors—literal theater—to pose as Secret Service agents around Bush, to make the candidate seem more important.

ID spots can be simple and subdued when the biographical material is sensitive. Tom Bradley made the runoff for Los Angeles mayor in 1973 without a large part of the electorate realizing that he was black. David Garth's solution was to stress Bradley's roots (appealing to local pride) and his police background (for the law-and-order vote). A Garth ad placed Bradley on the UCLA running track:

VIDEO	AUDIO
Camera up on track. A runner goes by the camera. In the distance is Tom Bradley, walking toward the camera, which simultaneously approaches him. He is wearing a blue suit, and walks with one hand in his pocket. Camera finally closes and holds on CU.	Bradley [SOF]: "When I was running track here at UCLA, I couldn't have dreamed that someday I'd be running for mayor. But it was possible because of the kind of city that Los Angeles is. It's a city that respects a man who makes it on his own, who works hard, who doesn't ask for favors. After twenty-one

Legend appears, white letters superimposed on bottom of screen: "ELECT TOM BRAD-LEY." Legend quickly changes to "LOS ANGELES NEEDS A *WORKING* MAYOR." It remains on the screen after Bradley finishes and the image fades to black.

years on the Los Angeles police force and ten years on the city council, I think the people of this city know where my heart is.

"I love this city. I want to keep fighting to make it better. That's why I'm running."

Mostly, though, the ID spots trace compact narrative histories of the candidate's life. Through film footage or stills, these spots frequently show the passages of childhood, school, military service, adulthood, family, and a life in politics. They may include interviews with people who know the candidate well—his mother (Miz Lillian in Rafshoon's 1976 work for Jimmy Carter) or high school football coach (in the Bailey-Deardourff spot for Ford in 1976) or family friends (Doris Kearns-Goodwin and others in Michael Kaye's 1982 spots for Edward Kennedy). These ID biographies are often designed for five-minute TV slots. Watching them, viewers may feel they have been allowed to flip through a family photo album. Sometimes, however, extraordinary sequences appear, as when Robert Goodman used film of young pilot George Bush being rescued from the sea after a World War II combat mission. No candidate had quite the dramatic story to tell in an ID as did John Glenn, and David Sawyer's 1984 bio inevitably showed astronaut Glenn riding into orbit in the Mercury spacecraft and later being greeted by the youthful President Kennedy. When good pictures cannot be found for IDs, imaginative spot making may occur. Ford's 1976 bio touched on his football

TECHNIQUES: ID'ING THE CANDIDATE

Tom Bradley "Running Track," 1973

"When I was running track here at UCLA, I couldn't have dreamed that someday I'd be running for mayor"

Barney Frank "Softball," 1982

"In 1981 Barney Frank's colleagues named him rookie of the year in Congress"

TECHNIQUES: THE ARGUMENT SPOT

**John Lindsay,
Confessional, 1966**

"I guessed wrong on the
weather before the city's
biggest snowfall last winter, and that was a
mistake"

**Linwood Holton,
Cinema Verité, 1969**

"What do you feel has
held you back more than
anything—it's black skin,
isn't it?"

playing days as a lineman at the University of Michigan—with film showing a running back on a spectacular open field dash (the Ford stand-in was at least a Michigan player). The more serious challenges to the bio spot creator may come when pictures are readily available but the candidate has no public record, an untelegenic demeanor (he or she simply looks bad on the screen), and/or a stumbling speaking style. The solution then usually is to let others—family, friends, recognized political figures—do the talking and the appearing. In Robert Squier's ID spots for Mike Sturdivant in the 1983 Democratic gubernatorial primary in Mississippi, for example, the gray-haired, bespectacled fifty-five-year-old farmer makes only a cameo film appearance in his own biography.

Incumbent presidents, their names, faces, and voices familiar after four years, frequently turn to the props of the presidency in their ID spots. The Hot Line, Air Force One, and the Oval Office are favorites. Footage of the Man at Work—Nixon in Leningrad, Ford puffing a pipe while listening to advisers, Carter greeting the Pope—is also a well-established standard, sure to be repeated. An emphasis on incumbency is nothing new (it was Abraham Lincoln, who, in the 1864 campaign, first used the slogan "Don't Switch Horses in the Middle of the Stream"), nor is it limited only to the presidency. Incumbent senators, congressmen, governors, and mayors frequently use spots depicting them at their desks (often with the U.S. or the state capitol building visible through a window in the background), or at legislative hearings, or talking with popular, recognizable officials. Mondale's 1984 commercials for Iowa and New Hampshire stressed his experience and what he would do as president. Because his name is well known, his ID is "presidential"—his commercials are shot in what looks like the Oval Office, complete with American flag on staff and pictures of family on wallboard behind the executive desk. In the 1984 primaries, too, Colorado Senator Gary Hart, a relative unknown at first, IDed himself in two ways: as youthful Westerner in denims in the great outdoors and as Washington force in dark suit at his Senate desk.

Phase Two: Argument Spots

Once the characters have been introduced, the complicating action begins. This is the argument stage of the media campaign. We have been told who the candidate is; now we are supposed to be told what the candidate stands for. The weight and worth of these arguments, their content, can be as varied as the kinds of candidates who put themselves forward. Nevertheless, our study of some 250 argument spots shot over the last thirty years discloses at least three common patterns of rhetoric, reflective of the accepted principles of electoral politics in a media age.

First of all, most argument spots don't get too specific. This is especially true of argument spots in general elections when, quite simply, the candidate is seeking wider support than in primary elections. Second, appeals to emotion—hitting the hot buttons of viewers—are more likely to be used than discursive arguments; the thirty- or sixty-second spot does not allow for extended development of ideas. Third and most important, despite both the vagueness of the content and the frequent short-circuiting of thought, many argument spots make serious, issue-oriented points. They can, in fact, offer useful information to voters, though it is also a fact that the majority of the commercials we studied do not measure up to the possibilities of the form. This may be sad, but no more surprisng than to learn that not every play produced on Broadway is intelligent or well made.

Specific argument spots and general argument spots are relatively easy to distinguish. The former take aim at some individual policy or interest group, say Social Security and the elderly. These may also evoke party loyalty or racial or class solidarity. The endorsement of a person, particularly a prominent person linked to the specific argument, is a frequently used style (borrowing from one of the evergreens of commercial advertising). Democratic liberals Eleanor Roosevelt and Adlai Stevenson, as we saw, did

TECHNIQUES: ENDORSEMENTS

**Henry Fonda For
Tom Hayden, 1976**

"Tom Hayden can bring
some hope back to Amer-
ica. God knows, we need
it"

**Pearl Bailey For
Gerald Ford, 1976**

"Oh, he's made some
mistakes, honey"

**Carroll O'Connor For
Edward Kennedy, 1980**

"I'm afraid Jimmy's
depression is going to be
worse than Herbert's"

**Mary Tyler Moore For
Jimmy Carter, 1980**

"Men and women truly
concerned about women's
freedom are going to vote
for President Jimmy
Carter"

**Jacqueline Kennedy For
John Kennedy, 1960**

"Viva Kennedy!"

**Eleanor Roosevelt For
John Kennedy, 1960**

"He is a man with a sense
of history"

**Elsie Frank For
Barney Frank, 1982**

"How can I be so sure
Barney will do the right
thing by us older people?
Because he's my son"

**Talking Fish For
Nelson Rockefeller, 1966**

"Next to a fish, I would
say that he's the best governor we've had"

endorsement spots for Kennedy in 1960. The actor John Wayne did spots for various Republicans, as well as for New York Conservative party candidate James Buckley, emphasizing the candidates were Wayne's Kind of Men. Nixon combined symbol (the White House) and celebrity (Duke Ellington) in a 1972 spot. Henry Fonda taped spots for his son-in-law, Tom Hayden, beloved American certifying suspect radical. In 1980 Kennedy spots aimed at working people were made by Carroll O'Connor (Archie Bunker), while Mary Tyler Moore (career woman Mary Richards) endorsed Carter, the supporter of ERA.

David Garth used a twist on endorsement spots in John Gilligan's 1970 campaign for governor in Ohio. The camera opens to show an older man, vigorous, about seventy, saying, "I've watched him get elected to city council six times. I've seen him elected to Congress—in fact I was there the day he took his seat. I know that he's familiar with the problems of the older citizens of Ohio, because he and I have discussed them many times. And so I'm going to vote for Jack Gilligan for governor of the state of Ohio. I think I should, because, after all, I'm his father." At that the camera pulls back and shows Gilligan and the father, laughing. "We did it mainly because we were having trouble with the elderly," says Garth. "Also Jack Gilligan was perceived as a kind of cold fish. He wasn't, but that's how he came across." In 1982 Dan Payne borrowed the technique, showing an elderly woman talking of her faith in Barney Frank: "How can I be so sure Barney will do the right thing by us older people? Because he's my son."

Emotions subtler than familial love infuse some argument spots. A sense of warmth can be evoked by creating a feeling of intimacy; the television sits in people's living rooms and bedrooms. The one-on-one style of appeal—sometimes denigrated as the talking head—has appeared and reappeared over three decades as a highly serviceable format. The candidate addresses the camera, sometimes with offscreen help, such as questions posed in a separate shot ("Eisenhower Answers America") or by an invisible announcer (Nixon, 1960, and Goldwater, 1964). More commonly the candidate talks to the voter directly, a style that Ronald Reagan has used from 1966 through the present. Because the talking-head spot reminds many media men of the product commercials they try to avoid, the device of a low-key, very soft naturalness may be used to heighten intimacy and emotion— and also visually to distance the political spot from the clutter of hard-sell commercial ads around it.

Naturalness and intimacy are commonly attempted with the cinema-verité style most often identified with Charles Guggenheim, who brought the format from filmmaking to politics. "I tend to use the candidate in real situations," Guggenheim told us. "This material shows the person in greater depth than just the fact that he's for or against an issue." David Garth used the technique in John Lindsay's first run for mayor of New York, in 1965. "We had tried to shoot him in a couple of different places," Garth told us. "We shot one inside a school, one inside a subway. The spots were well written, but the delivery looked staged and stiff. So we started following Lindsay around campaigning." Using two cameras, Garth shot Lindsay giving stump speeches and then talking to ordinary citizens. "We took that material back and edited it into spots. It became a 'slice of life' spot. We found out that people would say, 'We didn't see your spots, but we saw Lindsay on the news.' " Viewers had mistaken Garth's spots for news footage of the candidate. Later some media men would attempt to take avantage of that mistake with newslike spots.

In cinema-verité spots the natural looking moments are not artless. They are the result of an expensive and time-consuming process; producers can't know specifically what they are looking for until they see rolls of tape and envision how it might make an ad. Whereas a talking-head spot, filmed from a script, may take half a day and a dozen takes, a cinema-verité spot may occupy a film crew for weeks as they follow the candidate around. Some media producers save time by imitating others' work— what Guggenheim called "cookie-cutter" spots. A favorite cinema-verité shot in the late sixties and early seventies was the candidate, his coat slung over his shoulder, walking through mean streets. Another favorite on the West Coast was the candidate deep in thought as he walks along a beach, alone or perhaps with his faithful dog. Still, the apparent spontaneity of the form can make for emotional pictures. Robert Goodman, working for Linwood Holton in his 1969 race for governor of Virginia, approached a group of men standing outside a ghetto pool hall and asked if they'd ever heard of Holton. They hadn't. "He's running for governor of Virginia," Goodman said. "I don't know him well myself. He may be the biggest phony that ever came along, but I want you to find out." Holton then walked up and talked, forcefully and assertively, with the group. "What do you feel has held you back more than anything—it's black skin, isn't it?" he said at one point. The youths were skeptical but attentive. Properly edited, it made, in Goodman's words, "tremendous television."

Goodman says he uses emotional spots because "most people will agree that voting is a matter of the heart, what you *feel* about someone, rather than a matter of the mind." The mind, he adds, "takes what the heart feels, and interprets it." Moreover issue-oriented ads raise unnecessary risks: "The murky candidate wins. When you get hung up on one side of an issue, there's always fallout." Goodman claims that public opinion polls before the 1976 presidential race "showed that seventy-five percent of the people voting for Carter didn't know his position on one issue— which justifies where I am." Thus such Goodman ads as "Your Kind of Man/Ted Agnew Is" and "Ride with Us, Wyoming" are empty of political argument. "The reason I liked the Agnew theme," he freely admits, "was that it didn't say anything. You could pick out the reasons why he was your kind of man." Dan Payne offers a loftier argument against the primacy of specific issues in campaigns. "Voters put in a candidate their trust, their faith to act right—not to toe the line exactly on a certain set of issues. They're making an investment in the person as representing their general sense of things." Guggenheim, who has produced many of the most emotional spots in American politics (including the five-minute paraplegics spot for McGovern in 1972), argues that feelings play a legitimate role in elections. He describes an imaginary spot for the Democrats to use against Reagan in 1984; it's set in Youngstown, Ohio, where unemployment is high. "You talk to an unemployed steelworker. His unemployment compensation has been cut off, his health policy has been cut off, and it can be attributed to some insensitivity on the part of the opposition. You might get yourself a piece of film that's fairly emotional." But, Guggenheim continues, the emotion often present in his work also has a personal ingredient. "I often work for men I admire greatly, because of their devotion to issues, their relationship to people, their ability to work hard. . . . I see them taking part in the democratic process. I know enough about history that I'm very moved, sometimes, by the people I work with, and I have a strong inclination to try to communicate that."

Emotional spots have always formed an inviting target for critics, who lament the lost days of issue-based elections. Like much nostalgia, that vision of the past is selective. But beyond that, campaign issues frequently prove tangential to performance in office. The 1960 presidential election boiled over with discussions of hot content, due in part to the candidates' debates. Once John Kennedy entered office, many of these hot issues were heard no more. It is not that he broke campaign promises; rather, he—and Richard Nixon—campaigned on many ultimately irrelevant issues. Quemoy and Matsu returned to the obscurity they so richly deserved, while the campaigners did not anticipate the major issues of the Kennedy years, such as Berlin, Vietnam, and the Cuban Missile Crisis. Even if they had, outright position statements wouldn't have ensured the right outcomes. Because the kind of man the candidate is does matter to the electorate, those spots that convey some feeling for the subject also matter. In Agnew's case Goodman as well as the Maryland electorate guessed wrong about the kind of man they saw. But that is a risk we all run.

Partly in reaction to pure emotion in advertising, a form of high-content political ads appeared in the early 1970s, largely the work of David Garth and his colleague at the time, the writer Jeff Greenfield. Garth began using supers—superimposition of words, facts, and figures on the screen over the visual images. "Part of it was the distrust of politicians, generally speaking, in that period," he told us. "If you could actually super a fact, it would have more credibility than just a politician saying, 'I built something.'" To Garth's surprise, people picked up the supered information, even when it took effort and repeated viewings to do so. This went against expectation. The USP rule and various other advertising doctrines had always stressed simplicity: one ad, one idea. "Whatever you did," says Garth, "you were not to complicate up a commercial. We found that you could put more information into a political spot, that the printed word had more power on TV than it did, almost, in a pamphlet." High-content ads worked, Garth believes, by initially making voters uneasy: "When they first saw the spots, they missed it. There was too much information. So the next time they would look for what they missed. And in the process of straining to look for what they missed, they absorbed *more* information. By the time they saw the spot for the fourth or fifth time, they really had almost absorbed all the material."

Advertising in the argument phase of a campaign, whether emotion-rich or fact-rich, follows the campaign strategy and the campaign research. Robert Squier had his hands full in Mississippi in the 1983 Sturdivant campaign, handling an unknown candidate with no public record to run on. His task, however, was easy when compared to designing an advertising strategy for a well-known candidate with a very public record that must be run from. Typically this occurs in a reelection campaign. The most notorious example involves Governor Nelson Rockefeller of New York and his 1966 campaign. As Rockefeller neared the completion of his third term, his ID among New York voters stood near a hundred percent and his bio was familiar—too familiar.

His televised opposition to Goldwater at the 1964 convention had angered political conservatives, and his widely publicized divorce and quick remarriage hurt him with social conservatives. For just about anyone else he had the reputation of the man who raised taxes. His polls showed only twenty-one percent of the electorate would vote for him; "You couldn't be elected dogcatcher," Rockefeller's pollster supposedly told him. William Ronan, a Rockefeller adviser, told reporter James Perry, "Since people were down on the Governor, we decided to sell his accomplishments without using him at all."

The Rockefeller campaign hired Tinker & Partners to do the selling; one of the partners then was Mary Wells, who made the agency's presentation. Tinker used a New York fish to explain why Rockefeller was a good governor, in "Fish Interview":

VIDEO

Fade in on two puppets, a fish and a reporter. The reporter is simply a human hand beneath a hat labeled "Press," with a miniature microphone labeled "News" tucked into the puppeteer's shirt cuff; the hand opening and closing represents the reporter's mouth. The fish is a puppet, weaving back and forth as it floats, complete with opening and closing eyelids and mouth.

As the scene opens, there is a super in small white caps:

AUDIO

Reporter [SOF]: "You, sir!"

Fish [SOF]: "Uh-huh?"

Reporter [SOF]: "How do you feel about Governor Rockefeller's pure waters program?"

Fish [SOF]: "His pure what?"

Reporter [SOF]: "Pure water."

Fish [SOF]: "Oh, yeah."

Reporter [SOF]: "This program, sir, is wiping out water pollution in New York State within six years!"

"SIMULATED INTERVIEW
WITH A LARGE MOUTH
BASS."

Fish [SOF]: "Wait a minute.
He's supposed to be interviewing me!"

Reporter [SOF]: "Already one
hundred and thirty new sew-
age treatment plants are getting underway."

Fish [SOF]: "Yeah, well, it was
pretty smelly down here."

Reporter [SOF]: "State health
offices are working overtime,
trying to track down sources
of pollution."

Fish [SOF]: "Listen, they
should see what happened to
my cousin:
    "Ooo blu blu blu blub.
    "My cousin had a brilliant
career."

Fish takes a spiraling nose
dive out of the picture, then
resurfaces.

Reporter [SOF]: "By the end
of the summer, the government will have called in every
major polluter for a hearing."

Fish [SOF]: "Uh, I would say
that, next to a fish, I would
say that he's the best governor we've had."

Reporter [SOF]: "Over seventy cities and industries have
agreed to cut violations."

Fish speaks confidentially into reporter's ear.

Fish [SOF]: "Frankly, though, uh, my problem with Rockefeller is:

"Some of his best friends are fishermen."

Reporter turns and stares at camera. White super in two lines: "A PAID POLITICAL ANNOUNCEMENT BY FRIENDS OF THE ROCKE-FELLER TEAM."

Helped by the fish, Rockefeller later resurfaced in his own ads and won handily over his financially strapped, media-innocent Democratic opponent, Frank O'Connor.

Another way, in the argument phase of a reelection campaign, to deal with the burden of the past is for the candidate to use the confessional mode. Garth let John Lindsay speak for himself and directly to the camera in his 1969 spot, forthrightly called "Mistakes":

VIDEO

AUDIO

Fade in to ECU of Lindsay.

Birds are faintly audible in the background throughout.

Lindsay [SOF]: "I guessed wrong on the weather before the city's biggest snowfall last winter, and that was a mistake.

Slow zoom out, revealing his casual dress. He is sitting on a porch.

"But I put six thousand more cops on the street, and that was no mistake.

"The school strike went on too long, and we all made some mistakes.

"But I brought two hundred and twenty-five thousand new jobs to this town, and that was no mistake.

"And I fought for three years to put a fourth police platoon on the streets, and that was no mistake. And I reduced the deadliest gas in the air by fifty percent, and I forced the landlords to roll back unfair rents, and we did not have a Detroit, or a Watts, or a Newark in this city, and those were no mistakes.

"The things that go wrong are what make this the second toughest job in America.

Slow zoom to ECU. Fade to black, then fade in, white super: "Vote for Mayor Lindsay. It's the 2nd toughest job in America. Paid for by the Committee to Re-elect John V. Lindsay."

"But the things that go right are what make me want it."

"We looked at polls and concluded that Lindsay was in such trouble that, if you tried to put a positive record out on TV, nobody would believe it," Garth told us. "So we did what was to us the obvious thing." The technique wasn't obvious to the other Lindsay campaign advisers because, as Garth says, "the general inclination at the time was that a politician never admitted his mistakes."

Garth used a mistakes spot again, working for Brendan Byrne's reelection campaign as governor of New Jersey in 1977. Byrne had promised not to implement a state income tax, and then had done so. "Instead of walking away from that, once again we walked right into it," Garth says. The same idea was recycled yet again by Garth in Hugh Carey's reelection campaign for governor in New York in 1978. Roger Ailes did a variation for Republican Lew Lehrman in his candidacy for governor of New York four years later. Ailes's spot begins with Lehrman addressing the camera about taxes. He flubs a line and giggles—normally an outtake. But Lehrman continues: "That one blew me right off the chair. Holy mackerel! Too much energy." Then the frame freezes, and the camera pulls back to show the candidate sitting, watching himself on a monitor, a spot within a spot. Lehrman turns and addresses the camera. "Hey, I make some mistakes, even taping my commercials. I'll make mistakes as governor. . . ." The idea, Ailes says, was to show the candidate's human side. "He really was able to laugh at himself." When Ailes decided to use the outtake as a spot, he had a problem persuading the campaign: "People said it's undignified; that's not what we're selling for governor." But Ailes believes the voters "want their elected officials to show a wide range of emotion. People understand that politicians are human." The outtakes-as-final-spot idea also shows the campaign to be "human" and "real," the same thinking behind Gene Wyckoff's decision to let the woman shopper's quotes stand in his 1964 Rockefeller spot.

Like Wyckoff and Ailes, Ken Swope, a media manager based in Boston, has faced opposition to some of his campaign proposals. Swope contends that "almost all political advertising is very dull; it doesn't use any of the devices that commercial advertising is so good at." Swope spent two years with N W Ayer, and frequently brings in the commercial technique of humor in his

TECHNIQUES: HUMOR

**Republican National
Committee Spot, 1980**

"Congressman, I think
we're running out of gas"

"Congressman, this is getting serious"

"Hey! We're out of gas!"

"The Democrats are out
of gas. We need some
new ideas"

John Kerry Commercial, 1983

"Ever wonder what lieutenant governors do?"

"The lieutenant governor really ought to be part of the government"

Harold Washington Anti-Byrne Commercial, 1983

"She's hired some New York media experts to give her a 'new image' "

"But when the election's over, we'll be stuck with the same old Jane Byrne and the same old problems still piling up"

political ads. His goal, he says, is to create "Hey, Martha!" spots—
"Hey, Martha! Come in here and look, it's that crazy commercial
again." For John Kerry, a 1982 candidate for Massachusetts lieutenant governor, Swope wrote a script that ridiculed the office.
"Ever wonder what lieutenant governors do?" the voice-over
begins. The spot then shows a balding, middle-aged "lieutenant
governor" at work—unfolding paper dolls, talking to a stuffed
duck, and staring at the phone wistfully, awaiting an assignment
from the governor. The voice-over goes on to laud Kerry's accomplishments, as an antiwar activist and as a criminal prosecutor,
and concludes: "John Kerry really made something out of those
jobs, and he'll make something out of this one." "We almost
had fistfights in the campaign, to get that commercial produced,"
Swope says. Another 1982 Swope spot, for congressional candidate
Bruce Morrison in Connecticut, shows the candidate seated next
to an elderly woman. As he begins talking about the problems
of the elderly, the woman interrupts him and lashes out at the
incumbent Republican, Lawrence J. DeNardis. "I've got a few
choice words for you, Congressman DeNardis," she says. "Too
bad I can't say them on TV." She concludes by shaking her
finger into the camera and scolding, "You ought to be ashamed
of yourself, Lawrence J. DeNardis." Throughout the spot, candidate Morrison looks on, silently and haplessly, preempted by
a prop. Swope also produced a later spot for Morrison, visually
identical, in which the candidate speaks unhindered; at the end
he asks how he did, and the woman says, "Mine was better."
"The concept of humor is a very new one in political advertising,"
Swope says. "It's being done in product commercials, but most
politicians are wary." The politicians' fear of a backlash from
humor spots may be groundless: both Kerry and Morrison won.

Phase Three: Attack

Once the candidate's name, history, and something of his or her
personality and ideas are known, the campaign usually enters
its third phase, negative advertising. As soon as there were spots,

there were attack spots—Ike, for instance, comparing the Democrats to well-intentioned but reckless bus drivers. Name-calling and invective are themselves nothing new in American political life. Washington was called a "whore master" and would-be monarch; Jefferson, a coward and atheist; Lincoln, a "rail-splitting baboon." Franklin D. Roosevelt, Jr., as a surrogate for John Kennedy in the West Virginia primary in 1960, declared Hubert Humphrey was a draft dodger.

Direct personal attacks on TV had a run for a time during the mid-1960s to mid-1970s, when the wider society was shaken by confrontational styles. For example, after the fish interview spot aired in the 1966 New York governor's race, a young Rockefeller campaign aide named John Deardourff urged tougher materials, arguing in an internal campaign memo that "a greater anti-O'Connor thrust is likely to pay much larger dividends than anything else which could be done." Rockefeller did attack spots late in the campaign, saying: "If you want to help keep the crime rates high, O'Connor is your man." It seems O'Connor was adjudged soft on crime because he opposed a Rockefeller narcotics program that, among other measures, required mandatory treatment for addicts. In the 1970 Illinois race for U.S. senator, the incumbent, an appointee named Ralph Tyler Smith, ran a spot implying that his opponent and radical agitators were in league against the police. The voice-over quotes "Yippie agitator" Jerry Rubin as calling the police "pigs," with the adjective before it bleeped out, and then quotes Adlai Stevenson, III, as calling some policemen "storm troopers in blue." Smith, on camera, then makes his heavy-handed point: "I believe that the police are on our side. I simply don't understand how any responsible person could think otherwise." The voters were on Stevenson's side, though, and Smith lost badly.

By the mid-1970s, as the wider society quieted down somewhat, so too did the attack spots. In the typical late-1970s, early-1980s form, surrogates usually do the attacking. In the 1976 Ford effort, for example, Deardourff and Bailey made heavy, late-campaign use of "Georgia Papers":

VIDEO

AUDIO

Camera up on slide: white letters against black background, "Those who know Jimmy Carter best are from Georgia. That's why we thought you ought to know":

Sound of teletype underneath. Announcer reads script from slide and crawl.

Photo of Gerald Ford appears and holds underneath crawl: tough, unsmiling.

Script already on screen crawls upward, being replaced by new material:

"The Savannah, Georgia NEWS endorses Gerald Ford for President.

"The Augusta, Georgia HERALD endorses President Ford.

"The Atlanta, Georgia DAILY WORLD endorses President Ford.

"The Marietta, Georgia JOURNAL endorses President Ford.

"The Albany, Georgia HERALD endorses President Ford.

"The Augusta, Georgia CHRONICLE endorses President Ford.

"The Savannah, Georgia
PRESS endorses—"

The spot fades out midsentence, suggesting more papers to be named.

Most of the papers were small in circulation, and the state's
major paper, the *Atlanta Journal and Constitution*, had endorsed
Carter. But the list seemed impressively long.

In the same campaign Bailey and Deardourff popularized one
of the most widely used surrogate attack forms, the Man on the
Street spot. The idea—putting spot arguments in the mouths of
everyday voters—goes back to Thomas Dewey's 1950 reelection
campaign for governor of New York. Eisenhower brought it to
presidential politics in his 1956 campaign (which also featured
Woman on the Street spots, aired during daytime hours, and
even College Student on the Street spots). In this style the media
managers tape dozens of brief interviews with ordinary people.
Those that raise the desired point, in the desired language, with
the desired demographic mix, are then edited together into a
fast-paced spot. In 1976 one Bailey-Deardourff spot slides
smoothly from positive comments on Ford, none of them fulsome
beyond credibility, to negative remarks about Carter, all homing
in on Carter's major negative of the time:

VIDEO	AUDIO
Camera up on bald man, glasses.	Man [SOF]: "The thing that I like most about Mr. Ford is that he's steady. He is not erratic; we can count on him to do what's in the best interest of the country."

Cut to black man.	Man [SOF]: "I think he offers solidarity."
Cut to woman in scarf.	Woman [SOF]: "I think he's a strong person. I think he stands up for what he thinks is right."
Cut to well-dressed young man.	Man [SOF]: "I think Ford's been very stable."
Cut to blonde woman in turtleneck.	Woman [SOF]: "He takes things very gradually, very carefully. I don't think he's going to make any big mistakes. I'm afraid that Carter's too ambiguous."
Cut to man in leisure suit.	Man [SOF]: "Carter is not quite sure which direction he goes. He changes his mind on his stand every other day or so."
Cut to man in cap.	Man [SOF]: "He contradicts himself from one day to another."
Cut to young man in T-shirt.	Man [SOF]: "He has changed his opinions from one day to the next."
Cut to middle-aged woman.	Woman [SOF]: "He is much too wishy-washy."
Cut to man with mustache.	Man [SOF]: "He's very, very wishy-washy."

Cut to heavyset man.	Man [SOF]: "He seems to be a little wishy-washy."
Cut to earnest young man.	Man [SOF]: "If he'd stand up and say what he's for, he'd be a little bit easier to understand, and maybe to believe."
Cut to short-haired woman.	Woman [SOF]: "All the things we've read about Jimmy Carter, I think, are true—that he is fuzzy on a lot of the issues."
Cut to still photo of Ford at podium, smiling.	Same woman [VO, continuing]: "I like President Ford—the man who will tell you just exactly where he does stand."

Rafshoon learned from the opposition and used the Man on the Street technique in 1980. In the primaries, voters in Rafshoon spots criticized Kennedy's liberalism and stability; during the general election, Rafshoon spots labeled Reagan as trigger-happy. Several of the latter pointedly identified the anti-Reagan voters as residents of California, Reagan's home state. That too was borrowed from Bailey-Deardourff work in 1976, when one Man on the Street spot ends with the words of a woman on an Atlanta street corner (in a rich Southern accent): "It would be good to have a president from Georgia—but not Carter." Robert Goodman, as usual, has gone one manic step further; in 1972, he was running Arch Moore's campaign against Jay Rockefeller, a transplanted New Yorker, for governor of West Virginia. In one Goodman spot people on the streets of Manhattan are asked what they would think of a West Virginian running for governor of New York. One person waves the camera away dismissively;

others call the notion "preposterous . . . ridiculous . . . crazy." At the end, a woman says, "That makes as much sense to me as having the next governor of West Virginia be a New Yorker." Goodman admits that his "random respondents" were all paid actors or aides, "but, hey, they were all from New York."

Because even legitimate Man on the Street spots are shaped on the editing table, not everyone counts himself a fan of the technique. "They're hogwash, fake advertising," says Malcolm MacDougall. "The truth is, when you interview three hundred people, you can get them to say anything you want." Even when people don't say the right thing, skillful editing can help. In a Goodman spot for New Mexico Senator Pete Domenici, a woman says, "We like Mr. Pete 'cause he answers our letters when we write to him." Left on the cutting room floor, Goodman says, was the rest of her comment: ". . . especially when we send him money."

Skillful editing can permit greater subterfuge. In his 1964 Senate race from Texas, George Bush ran spots in which he "debated" his opponent, Ralph Yarborough. Actually the Yarborough clips were from filmed speeches, permitting the Bush campaign wide discretion. That same year, as we've seen, Henry Cabot Lodge's aborted primary campaign aired a spot that implied (wrongly) Eisenhower's endorsement. Such incidents are rare now; the news organizations, increasingly attentive to the inner workings of campaigns, are too likely to publicize an unfair attack, creating publicity that can weaken the candidate's existing support.

Yet it doesn't take tricky editing to create a spot that the press, and frequently the electorate, judge to be a low blow. In 1982, Republican Robin Beard used an actor portraying Fidel Castro, in a spot attacking incumbent U.S. Senator James Sasser of Tennessee:

VIDEO	AUDIO
Camera up to show wooden crate labeled "U.S. Aid," with	Announcer [VO]: "When it comes to spending taxpayers'

hands holding crowbars prying lid open. Hands grapple for stacks of dollars.	money, Senator James Sasser is a master. Take foreign aid. While important programs are being cut back here at home, Sasser has voted to allow foreign aid to be sent to committed enemies of our country—Vietnam, Laos, Cambodia, Marxist Angola, and even Communist Cuba. You can bet James Sasser is making a lot more friends abroad than he is here in Tennessee."
Cut to actor dressed as Fidel Castro. Holds up a dollar bill aflame, lights his cigar.	"Castro" [SOF]: "Muchissimas gracias, Señor Sasser."

The distortion of Sasser's record backfired; the senator won handily and could feelingly say much thanks, Mr. Beard.

While many negative polispots, like the Castro one, carry their entire message, others seek to activate existing attitudes in the audience. As Tony Schwartz, the leading advocate of this approach, has written in *The Responsive Chord*, "Commercials that attempt to *tell* the listener something are inherently not as effective as those that attach to something that is already in him." Schwartz's Daisy spot sought to evoke existing fears about Goldwater; similarly several Schwartz spots have aimed at voters' doubts about Republican vice-presidential candidates (the laughter and heartbeat spots against Spiro Agnew, and the "MonDole" spot against Bob Dole). In the 1980 Democratic primaries Gerald Rafshoon produced spots lauding Carter's wholesome family life and tying it to the presidency (much as Squier tried to connect the National Guard to the job of governor). "Husband, father,

TECHNIQUES: SYMBOLS AND PROPS

Foreign Leaders

Ford, 1976

Hot Line

Johnson, 1964

Oval Office

Carter, 1980

Air Force One

Ford, 1976

Social Security Card

Johnson, 1964

Riots and Disorder

Nixon, 1968

president. He's done these three jobs with distinction," ran the tag line on some Rafshoon spots. Taken alone, they are standard argument spots; but, in the context of the campaign—with opponent Edward Kennedy's rocky marriage—the attack becomes clear. Rafshoon resists the label negative, calling them "comparative." "Carter certainly is a family man," he insists. "It has always been part of his campaigning." David Garth used an evocative approach in his 1982 work for Edward Koch against Mario Cuomo in New York's gubernatorial primary—"the toughest spot we ever did," Garth says. The camera comes up on a stopwatch that looks like the watch on CBS's *60 Minutes*. Then the announcer's voice-over says: "You have the following twenty seconds to think of one single thing that Mario Cuomo has accomplished as lieutenant governor." The clock ticks loudly away. "Mario has not forgiven me yet," says Garth, "but it was really a fair commercial, because he had no record."

The stopwatch is not yet a standard prop in political commercials, but other symbols have become clichés, principally in negative spots: the dollar bill shrinking to show inflation; a Social Security card being torn or cut; a photo of the opponent with his nose growing Pinocchio style. The most common is the flip-flop spot, showing the candidate's profile reversing (Johnson against Goldwater in 1964; Nixon against McGovern in 1972) or a weather vane (Humphrey against Nixon, 1968). An empty chair or podium is a favorite of candidates whose opponents refuse to debate. One 1980 spot, financed by the Republican party, employs humor and symbolism, with a car running out of gas to symbolize the energy crisis; the driver, an actor strongly resembling Democratic Speaker of the House Tip O'Neill, jovially ignores the warnings of his Everyman passenger until the car sputters and dies. In a 1980 spot for Edward Kennedy, David Sawyer used sports as a metaphor in order to attack Jimmy Carter:

VIDEO	AUDIO
Camera up on Jimmy Carter at bat during softball game, smiling, casual dress. Ball goes by. Cut to ticker tape running by over stock exchange. Zoom out. Cut back to softball shot. Ball goes by, Carter's bat still on shoulders.	Announcer [VO]: "When it came to inflation, his attitude was: 'I'll keep my fingers crossed.' Today we have twenty percent inflation. "On housing, interest rates, even foreign affairs his attitude was: 'I'll keep my fingers crossed.'
Cut to Kennedy approaching lectern, crowd cheering. Cut to Kennedy at podium, giving speech.	"This man's attitude is: fight until the job is done. His colleagues have named him one of our most effective senators. We have a choice. We can choose a man who will do the job, or we can keep our fingers crossed. Take a stand.
White super fades in: "KENNEDY FOR PRESIDENT."	Kennedy for President."

Some symbol spots function reactively, trying to characterize an opponent's attack as unfair. When his 1982 opponent had accused him of big spending, Congressman Les AuCoin of Oregon aired a spot, produced by Dan Payne, showing mud being thrown against a campaign poster (Payne admits AuCoin *was* something of a big spender). In the 1982 congressional race against Barney Frank, Margaret Heckler's campaign aired this spot:

TECHNIQUES: THE FLIP-FLOP

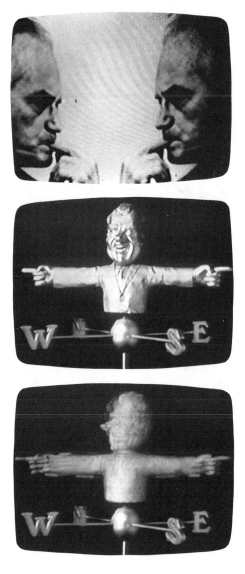

Johnson Anti-Goldwater, 1964

Humphrey Anti-Nixon, 1968

**Reagan Anti-Carter,
1980**

VIDEO   AUDIO

Camera up on black-and-   Announcer [VO]: "Barney
white photo of Frank,   Frank says you can trust him.
unflattering.   But look at his record.
Supers over Frank photo: "As a state legislator, he
"Prostitution,"   sponsored a bill to permit le-
"Pornography."   galized prostitution and allow
                              combat zones in every city
                              and town in Massachusetts.
                              He introduced a bill to per-
                              mit legalized prostitution—
                              four times in four years. He
                              voted against increased pen-
                              alties for criminals who dis-
                              tribute pornography to
                              minors. And last year he
                              voted to reduce the sentence
                              for violent rape.
Cut to Heckler and her fam-   "Keep Margaret Heckler.
ily walking toward the cam-   She has a record we can be
era with an American flag in proud of."
her hand.

Payne, working for Frank, produced this in response:

VIDEO   AUDIO

Camera up on still photo of   Announcer [VO]: "Barney
Barney Frank, black and   Frank's been in politics long
white. Hand enters picture   enough to know your image
and, with black felt-tip pen, suffers a little at election
draws mustache and then   time.
goatee on photo.

Hand disappears, then re-
turns with wide red marker;
slashes across photo, nearly
obliterating it.

"But this time, things have
gone too far. Margaret Heckler's so worried about her
own record, she's painting a
distorted picture of Barney's.
There's a name for this
tactic—

White, bold letters supered
across bottom of photo:
"SMEAR."
Super and pen markings
slowly fade, leaving photo
untarnished.

"The truth is, Barney
Frank's always fought against
crime and vice, and to protect families, from students to
senior citizens. Wipe away
the smear, and you see why
Barney Frank is still a congressman you can trust."

Cut to slide: white letters
against black background,
"Barney Frank. The Demo-
crat. A Congressman you can
trust."

The commercial, like the Heckler attack that prompted it,
begins with a black-and-white photo of Frank. "We wanted people
to see our spot and, when they saw the Heckler commercial,
automatically remember the response," Payne says.

Negative spots sometimes reach beyond (or behind) the opponent to attack the campaign advisers or contributors instead.
Senator John Melcher of Montana, under attack by a conservative
PAC in 1982, aired a commercial reminiscent of Rockefeller's
1966 fish interview, with a group of animated cows complaining
about the opposition's excesses (Melcher is a former veterinarian).
"Didya hear 'bout those city slickers out here bad-mouthin' Doc

Melcher?" asks one cow. In the 1983 Democratic primary for mayor of Chicago incumbent Jane Byrne hired David Sawyer to do her media, inspiring an opponent to air a spot with a Byrne look-alike mannequin seated at a desk. Four men enter the frame and apply makeup to the mannequin. "She's hired some New York media experts to give her a 'new image,' " the voice-over says. "But when the election's over, we'll be stuck with the same old Jane Byrne. . . ." In the 1984 Illinois primary a Gary Hart attack ad linking Walter Mondale to Chicago machine leader Edward "Fast Eddie" Vrdolyak backfired seriously.

Because attack advertising produces such mixed results, the media men have mixed feelings about it. Charles Guggenheim is the wariest: "What we refer to as negative advertising is fundamentally inferences, innuendoes, half arguments. Some negative advertising is constructive; some is not, and the second kind has proliferated. It's much easier to produce. In a short time segment it's much easier to say something bad about a person than something positive about yourself." Guggenheim did harsh negative advertising on behalf of California Governor Edmund G. "Pat" Brown against Ronald Reagan in 1966, with lines including, "An actor shot Lincoln," "Vote for a *real* governor, nor an acting one," and, "Over the years, Ronald Reagan has played many roles. This year he wants to play governor. Are you willing to pay the price of admission?" Guggenheim has called them "the most entertaining spots we ever did . . . and I think they were among the most destructive for our candidate." He has been far more restrained since. In 1972 he refused to do the tough negative ads some McGovern managers wanted (Tony Schwartz was brought in for the job). Guggenheim now says he does negative ads only on occasion, "to show where your opponent has gone wrong, what he has done that is not useful, attractive, admirable, or in the public interest. I think you can make an argument for that."

David Garth agrees: "Where it's on the record that a man or a woman voted wrong, negative ads are legitimate. Negative

spots that are not based on facts or issues are not legitimate."
Michael Kaye also dislikes attack ads but uses them when necessary. Kaye, who did the Edmund G. "Jerry" Brown presidential
campaign in 1976, told us, "My own style is a kind of consensus,
trying to bring people together instead of dividing them. Negative
advertising helps put someone down so someone else gets elected.
But when it's all over nobody has really benefited. Consequently
I hate it. But I'm not a dummy. Politics is important, and I want
to win." Kaye did negative spots for Alan Cranston's reelection
campaign in 1980 and Howard Metzenbaum's reelection campaign in 1976, "but with a velvet glove. I've never done a spot
where somebody has cringed, said it's below the belt, or written
an editorial against it." Robert Goodman sees attack advertising
as part of the "kind of society" we live in: "We've always known
that people like a fight. It's more newsworthy when one candidate
calls the other a son of a bitch than when he puts out his white
paper on education." Goodman's negative spots—he calls them
"competitive advertising"—frequently contain humor to reduce
the chances of a backlash. "People sometimes think you're coming
into their living room and spoiling their carpet with mud. It has
to be done carefully." John Deardourff's views on attack ads
haven't changed in the years since his Rockefeller memo of 1966.
He argues that negative spots are a legitimate, even essential
element of political dialogue: "One school of thought holds there
is something wrong with negative advertising; to me quite the
contrary is true. The burden on any challenger is to establish
not only that he is himself a good person, in a political sense,
but that there is something wrong with the job that has been
done by the incumbent. What other reason is there for people
to change their voting habits? If they voted for him once, why
not vote for him again? They have to be persuaded that he hasn't
measured up to the job in some way."

Negative advertising campaigns attract considerable attention—
as Robert Goodman says, people watch conflict—and in almost
all major campaigns at least one candidate goes through this

attack phase, though its intensity and length may vary greatly. Some candidates have built up such good reputations that, in Deardourff's words, there is "automatic voter resistance to any negative information." In such cases—and despite the general skepticism about the quality of contemporary public officials, there are such people—the campaign skips the attacks in favor of lengthening the argument phase.

Phase Four: "I see an America . . . "

At the very end of the modern media political campaign, as in conventional theater, there usually comes the quieter moment of resolution and reflection. This final phase is short and saccharine sweet. The candidates have been introduced and IDed in their advertising. They have stated their arguments and sketched an outline of their characters, albeit all highlights and brilliant glow. Their attack spots have provided some unfavorable details, the shortcomings and the shadows, of their opponents. It remains now for each candidate to sum up, to appear on camera in repose, thoughtful and dignified without the overpowering visuals and the strident noises of the campaign. In higher-level campaigns, particularly for the presidency, this has come to mean an election-eve program of thirty or sixty minutes (lower-level campaigns frequently return to positive advertising during the final week). In the past such election-eve specials usually offered hoopla and Hollywood (Tykes for Ike, 1952; Ginger Rogers for Nixon, 1960). In 1976 Bailey, Deardourff, and MacDougall hoped to produce an election-eve special with Gerald Ford, his family, dozens of celebrities, and thousands of supporters gathered at the Lincoln Memorial in Washington. Ford would speak, the celebrities would praise him, and the program would end with the assembled throng singing the "Feelin' Good" song. The logistics problem would have been a "nightmare," MacDougall later concluded, and the idea was scrubbed in favor of the Jerry and Joe Show. By 1980 the more subdued format of the candidate talking one-on-one with the voter was established. In our analysis this seems more likely to be the model of future final acts than high production extravaganzas.

We have classified political advertising into four rhetorical modes, or acts, roughly following the chronology of the campaign. The classification to an extent is arbitrary. Although campaigns usually begin with ID or bio ads, proceed through the argument and attack phases, and end with visionary appeals, the exact length of each act may vary depending on campaign strategies; the four acts may overlap as well, again in response to campaign developments and strategies. Sometimes too one polispot or polispot series may be intended to accomplish two or more rhetorical tasks—for example, when a candidate has limited funds. Senator Gary Hart's low-budget primary spots in New Hampshire combined his ID and his "new ideas" pitch. The classic example is Richard Nixon's Checkers speech. It has been widely admired for its effectiveness, as measured by the outpouring of support that ensured the beleaguered Nixon's place on the Eisenhower ticket in 1952. Looked at in terms of our classification, Nixon's presentation combined four rhetorical modes in one inspired act: Nixon identifies himself as hardworking and gives details of his family's financial life; he argues his case with specific facts and figures, using documents when necessary; he attacks the Communist-coddling, big-spending opposition; and he ends with an appeal for support so that Eisenhower can do the job of saving America. In pure technique Checkers is a model of political advertising. Rather than bathos for the yokels, to use Garry Wills's phrase, Checkers offers a textbook case for political rhetoricians to study. And, oh yes, it worked. Explaining how and why political advertising succeeds, is the next and final task of our study.

EFFECTS

PART IV

IT WAS THE TRUCK: JUDGING THE EFFECTS OF POLISPOTS

CHAPTER 15

The weekend before a presidential election, as the political commentator Mark Shields tells the story, a lowly Democratic party hanger-on in the second ward of a small town in Iowa worried about the outcome. "Our voters don't know there's an election coming up," he complained to the ward committeeman; "we need a truck with a big sign and music to get people to notice." The committeeman brushed him off, but the man persisted. And, finally, the committeeman gave in: "Here's a hundred bucks to rent a truck from your brother-in-law down at the garage, if that's what you want to do." Off rushed the man, and on Saturday afternoon, as Iowans shopped, the truck rumbled by, music blaring, placards urging a vote for the Democratic party. On Tuesday Democrats across the nation swept into office, winning the presidency, fifteen U.S. Senate seats, ten governorships, including Iowa's, the local congressional district as well as control of the U.S. House of Representatives, the city manager, and three out of five ward alderman races. At second ward headquarters, amid all the joy, the hanger-on came up to the committeeman and with a big smile, punched him on the arm and exclaimed: "What did I tell you! It was the truck!"

The media managers would never behave that way in public when talking about the effectiveness of their trucks in the making of political victory. They have little choice in the matter: because just about every major campaign now has media specialists working for each candidate, necessarily less than half of the advertising done in any specific election year will be for successful candidates and more than half for unsuccessful candidates. Just as obviously, many elements go into electoral success or failure besides paid media and communications strategy, including, but not restricted to, the nature and disposition of the voters, the strength of incumbency, the character of the candidates, and the unpredictable events of the campaign and of the wider society. There is, in short, a real world outside the artfully arranged realities of the media campaign. While many media managers will claim their particular truck played a part in victory, few will acknowledge their role in defeat, for they can point, justifiably, to these other dynamics. Rosser Reeves helped Ike and Daisy helped Lyndon Johnson, but both men would have been elected without advertising. Checkers, just as clearly, saved Nixon; without those thirty paid minutes it seems certain he would have been dropped from the ticket. Again, in 1968, Nixon needed TV; by 1972 he didn't. Gerald Rafshoon helped Carter against Gerald Ford in 1976; by 1980 no advertising could help Carter against Ronald Reagan. ("If we had it to do all over again," Rafshoon told us, "we would take the $30 million we spent in the campaign and get three more helicopters for the Iran rescue mission.")

Beyond these obvious home truths, are there any other definitive answers that can be given to the question of the effectiveness of paid political television advertising—which spots work, and why? The answer depends on (1) who is being asked, (2) what evidence is cited, and (3) which one of three effects is analyzed—the specific effects of the direct vote-getting campaign, the indirect effects of the metacampaign, or the general systemic effects on the overall electoral process and choice of candidates.

What the Experts Say

Social scientists tend to be cautious about the effects of television campaigns. Kay Israel did a 1983 survey of the existing academic literature on political advertising and found little that went beyond the standard textbook conclusion offered by Bernard Berelson of the University of Chicago in the pretelevision 1940s. Berelson wrote that "some kinds of communication on some kinds of issues, brought to the attention of some kinds of people under some kinds of conditions, have some kinds of effects." For this cautious adagio we are tempted to say to Berelson, "Thanks a little," except that Berelson's words were a welcome counterpoint to the then-existing, overwrought ideas of the powers of political persuasion and propaganda. Messages sent, it was thought in the years between the great wars, were messages received, understood, and acted on. By Berelson's time, however, the verdict had begun to move the other way. Social scientists, using survey research techniques, reported that most messages didn't get through at all, and few of those that did had an appreciable effect on attitudes.

The academic research now suggests that people pay attention principally to messages that reflect their preexisting views; that is, the most attentive audience for a Reagan spot will be people who have already decided to vote for Reagan. As Marshall McLuhan argued two decades ago, people attend to those advertisements extolling goods they already own. Supporters of Reagan's opponent, on the other hand, may ignore the message, or they may receive it, argue with it, and reject it. Several studies have found that some supporters of a particular candidate tend to project their own views onto the candidate's advertising—they will hear what they want to hear, almost regardless of what the favored candidate says. And a number of studies have concluded that few people actually change votes due to political advertising.

Conversion, certainly, is the obvious goal for a polispot. But it is not the only goal. There is evidence that polispots may be better at reinforcement—keeping the committed in line. Polispots also seem suited for activation—prodding the already committed to go out and vote on the basis of their commitments. The academic consensus is that advertising can matter in campaigns, as one of several variables. Some of the best purely statistical work, including studies by Gary Jacobson, found that incumbency and voter partisanship explain more electoral outcomes than broadcast expenditures. In cases where these factors are nullified—in primaries for vacant seats in Congress, for example— broadcast spending seems to be a significant determinant of outcomes.

The findings that political commercials only occasionally convert, reinforce, or activate tend to devalue their worth. When the informational content of polispots is surveyed, however, more positive qualities emerge. Thomas Patterson and Robert McClure studied the 1972 Nixon-McGovern campaign and concluded that polispots provided significant information to voters. They found that forty-two percent of spots during the general election focused primarily on issues, that another twenty-eight percent focused substantially on issues, and that "the two candidates' advertising campaigns reflected what each felt should be the nation's policy priorities." Patterson and McClure also reported that the information coming across in spots was greater than that received from the news media. Two years earlier, though, Walter DeVries and Lance Tarrance found that voters got little information from spots. Their book *The Ticket-Splitter* reported the results of a poll that found that political ads ranked twenty-fourth in campaign influence. (News reports ranked first, encouraging some media managers to create polispots resembling news stories, and to place them next to newscasts.) The Patterson-McClure and DeVries-Tarrance findings aren't necessarily contradictory. Perhaps the information is present in spots, but voters don't recognize it. More likely, many of the DeVries-Tarrance respondents be-

lieved, as Robert Goodman says, that good citizens shouldn't
admit that they get campaign information from TV advertising.

Several of the media managers we interviewed keep up with
the social science literature. Indeed, they often sound like academics themselves, when talking for the record about the effectiveness of political advertising. We hear echoes of Bernard
Berelson in Stuart Spencer's answer, when asked if spots work:
"Some do, some don't. Not everything you put on the air is
going to move somebody. But if you have the right issue and
it's handled in the right manner, and you're getting it to the
right audiences . . . media can have an effect." John Deardourff
was equally cautious. "I think everybody believes, in a very ill-
defined, inarticulate kind of way, that television is incredibly
important," he told us. "The problem is, nobody has made any
serious effort to quantify its importance." One reason, as Deardourff says, is the difficulty of "isolating and identifying the impact
of paid advertising on television, as opposed to any other of a
dozen independent variables" involved at the same time. Charles
Guggenheim says, "In some cases you can identify television as
being the reason people have won elections, and you can also
identify elections where television has, because of certain circumstances, not had much effect." He adds: "No one in his right
mind, in a senatorial or gubernatorial or presidential election,
cannot use television—if for no other reason than self-defense,
to neutralize what will undoubtedly be coming from the other
side. It's like air power in a battle. Can you fight a major campaign
without air power? The North Vietnamese showed you could.
But I don't think you want to do away with your air force."

"The very best people in this business," Bob Squier told us,
"probably understand only about five to seven percent of what
it is that they do that works. The rest is all out there in the
unknown." Robert Goodman also sounds a little like Berelson:
"The crime in our business is that we never know why the
candidates win or lose. I did work for Dave Owen for governor,
in a primary in Kansas, which we lost—and I thought some of

that work was the prettiest I'd ever done. I would say the best spots we've ever done are equally divided between those who lost and those who won." Of nearly a hundred statewide races he has worked on, Goodman adds, "there are maybe three or four where I really feel we did it."

"The most important thing today is not the David Garths of the world," says David Garth, placing himself in the company of DeVries-Tarrance. "It is the free media." Garth cites the 1980 polls showing Kennedy leading Carter in August by thirty-six points. "In December Kennedy was trailing by thirteen"—with not one paid commercial, but with the intervening interview that a stumbling Kennedy gave to Roger Mudd on CBS News. Garth also argues that George Bush "went up something like thirty points in the national polls in 1980. He didn't do national spots; all he did was local spots. Bush went that far up nationally because the influence of free media far surpasses the influence of TV commercials." A controlled situation, with no paid national media and plenty of free national media, would seem proof of the primacy of the latter, except that Deardourff offers a second example with controlled variables where the results were the opposite. At the start of the 1982 governor's race in Illinois, Deardourff says, his client, the incumbent James Thompson, scored low on personal ratings in the polling. An ad campaign for Thompson's reelection began over the summer when news media carried relatively few stories. The paid media campaign, Deardourff claims, "shifted the focus away from Thompson's personal problems and onto the question of his record and his issues. Before-and-after polling showed a clear shift in favorability toward Thompson, both generally and in terms of his ability to deal with those issues we were showing on television. The shift happened at a time when there wasn't enough other outside coverage of the campaign. You could have no doubt about where it came from."

Rules of the Game

The media managers we interviewed were willing to live with these ambiguities. They can have it both ways, putting a lot of time and energy into trying to influence the putatively important coverage of news organizations—the metacampaign—while gaining a validation for their work in those academic findings that show polispots to be informative. The media managers also do their own extensive, and proprietary, research, not for publication in academic journals but meant for guiding clients' campaigns—and for sharing with prospective clients during presentations for new business. Videotape screenings, polling data on flip charts, focus group results, and testimonial letters from past winners—the big payoff—go into these presentations. Each of the media managers we interviewed at length shared at least some of his work with us, while others provided examples of their presentation materials. Based on the evidence of these interviews and research materials, we have tried to write down some of the "unwritten rules" of political advertising that the media managers follow.

First of all many major campaigns now pretest spots, typically with focus groups, before releasing them, and most managers have a moderate degree of confidence in the value of such testing to measure advertising effectiveness. In the 1972 Nixon campaign Peter Dailey produced and pretested several negative spots. A given spot was found to be much more effective, he later said, when it was identified as sponsored by the group called Democrats for Nixon rather than by the Committee to Re-Elect the President. Such sponsorship, Dailey said, reinforced the idea that people like John Connally, who were highly credible Democrats (at the time, at least), "were doing the same thing."

In 1976 pretesting by the Ford campaign led to the shelving of several spots. Malcolm MacDougall had made a commercial arguing that agribusinessman Jimmy Carter had taken advantage of tax loopholes, paying $1,375 in federal tax on an adjusted income of over $120,000—while candidate Jimmy Carter was

railing against tax loopholes and three-martini lunches. It begins
with Carter (in footage borrowed from a Rafshoon spot) calling
tax laws "a disgrace." The announcer then says: "Jimmy Carter
and his family took advantage of the tax loopholes to reduce
their taxable income below that paid by a family of three earning
$15,000 a year." In pretests with focus groups gathered in a
Cleveland motel, the viewers reported that the tax spot was too
complicated. They also thought that the tax laws were complex—
and that most people tried to pay as little taxes as possible.
Viewers also found the "commercial within a commercial" idea
too confusing. The spot was shelved. In the same campaign,
Douglas Bailey made a five-minute spot, showing Ford campaigning in an open car in Dallas, evoking comparison with John
Kennedy and 1963 and playing on the "Feelin' Good" theme.
The media men agreed it was terrific stuff, very emotional, but
also risky: no one could predict how the voters would react to
being reminded of the assassination. In pretesting, viewers found
the spot upsetting, and it too was shelved (though Bailey later
said that, had he been certain Ford was losing, he would have
aired it).

On the other side, Gerald Rafshoon also made similar judgments about the effectiveness of various negative spots. Tony
Schwartz made two dozen spots for Carter, about half of them
in the attack style. Only a few were used. Rafshoon rejected such
spots as the one using an off-camera voice to list all the Ford
"against" positions—against Medicare, against job training,
against school lunches, against food stamps, against day care.
The voice-over asks: "Who'd believe a nice man like Gerald Ford
would vote against or oppose all these?" Another no-show opens
on a white sheet of paper titled "Résumé for Gerald Ford." The
page turns and the résumé lists all of Ford's "against" positions,
once more a long series. Finally, a Schwartz spot shows the
glistening skyline of New York; the voice-over says, "How can
anyone say to this great city, 'Drop dead'?"—a reference to
Ford's reputed attitude toward New York City's efforts to obtain

federal aid to avoid bankruptcy. Rafshoon rejected it and the others, he told us, because the Schwartz spots were trying to show that Ford was inhumane and "people didn't think he was inhumane; they thought he was kind of bumbling and stupid." Anti-Ford ads in general wouldn't work in 1976, Rafshoon added, "because people didn't think of Ford as a bad guy." But when Rafshoon produced attack spots against Kennedy and Reagan in 1980, his justification became: "People had negative perceptions of these people already. We didn't invent them."

Pretesting measures some effects better than others. Focus groups, for example, are more useful in looking at positive media than at negative media. Robert Squier says, "No focus group I've ever seen liked a negative spot. They think it's dirty politics." Charles Guggenheim adds that pretesting is "more useful to tell you what spots are really bad than to tell you which ones are the best." Guggenheim cites an example, a spot he produced for U.S. Senator John Danforth of Missouri in 1982. Guggenheim's crew accompanied Danforth to a car plant. The spot begins when workers ask him to "stuff an engine," to push the engine into the car. Danforth bends to the task with the workers. Finished, he says, "Thanks, team. You've taught me everything I know." Everyone smiles. "I thought it was terrific," says Guggenheim. "But there was something in there that people didn't like. I had it tested twice. People thought it was sort of talking down to them. I didn't see it, but the previewers did."

John Deardourff also does extensive pretesting and agrees that the technique "helps eliminate the clinkers, the commercials which are relatively ineffective, or maybe even dangerous in some un-anticipated way." As for the reverse—measuring the positive effects—Deardourff says, "We are not even close to being able to do that." Robert Goodman also agrees that focus groups aren't always reliable, "but they can sometimes keep you from making a terrible mistake." Roger Ailes believes focus groups work best at the extremes, positive as well as negative. "If you get a hundred percent negative reaction from people, chances are that something is wrong with that spot." And Michael Kaye finds pretests are toughest on "commercials that are clever, that have twists. The previewers will say, 'Those are gimmicky; we just want the candidate looking us in the eye, telling us what he stands for.' " Kaye adds that the interviewees—perhaps like the DeVries-Tarrance respondents—"think that's what they should say, and that's what they will say." Focus group leaders use various methods to plumb beneath such automatic responses to the truth. Still, focus groups and other pretesting methods that are tools for measuring effectiveness themselves prove ineffective at times.

The second rule we found is that ID commercials work in getting the candidate known. With the driving force of enough dollars, the name and face of a low- or zero-recognition candidate like a Lew Lehrman or a Frank Lautenberg can become familiar to just about every likely voter. The money buys enough air time so that no individual viewer can eventually escape seeing the candidate several times. The advertising rule of thumb is to buy enough gross ratings points to make a half-dozen hits per viewer. Name recognition alone is not enough; but if advertising can associate the candidate with attributes desired by the electorate, that translation may take place. Both Lehrman in New York and Lautenberg in New Jersey, for example, were millionaire business entrepreneurs who had never held public office.

Roger Ailes's polls for Lehrman showed that some of the candidate's issues would be most effective—for example, Lehrman was for capital punishment whereas his opponent, Mario Cuomo, was against it, and Lehrman favored "holding the tax line." The fact that Lehrman was a businessman and an outsider was also a positive in the polls. Ailes stressed these factors in his ads for Lehrman, spending over $1 million a month to buy four to five hundred gross rating points a week throughout the state, and continuing to ID Lehrman as "not a politician." Lehrman lost to Cuomo, and some of the reasons are a matter of litigation— literally. Ailes and the TV time-buying service are still, as of early

1984, tangled in lawsuits about the time buyer's alleged failure to buy enough air time upstate for Lehrman.

David Sawyer, working for Lautenberg, hit upon a similar outsider ID strategy. "The quantitative research showed that nobody knew who Frank Lautenberg was. But qualitative research showed that a spot strategy emphasizing his executive qualities could work," says Sawyer. "When we began to describe a candidate who had been successful at a high-tech industry, a poor boy who had made good, we found Lautenberg was the ideal candidate." Lautenberg got the phase-one ID he needed and won the primary, and then dropped Sawyer in favor of Squier (Lautenberg's business style included bargaining for the best price in media managers, and the managers themselves bid competitively for work, in the marketplace tradition). In the general election against the popular incumbent Millicent Fenwick, Squier's polls showed Lautenberg moving up only four points in his vote percentage in the first half of the campaign, but other indicators showed that Squier's phase-two, issue-oriented spots were working: "His positive rating, the idea that jobs were the most important issue, that his opponent was not sensitive to jobs—all that was moving up. You could plot it at a forty-five degree angle. Yet the vote had moved four points, which is relatively small." Squier's explanation is that "voters come to conclusions about pieces of the voting decision; they begin to form specific opinions, then they finally make the voting decision." The opposite is true too, says Squier: "The internals may be moving away from the candidate, even while support remains steady in the polls. You have to recognize that early, and solve it with media."

Third, as a rule negative advertising is the riskiest element of the campaign. The candidate, as John Deardourff told us, must be defined "in the most positive possible terms" before the campaign goes on the attack. Also any implicit messages in the negative spot must work to the campaign's advantage. Implicit in Goodman's "Porta-Potty" is the issue of high taxes and government waste, the thrust of Malcolm Wallop's candidacy. But the negative themes implicit in the unused Tony Schwartz spots for Jimmy Carter in 1976 would be counterproductive, or so Gerald Rafshoon believed when he shelved them, convinced that viewers would see Ford as fiscally responsible rather than as lacking compassion. Further, negative advertising tends, as Deardourff told us, to "harden the lines quickly—people leaning heavily toward a candidate will probably be firmed up in his favor by any attacks on him." It also tends to incite the opposition to let loose with its attack spots, perhaps more effective ones. Besides, there is the risk, especially for incumbents battling less-known challengers, that negative advertising will increase the opponent's ID without reducing his support. Also, negative advertising must be seen as credible. Margaret Heckler's ads accusing Barney Frank of wanting to establish prostitution zones didn't ring true; neither did a 1972 Nixon spot that accused McGovern of wanting to put half of the country on welfare, nor did the 1984 spot in the Illinois primary making Mondale out to be a tool of the party machine.

Most important, the attack must be seen as fair. Fairness, to paraphrase Potter Stewart's remark about obscenity, may be something we can't define, but we know it when we see it. Some of the underlying factors, though, can be listed. An extreme attack, saying that Barry Goldwater might push the button, can best be made indirectly, as in Daisy, a spot that never mentions Goldwater's name—though even that was widely viewed as unfair. Humor dilutes some attacks (the actor playing Tip O'Neill) but fails to soften others (the actor playing Fidel Castro). Certain personal themes are so touchy as to be considered unmentionable in negative spots (Chappaquiddick), though they can be raised implicitly ("You may not agree with President Carter, but you'll never find yourself wondering if he's telling you the truth"). Even nuances can make a major difference in whether an attack seems fair. In his work for Edward M. Kennedy in 1980, David Sawyer found that voters rejected as unfair the message that Carter, perceived as a decent man, had broken his promises, but they were receptive to the message that Carter was incapable of keeping his promises. Consequently the Kennedy campaign, Sawyer told us, "changed the argument from morality to competence." Sawyer's caution was justified, for voters tend to resent unfair attacks on an incumbent president. But the opposite is true too: voters may feel uncomfortable when the president goes on the attack. As Gerald Rafshoon—who successfully challenged a sitting president but failed to defend one—told us, "There's a different standard. You can play fast and loose if you're a challenger, but if you're president, they expect you to act presidential. You can't be irresponsible." Also, and sometimes in conflict with the risks or benefits for an incumbent president, voters seem more tolerant of attacks by an underdog. Thus President Ford in 1976 could freely attack front-runner Jimmy Carter, while Carter had to be more restrained.

To complicate the situation further, attacks are judged by the press as well as by the electorate. Political scientists are divided on whether press comment alone can affect voter attitudes, but most media managers believe it can; therefore they try to anticipate the press's likely response to an attack commercial. Deardourff told us that he sometimes gives reporters memos, substantiating the charges made in spots—"footnotes, in effect"—in order to forestall criticism. But, as Deardourff discovered in Chicago in 1983, footnotes sometimes aren't enough, for press or public.

In January 1983 Bailey and Deardourff went to work for the Republican mayoral candidate after Harold Washington won the Democratic primary. The GOP candidate was Bernard Epton, liberal, Jewish, and white. While Chicago had not elected a Republican as mayor since the 1920s, the Democratic nominee Washington had a number of liabilities on his record, including a conviction for failure to pay his income taxes, suspension from his law practice, and a string of lawsuits for nonpayment of all sorts of personal bills. Washington also was black, in a city that still has segregated neighborhoods. Deardourff now says that "the Epton media campaign had to be against Washington on a personal basis; his character was the issue. We had just six weeks to go so we did an indictment of Washington, and wrote a tag line for the commercials." The tag line was, "Epton: Before It's Too Late." As Deardourff sees it, "The whole idea was to summarize the notion that there were a few weeks remaining before Chicago was going to have a new and entirely different kind of mayor. Our message was, wake up, Chicago—look what you're getting here." Deardourff professes not to have seen the racial play in the line: Before it's too late—before a black becomes mayor.

The effort to frame the campaign around Washington's record framed the campaign instead around race. Black voters turned out in record numbers to vote for Washington on election day; thousands of white voters deserted the Democratic line to pull the lever for Epton; a smaller swing vote of white Democrats and some white Republicans voted Washington, as much out of a civic-minded desire to repudiate the aura of racism in Chicago— no Rose Garden but still their city—as anything else. The Deardourff strategy managed to make Washington-Epton a race, in both meanings of the word; it failed ultimately to win.

The fourth unwritten rule we found is that political advertising can polish a candidate's image considerably. Especially since Jimmy Carter's come-from-nowhere success in 1976, it has been widely believed that image-making is easier than image-remaking and that unknown challengers, if they're well heeled, have an advantage over familiar faces. We found otherwise. A well-planned, well-executed media campaign can shift voter perceptions of a candidate, even a highly visible incumbent. One of the best examples is the remaking of Chicago Mayor Jane Byrne.

Byrne had been elected in 1979, replacing a party machine hack who couldn't get the snow off constituents' streets after a big winter storm (he did clear those streets leading to a party fund raiser). Once in office, however, Byrne's strength dissipated. She had run as a reformer and then had brought in the old

machine gang she had run against. She supported Carter for
reelection one day and five days later supported Kennedy. She
was seen on television being abusive to the press. She raised
taxes by more than $400 million. She offended blacks by removing
black officials from the Chicago Housing Authority and replacing
them with whites. For her 1983 reelection effort, she hired David
Sawyer & Associates.

After studying poll results, Sawyer, in a confidential memo of
October 15, 1982, stated: "Both the qualitative and quantitative
data indicate that the Mayor is perceived to be unconcerned,
vindictive, erratic, impatient, someone who does not keep her
promises, and who is not 'concerned about me.' The Mayor is
also thought of as a smart, able, competent person, and there
is confusion, a lack of understanding, even embarrassment when
her behavior is inconsistent and uncontrolled." The theme of the
advertising effort would be "to soften the Mayor's image so that
she always appears to be listening to people, understanding their
concerns, and responding with appropriate actions. . . . While
working to soften the Mayor's image we must watch that visible
symbols reflect our message. The Mayor should be seen as a
hard worker, in the neighborhoods, listening and talking with
ordinary people." Day-to-day deportment would have to match
the advertising message. This meant, among other things, no
more mixing it up with the press, more attention to black sensibilities, and renewed emphasis on Byrne's credentials as a good
Democrat (after her back-and-forthing with Carter and Kennedy,
she had cozied up to the Reagan White House). "In order to
establish herself as a loyal Democrat, the Mayor should begin
to speak out on the impact of national policies on the lives of
the people of the city. With great emotion the Mayor can explain
the impact of Reagan policies on Chicago, how they have created
unemployment, less federal funding for schools, housing, and
aid to the city. The Mayor can acknowledge that she has had
to maintain cordial relations with Washington and Springfield in
order to get help on key financial issues. However, now is the

MEMORABLE IMAGES: FORD, 1976

Ford Anti-Reagan Spot

"Ronald Reagan said he would send American troops to Rhodesia"

"Remember: Governor Reagan couldn't start a war; President Reagan could"

MEMORABLE IMAGES: CHICAGO, 1983

Framing Bernard Epton

The tag line produced a
backlash

Remaking Jane Byrne

Her media managers
closed the gap, only to
have it reopen

time to vote Democratic." Sawyer aired Byrne spots prior to the
November 1982 midterm elections, ostensibly to show her en-
dorsing the Democratic ticket, but actually as the first part of
the reelection effort.

The second phase of the remaking of Byrne, mid-November
through the end of the year, would use several five-minute spots
to address issues as they relate "to the city's past and the Mayor's
personal past," as well as thirty- and sixty-second spots to "emphasize key points" in the budget. "Our objective for this Phase
is to share with the people of the city a sense of accomplishment
and hope. . . . It is like the feeling of having made the last payment
on a personal loan. . . . Now the worst problems are over, many
difficulties have been surmounted, she has learned the job inside
out, and knows how to make things happen." The final phase,
to run through the primary, "will continue to develop a personal
portrait of the Mayor. We will show her vision of what it means
to be Mayor of Chicago, her vision of Chicago's future." Specifics,
the memo humbly notes, will have to wait for "poll results and
other research" closer to air time. The memo included a campaign
budget of $3.5 million, of which $2.3 million was for "electronic
media" (the next largest item, organization, received $500,000).

The first flight of Democratic theme spots were followed by
a second flight of New Byrne commercials and a poll surveying
their impact. "Mayor Byrne's image has improved dramatically
in almost every area," writes Richard Dresner, an opinion researcher working with Sawyer, in a confidential memo dated
December 20. Her favorability was sixty-four percent, up from
fifty-six percent in August. Her job rating was a thirty-three, up
from twenty-seven. Her credibility remained a problem, with a
twenty-four percent positive against a thirty-eight percent negative
rating. But that too was an improvement: in August her credibility
had been twenty percent positive, forty-two percent negative.
According to Dresner, two out of three respondents had seen
Byrne's TV spots, and, among those people, Byrne held a sixteen-
point lead over Richard Daley, who had been favored to beat

her. So, concludes Dresner, "We moved up because of our commercials—this one's obvious. . . . It should be noted that the Mayor's standing has increased dramatically on the themes stressed in our commercials—'fiscal improvement,' 'the city that works again,' and 'the first Byrne Budget.' " Spots weren't the whole story. Byrne had also "carried out some popular policies which have then been publicized in the free media," and—Dresner lists this last but underscores it—she had been endorsed by the Democratic party organization in the city.

The third candidate in the Democratic primary race, the black U.S. Congressman Harold Washington, doesn't appear in Dresner's favorability ratings. But in a section titled "Minority Politics," Dresner points out that voters, black and white, felt too little attention was being paid to minorities (by a four-to-one margin), and that they supported more black appointments to the school board and housing authority (by more than two to one); moreover thirty-nine percent of black voters and thirteen percent of white voters said that Chicago ought to have a black mayor. Further, "If everyone who said they very much wanted a black for Mayor acted on that behalf, Washington would actually lead in our poll with thirty-four percent to thirty-two percent for Byrne and twenty percent for Daley." Dresner calls this the "real Washington potential" and concludes: "We have to watch Washington voters extremely closely, and be ready to put on some commercials which go after Harold Washington directly come the end of this campaign."

Sawyer and associates did not listen to Sawyer and associates, and did not go after Washington at the end. Instead, an ill-considered whites versus blacks statement by one of Byrne's political operatives the weekend before the election helped realize the "real Washington potential" predicted by Dresner. On primary day Harold Washington won with thirty-six percent of the vote, to Byrne's thirty-four and Daley's thirty percent.

The intrusion of such reality as racial politics into campaigns sets limits on what paid media can accomplish, and all evidence of effectiveness must be read in the light of these real-world events. Earlier we referred to the Ottinger Effect — the dissonance between the image of the candidate and the substance of the candidate. Gerald Ford had been moving up in the polls against Jimmy Carter in 1976 until Ford's Eastern European stumble in the second debate produced a Ford model of the Ottinger Effect. The real Ford seemed at odds with the advertised Ford. It was, as Deardourff told us, "the tragedy of the campaign from a media adviser's standpoint." The extensive news coverage of the episode negated the Ford spots and all their "good feelings," says Deardourff, because "advertising cannot introduce ideas or concepts that are at odds with what is being seen on the news." The media managers were spending millions on TV spots to convey the notion that one of the major differences between the candidates was Ford's experience in international politics, the man who had sat at the bargaining table with Brezhnev. "Suddenly, eighty million people are exposed to a new reality," says Deardourff. "What good is your television, showing Ford riding a railroad car with a bunch of Russians, when he can't correctly position Poland?"

The fifth rule, then, is that the best advertising in the world can't paint the face of victory on a moribund campaign. The attentive, honest George McGovern of Charles Guggenheim's spots made excellent television but couldn't cover over the candidate's self-inflicted wounds. Good advertising couldn't compensate for a faltering public performance, like Edward Kennedy's in his interview with Roger Mudd in 1979; Rose Garden advertising couldn't overcome the intrusion of the prolonged Iranian hostage crisis in the 1980 general election. In 1984 John Glenn's ads soared; his candidacy stayed earthbound.

Spots in the Metacampaign

Not all polispots, as we've indicated, directly aim at winning votes. One target of spot advertising is the elites of the metacampaign, the campaign within the campaign. Media managers often preview their next flight of commercials at special screenings for reporters, likely contributors, or other elites, to convey a sense of movement, strategy, and organization. Political consultant Eddie Mahe argues that a spot campaign is now expected by both the insiders and the public. "You can, for example, use direct mail appeals until hell freezes over," he says. "But broadcast media buy authenticity. I might be persuaded by the seventeen direct-mail letters you send me, but if I never see your campaign on TV, I wonder if I'm the only who got those letters." Beyond legitimizing the campaign in the eyes of its audiences, television ads also can be used to attract contributors' dollars in a more direct sense. Humphrey in 1968, McGovern in 1972, and Reagan in the 1976 primaries, as we've seen, all used longer form paid media to raise money. No campaign that we know of, however, aimed such a program at so small a group as the liberal Republican (who later switched to Democrat) Don Riegle did when he went against the wealthy Arthur Summerfield, the former Postmaster General, in Michigan's seventh congressional district in 1966. Stu Spencer, working for the strapped Riegle campaign, had concluded that potential contributors "had certain philosophical beliefs not really important in the election process, but important to them." Because Riegle wasn't coming out strongly on those issues, he was having difficulty raising money. Spencer developed a half-hour show featuring Riegle and incorporating all the ideas of the fat cats: "It was a trash job. We bought some half-hour on a Sunday afternoon, the cheapest time we could find in Flint. And, of course, we notified the people that counted that it was going to be on. We ran that show for those guys. Money started coming in."

Some spots—particularly negative spots—may be aimed partly at the strategists of the other side. Gerald Ford in his memoirs recalls that the attacks on Carter in 1976 were intended "to provoke him into a serious mistake." One such mistake, Ford's advisers agreed, would have been commercials attacking Ford. But, as Rafshoon says, the Carter camp didn't allow themselves to be baited. In the 1978 Democratic gubernatorial primary in Florida, Robert Shevin, the attorney general, attacked Robert Graham, a state senator and a client of Bob Squier's, as a profligate member of the legislature. One Shevin spot showed an adding machine spewing out tape, while a voice-over told of Graham's big-spender votes. Squier's polls showed that Graham's steady lead had abruptly flattened, and overnight Squier produced his own "Adding Machine," visually identical to Shevin's spot:

VIDEO	AUDIO
Camera up on adding machine punching out long tape.	Announcer [VO]: "Bob Shevin is an expert on spending the taxpayers' money. Year after year, Shevin's overspending got worse. To cover the difference, Shevin would dip into the general fund to bail out his office. We'll never know how much Shevin would have spent, because finally the legislature stepped in and put a stop to it. We couldn't afford Bob Shevin as attorney general. Imagine what he would cost us as governor."

Squier ran the "Adding Machine" spot for three days, until "theirs went off the air, so ours went off the air."

Perhaps the major target of the metacampaign is the press. News coverage closely follows the shifts in opinion polls, and early advertising often attempts to get the survey numbers moving in the right direction in order to establish a candidacy as serious. The least successful, though most expensive, example of such a poll-vaulting effort was attempted by Nelson Rockefeller in 1968. The Tinker agency launched a $4.5 million nationwide publicity campaign just before the Republican convention in order to boost the governor's standing in national polls and to show that the front-runner, Nixon, couldn't win. The ads failed to move the Gallup poll or the GOP delegates.

Sometimes spots by themselves generate news stories that can affect the campaign. During the 1976 campaign a Ford negative spot received heavy press attention and comment:

VIDEO	AUDIO
Camera up on CU of blond woman, around thirty, smiling slightly.	Woman [SOF]: "If you've been waiting for this presidential campaign to become a little clearer so that you can make a choice, it's happened. Last Wednesday, Ronald Reagan said that he would send American troops to Rhodesia. Thursday, he clarified that. He said they could be 'observers' or 'advisers.' What does he think happened in Vietnam? Or was Governor Reagan playing with words?
Camera pulls back: to woman's left in background is a campaign poster showing Ford in dark suit.	The President of the United States can't play with words. When you vote Tuesday, remember: Governor Reagan couldn't start a war; President Reagan could."

Freeze frame; white super ap-
pears at bottom: "PAID FOR
BY THE PRESIDENT FORD
COMMITTEE."

Ford lost the California primary badly, and most metacampaign
observers thought that his harsh attack on a native son hadn't
helped. But Ford strategist Stu Spencer claims the campaign had
already written off California. Spencer knew that the press would
jump on the spot, effectively providing national exposure for the
price of statewide exposure. "They all watched in the East," says
Spencer. "Newspaper reporters all had to write about it. That
ad accomplished our purpose—it ensured us those other states."

A spot need not be so hard-hitting to generate press coverage.
The 1980 spot that shows Howard Baker shouting down an
Iranian student, Deardourff says, attracted "fifty times more
coverage" than the actual speech. Today, news coverage of a
campaign's paid media has become routine. Indeed, for the
indolent (or overworked) journalist, it can be easier than rolling
out of bed in the morning—flip the candidate's new videotape
into the home VCR and write the story of the new ads right there,
or at most attend the news conference screening and file the
media story. As David Broder pointed out in the 1986 campaign,
"Candidates complained with justification that the only way to get
coverage was to introduce a new TV ad."

Finally, metacampaign spots can frame the overall electoral
dynamics, to tell voters and elites alike: "These are the points
that matter." The first polispot strategy in 1952 succeeded in
this respect, when Eisenhower convinced voters that the election
centered on whether it was Time for a Change. In 1956 Stevenson
tried, unsuccessfully, to make the election a referendum on Richard Nixon, given Ike's presumed failing health. In 1980 Carter
tried to make "cowboy" Reagan the issue, while Reagan ran
against "ineffectual" Carter. In 1984 Reagan succeeded in focus-
ing attention on the "springtime of hope for America" that his

administration represented; Mondale tried, and failed, to focus on fairness, the deficit, and "killer weapons in space."

The Trouble with Spots

So far we have been analyzing the effects of a given spot in a given race. More significant, ultimately, are the systemic effects of political advertising on the general strategy of campaigns, the overall styles of electoral politics, the kinds of candidates chosen, and the shifting sources of their support. The media men argue that they have helped displace at least some of the old politics and party power—the political bosses, in Robert Goodman's words, who "handed all the money around." Now, says Goodman, "Anybody can run for office if they can get enough backing to get on the tube. They don't have to pay party dues any more; they don't have to come up through the ranks; they don't have to kiss the butts of party bosses or newspaper publishers. They can do their own thing." Gerald Rafshoon also claims that the media campaigns have opened up politics. "I think it is better if you can raise some money to be able to go directly to the people, through television, than to have to go through middle-men." While there are abuses in the system, Rafshoon says, they are not as great as they were before, "when people didn't really know the candidates."

Charles Guggenheim, however, thinks we only have traded one set of troubles for another. We asked him, is the system of campaigning better or worse than when Guggenheim began working in presidential politics in 1956? "Better *and* worse," he replied. "Adlai Stevenson was not nominated by going through the primaries. He wasn't nominated by a bunch of kids who worked like hell for him in New Hampshire. Harry Truman made up his mind he wanted Stevenson nominated, and he was nominated. One man decided. Who was going to be his vice-president? That decision took place in some smoke-filled room. Who knows what was traded off. If we were there in 1956, we'd be talking about that problem. Now we're talking about new problems."

In our interviews, monitoring, and analysis we found that these new problems within the campaign system group under seven headings:

1. *High Costs of Campaigning.* After the 1950 congressional elections, in which television played a relatively minor role, William Benton, who founded a major advertising agency before he became a U.S. senator from Connecticut, told a reporter: "The potentialities of television are so great that they could revolutionize politics. The terrifying aspect is the high cost, the expense of which could well determine election or defeat." In 1968, a few weeks before his death, Robert Kennedy was interviewed by Walter Cronkite. The CBS newsman asked Kennedy to respond to charges that he had tried to buy the Indiana primary election. A testy Kennedy responded, "We would all cut down eighty percent of our expenditures if television wasn't so expensive. If television would make all of this time available to us, as a public service, then there wouldn't be any great expense in a political campaign."

The exact numbers are elusive and often resist comparison, but clearly campaign spending has risen sharply, and television advertising has contributed to the rise. From 1912 to 1952 each national party committee spent about the same amount of money per vote cast in national elections. Thereafter, concurrent with the introduction of television, campaign expenditures skyrocketed; by 1968 the committees were spending three times as much per vote as they had sixteen years earlier. Moreover the share of campaign spending going to television has increased at an even faster rate, at the expense of other campaign methods: while total political spending (adjusted for inflation) has tripled since 1952, the amount spent on television has increased at least fivefold. Many local campaigns of course don't use TV—the district is too small, the cost too high, and/or available stations reach beyond district boundaries. In local or statewide races using television heavily, the proportion of the budget devoted to TV can go as high as ninety percent.

Is this too much? For perspective, United Airlines spent more to advertise its friendly skies in 1986—$110 million—than was spent by all the candidates for House and Senate seats in the same year—$97 million. Herbert Alexander, the political scientist and campaign-spending specialist, argues that "election dollars should be regarded as the tuition Americans are willing to pay for their education in politics." David Garth believes the only place where political campaigns may be cheaper is England, "because they only last three weeks." In Israel, Garth says, $9 million was spent for the election of a prime minister—in a country with only three million people. (Some of that money was spent for Garth's services; he worked as a media consultant to Menachem Begin.) If the major function of a political campaign is to educate the electorate concerning the alternatives available, then perhaps we should more properly ask whether enough money is being spent. In a 1982 report commissioned by the U.S. Senate, Harvard's Institute of Politics asked that question and concluded that, at least at the presidential level, candidates lack the financial resources to meet "the vast demands of a national campaign." Of the many problems related to campaign finance, the Harvard study termed this insufficiency "the most troublesome."

Some critics argue that, total spending levels aside, campaigns spend too much on television. But again, viewing a campaign as an educational process, TV is a good buy in political campaigns when compared to alternatives. By one estimate, reaching a TV viewer in 1983 cost less than half a cent, reaching the same person by a newspaper ad cost one and a half cents, and reaching the same person by direct mail cost around twenty-five cents. In primaries, and especially in the highly contested Iowa and New Hampshire curtain raisers, the education process proceeds with a vengeance; *Congressional Quarterly* estimates that the presidential candidates in 1980 spent $13.89 a vote in Iowa and $8.90 in New Hampshire. For the 1988 primaries, a Federal Election Commission official told us, each candidate would be allowed, by the formula of congressional law, to spend around $1.2 million in the two states ($745,000 in Iowa and $445,000 in New Hampshire). Still, we believe that restricting or abolishing polispots would by itself not reduce overall spending levels. The money would go into other, less efficient forms of communication.

The more pointed question about the high cost of running for office has to do with the sources of money rather than the amounts. Can only the well-to-do or the well-connected compete? At times it seems that politics has become solely a rich man's game. This idea was driven home by the best bumper sticker of 1980, distributed by Arch Moore's gubernatorial campaign against Jay Rockefeller in West Virginia: "Make him spend it all, Arch." Money is and always has been, in Jess Unruh's phrase, the mother's milk of politics. Campaign finance reforms have sought to lessen its preeminent role. An individual's political contributions, for instance, are now restricted to $1,000 per candidate in federal elections. But the Supreme Court overturned the part of the reforms that would restrict a candidate's contributions to his own campaign. The unintended consequence, then, has been to make individual contributors less important relative to a candidate's own wealth. Politics, as a result, is at least as much a rich man's game as ever—a problem that reaches well beyond political advertising.

2. *The Death of the Parties.* Candidates used to need the blessing of party leaders in order to run, and once running, they needed the help of party workers. That began to change in the 1950s, with the entry into politics of people like Rosser Reeves from ad agencies and later with the rise of the independent media specialists. Expertise slipped from the party's grasp as new political tools became available, and the parties failed to adapt. Candidates no longer need parties in order to run, and if they can be elected without their party's help, they may see little need to be loyal. A certain political cohesion is lost, and governance becomes more difficult.

Like the problem of money, the problem of weakened parties predates television. The decline of the parties began with the

Progressive Era, when reforms cut into one of the parties' strongest tools, patronage (incumbent parties still have prizes to pass around, of course, as readers of New York City newspapers were reminded by the Koch administration's scandals of 1986). But television certainly has contributed. Candidates and elected officials can now reach the public directly, through newspapers and the evening news as well as advertising. News coverage in particular has encouraged a move toward "democratization" of the presidential nominating process. Voters—in some states they need not even be registered Democrats or Republicans to participate in primaries—increasingly have selected the delegates to national conventions and, by extension, the parties' nominees. In the process incumbent officials have often been shut out —officials who have a particular stake in the outcome, in that they must run on the same ticket with the presidential nominees. As with campaign finance reforms, the adjustments to the party system have created several unintended consequences. Reforms designed to eliminate corruption and to open up the process to the public have instead continued to weaken the parties. In 1988 the process may be reversed, as both parties have taken measures to give elected officials greater influence on party matters.

While television has contributed to the problem, we believe it can also contribute to the solution. Both parties, but especially the Republicans, have adapted the television medium and the newer communications technologies to the changing politics. The Republican National Committee sponsors seminars for Republican candidates on television techniques, direct mail, polling, and other media tools. It also now maintains a résumé videotape from each of several Republican media consultants, so that candidates can get a feel for the work done by different media firms. The committee also sponsors TV advertising of its own, including the 1980 spot starring the Tip O'Neill look-alike and 1982 ads urging midterm election voters to "give the guy [Reagan] a chance" by sending more Republicans to Congress. The Republican Senate Committee now produces programs featuring

Republican senators, for cable systems and local TV stations. All these signs of life suggest that television can have a reviving effect on the parties.

3. *The Rise of the Hired Gun*. Beginning in the 1960s candidates turned to independent consultants. The consultants, as their critics say, get paid to win; they have no incentive to worry about the behavior of their candidates once in office, or about the level of political debate, or about the quantity of voter participation. One such critic, Curtis Gans, says that many of the media managers are "very nice, very bright, but not responsible to anybody. They do twelve campaigns at once, and they do the same for each person." Politicians have always had aides, coat-holders, advisers, hangers-on, and kitchen cabinets. But, while the retinues in the old days stayed with the politician in office, the new consultants serve the candidate only through the election, and then again, two or four or six years later, should they be called on. The media managers have a guaranteed payday, win or lose. The political retinue get their payday only with victory, in the form of jobs and influence. The media managers need victory also, though: too many losses and their business phones stop ringing.

On the whole, then, are outsiders more likely to counsel a winning-is-the-only-thing strategy, while insiders, or the candidate's conscience, urge the candidate to hold true to principles? Will they behave like amoral mercenaries? Not usually, we believe. The media managers are less involved in the petty rivalries, the jockeying for power, the ego contests (including the inner struggles of the candidates themselves), the backstabbing—and they are more likely to be objective in their judgments. The consultants often perform more responsibly than the retinue. And in any case, the voter can only judge candidates on the basis of their campaigns—*vide* the faltering John Glenn campaign in early 1984—or of their characters—*vide* Hart and Donna Rice in 1987. The voter doesn't know the inside-baseball details of which adviser did what to whom, or whether Hart left his townhouse during the night, nor should the voter care about

the details. It's the candidate's campaign and overall persona
that count. Responsibility, finally, for strategy and tactics rests
with the name on the ballot. We talked personally with two
dozen of the best-known political consultants, media and
otherwise. There are dozens more, many of them talented,
unknown, eager for experience and exposure. Candidates need
not bend themselves and their candidacies to suit a particular
consultant. They can always get a new helper.

4. *The Arrival of the Outsider.* The media consultant isn't the
only new player in politics. Candidates themselves, no longer
beholden to party leaders, find that they need not work their
way up through party ranks—or in fact up through any particular
ranks at all. The potential has always been present, but mainly
for military leaders (Presidents Jackson, Harrison, Taylor, and
Grant, as well as, posttelevision, Eisenhower). But today men and
women with no previous electoral experience run for office more
and more frequently, coming from business (Frank Lautenberg,
Lew Lehrman), from academe (Daniel Patrick Moynihan, S. I.
Hayakawa), from the space program (Harrison Schmitt, John
Glenn), and from Hollywood (Shirley Temple Black, Clint
Eastwood, Ronald Reagan). The most consistently effective political advertising, as we saw, is that promoting name identification. A
candidate can, with sufficient funds, swamp the electorate with his
name and face; some can go on to win office. If the concept of
political outsiders in government seems unappetizing to us today,
the opposite would have been true for the Founding Fathers—for
them, political insiders were to be guarded against. The national
legislature, in their vision, would be composed largely of farmers,
leaving their fields for a couple of years to serve their country. The
principal difference today is that media-propelled outsiders rarely
return voluntarily to their fields.

5. *Reduced Political Participation.* Turnout in presidential elections had declined since 1960; only 53.3 percent of eligible
citizens voted in 1984, the lowest since 1948. This is the same
period when the amount of money spent on television political
advertising has tripled (in constant dollars). The national and

the big state campaigns have taken money from participation-oriented activities such as canvassing and phone banks and put it into political spots.

But it is extremely difficult to untangle the various factors that may relate to voting decline. There is evidence, for example, that other forms of political participation, such as letter writing, petition signing, and protesting, have increased while voting has gone down—people may be turning to other means of political expression. Some consultants we interviewed, notably Eddie Mahe, argue that the decline in voting is more apparent than real, a temporary artifact of the demography of the country. In the 1960s and 1970s the baby-boom generation reached voting age and reduced turnout figures (a reduction that increased when the voting age was lowered from twenty-one to eighteen, swelling the ranks of younger voters), because young people traditionally vote at a lower rate than older people. As that population bulge grows older, by this reasoning, voting turnouts will begin to increase. Still others argue that television campaigns alert apolitical people to the major event of an election and get them to come out; thus Nixon's media blitz of 1968 has been credited with sending poorer, less-educated Democratic voters to the polls. Perhaps, too, nonvoting may be an implicit declaration of satisfaction with the status quo. Or perhaps nonvoting reflects the judgment that candidates are indistinguishable. Jesse Jackson's early 1984 successes showed that blacks will register and vote when they perceive that a candidacy represents them. Finally, some evidence suggests that the problem is not turnout among registered voters, but rather getting voters registered to begin with. Among registered voters, according to Derek Shearer, turnout in the United States isn't much different from turnout in other Western democracies. "The significant fact," Shearer adds, "is that we are the only country where the entire burden of registration falls on the individual rather than on the government."

Television has been blamed for a variety of developments in American society. But correlation—the simultaneous expansion of television and of nonvoting—does not indicate causation. For now, at least, the vote is still out on whether media campaigns have contributed significantly to lower voter turnouts.

6. *The Debasing of Political Argument.* The examples should be familiar by now: Daisy, "Castro" thanking Señor Sasser, "Governor Reagan couldn't start a war; President Reagan could." We have talking fish and talking cows praising incumbents, instead of Lincoln and Douglas debating slavery. Again, the past is being romanticized considerably. Television has changed some of the conduct of the political game; the attack that once might have been carried out through crude leaflets or street-corner whispering campaigns can now be broadcast in a high-gloss, thirty-second flash to millions. But there is a self-correcting mechanism. Because of television's large, undifferentiated audience, candidates' messages are transmitted to everyone—supporters, leaners, and opponents alike. The cheap shot that attracts ill-informed fence sitters, for example, may repel previously solid voters.

The case about debasing frequently focuses on the brevity of spots: What can possibly be told in thirty seconds? In our studies of over 850 such spots, we found that a great deal can be said, though relatively few candidates do so. Straightforward positions can be made. Eisenhower's promise to go to Korea took less than thirty seconds. So did McGovern's promise to end the Vietnam War. John Deardourff, tired of the debasing criticism, once wrote this script as an exercise:

I believe that the question of
abortion is one that ought to
be reserved exclusively to a

woman and her doctor. I favor giving women the unfettered right to abortion. I also
favor the federal funding of
abortions through Medicaid
for poor women as an extension of that right to an abortion, and I oppose any
statutory or constitutional
limitations on that right.

As Deardourff explained, "That's twenty-four seconds. I don't
know how much more one needs to know about that subject in
order to form an opinion if that's an issue about which you're
concerned."

Most campaigns avoid such specifics, but that has less to do
with the thirty-second spot format than with campaign strategy.
John Lindsay's 1972 presidential campaign ran a thirty-second
spot in Florida that gave the candidate's position on, among other
issues, gun control (for), abortion (for), and school prayer (against).
"He probably lost the entire population of Florida in that one
spot," Lindsay's media manager, David Garth, later said. The
risks and benefits of an issues strategy have little to do with the
polispots form per se. Pretelevision, those same voters would
have found something to dislike in the candidate's positions—
if, that is, they learned about them to begin with. As for the
length of spots, Carroll Newton, the ad agency executive who
worked in the Eisenhower campaigns and the first Nixon campaign, once calculated that a half-hour speech would lose a third
of the time slot's normal audience; a fifteen-minute speech would
lose a quarter of the audience; a five-minute speech would lose
from 5 to 10 percent; and a thirty- or sixty-second spot would
lose nothing. Long form telecasts usually end up preaching to
the already converted—which is important, but not the only goal.

A variation of the debasement of debate indictment holds that with television campaigns physical good looks have become more important in the selection of candidates or, in another variation, that the dramatic performer's skills of presentation and projection are now paramount. With the rise of television campaigns, the fear is that candidates now pose for office instead of run for office, and that "homely men of stature and capability," as filmmaker and consultant Gene Wyckoff once put it, will inevitably falter. The vivid examples of the slim, handsome John Kennedy, or the tall, chiseled features of John Lindsay, or the smooth demeanor of Ronald Reagan would seem to prove the case, except that for every matinee idol on the screen we can also spot a cartoon character like Jesse Helms, Spiro Agnew, or George Wallace (the late Walt Kelly in fact drew an anthropomorphic Agnew and a Wallace in his *Pogo* comic strip). In our view television, paid and free, does show the voters those candidates who might once have been invisible, and in the process perhaps potential candidates with physical deformities or speech impediments may be discouraged from running. But polispots can present the candidate in still photos (getting past speech impediments) or, occasionally, not at all. And candidates may be able to address the issue directly, as when a 1986 Alan Cranston spot told voters: "Don't be fooled—we're electing a senator, not a commercial." Voters, all else being equal—and all else never is equal —probably prefer an attractive candidate, but that is nothing new. The political scientists Steven Chaffee and Jack Dennis surveyed the evidence and concluded that the electoral advantage of a good-looking face has remained approximately constant from one election to the next. For every hunky Jack Kemp, it seems, there has also been a rumpled Barney Frank in the House. After election, the rumpled may decide to shape up for personal reasons (health, vanity) if not for political reasons—Frank lost seventy pounds in office.

7. *Politics as Entertainment, Entertainment as Politics.* This begins with the criticism that polispots tend to emphasize the diverting

over the cerebral. The element that helps make polispots "watchable" is production values, all the visual elements we have been writing about. If these elements distort political discourse, then perhaps they should be controlled.

On September 29, 1983, Curtis Gans, testifying before the Senate Committee on Rules and Administration, asked the senators "to require that all paid political advertising be without production material." He summoned up a world of political commercials without "voice-overs; anonymous faces; actors playing the part of politicians; demagogic scene settings; devices such as graphs, charts, and the like; talking cows; nuclear weapons and any other paraphernalia that would tend to provide unnecessary emotive content to a political message." Instead, spots would consist solely of "the candidate, party chairman or interest group leader" addressing the camera "full face for the duration of the advertisement."

Gans ran Eugene McCarthy's campaign in New Hampshire in 1968. "I didn't need demagogic television," he says. "All I needed was the war in Vietnam to be going on, and Lyndon Johnson to appear on the tube. All Ronald Reagan needed was Jimmy Carter's performance, and the public perception of it. Where there is real dissatisfaction with the incumbent, the incumbent can get ousted without these devices. And where it is created dissatisfaction, he probably shouldn't be ousted." Gans's Committee for the Study of the American Electorate focuses in large part on declining voter participation, and he and the committee single out the polispot as one reason for the decline. He recognizes that total abolition of polispots would be "a political impossibility." But he thinks that the no-production proposal would eliminate a great deal of political advertising because talking heads are considered boring; the ad money freed up, he hopes, would go into "people-oriented" activities like field campaigns. Gans argues that "the demagogic trappings, the props, are not intrinsic to free speech, and may indeed crowd out free speech and the rational discussion that was intended by the First Amendment."

John Danforth, the Republican senator from Missouri who cosponsored the Gans legislation in 1985, has argued that the effects are even broader. Negative ads, he said, not only create "apathy and cynicism among the voting public;" they also distort the Senate's atmosphere. "I sense an increasing mood of defensiveness, or testiness, and a breakdown in the comity and collegiality that we need to function as a deliberative body," Danforth told a reporter. When the Senate Commerce Committee held hearings on "The Clean Campaign Act of 1985," support for the bill was voiced by Howard Baker, Common Cause, the League of Women Voters, and the American Bar Association's Election Law Committee. Political consultants, almost alone, opposed it. Bob Squier said the bill should be called "Incumbents' Preservation Act."

The bill died without ever being brought to the floor for a vote, and (as of late 1987) no one plans to reintroduce it. The goal from the start seemed largely to publicize the problem rather than to legislate its solution. Constitutional concerns in any case probably would have doomed the legislation. The Supreme Court once ruled that a state could not require handbills to include the name of their sponsor. Although the media are different, the precedent raises at least constitutional questions about the Gans proposal to require polispots to include the face of their sponsor.

Constitutional questions aside, politicians have always gone duck hunting where the ducks are, and today that means buying television time. A century ago a few thousand people might learn a candidate's arguments directly, through speeches or leaflets (fewer than twenty thousand people witnessed one of the Lincoln-Douglas debates of 1858); today spots can bring the candidate and his message to hundreds of thousands, even millions of voters, repeatedly. This is the meaning of the term "living-room politics." "A political rally in California," consultant Robert Shrum has said, "consists of three people around a television set." The same is true around the country. On any given autumn night during the week, a hundred million Americans are watching television—they can be found between *Dallas* and *Falcon Crest,* as Michael Barone has said. This does not mean they can be sold the Brooklyn Bridge, or Gary Hart's "new ideas" of 1984. After thirty years of experience with television, Americans are largely inured to the razzle-dazzle of production values. A jump cut may sustain some viewers' interests, but it won't suspend their disbelief. Most voters, we believe, are qualified to judge the candidates' assessments of the electorate, as reflected in their media campaigns.

But, as Gans argues, television has not only amplified the candidate's voice; it has also changed the nature of political discourse. That raises a more difficult problem: the prevalence of high-gloss, high-tech media campaigns may be trivializing electoral politics. Certainly there is nothing trivial about the Deardourff pro-abortion script, or about Garth's Lindsay commercial for Florida, but spots that explicit are the exception. To the extent that polispots are made to look like, for example, life-style cola commercials, they may be taken no more seriously than the rest of television advertising. When the polispots become just one more entertainment to watch, it will become harder and harder for the audience to regard them as important—especially if there is no other campaign visible to the viewer. The result may be a distancing between candidate and citizen; voting may become just one more activity being commended to us by television purveyors of goods and services. We watch the free show, but we don't necessarily get involved; we are passively entertained. Although quantitative evidence for this is hard to produce, the criticism can't be dismissed.

The problem may be more basic than any one spot or series of spots. Thirty years of television experience may have inured us not only to production values but to the immediacy of politics as well; something fundamental may have been lost when campaigns switched from live to taped. However, the obvious solution—to divorce politics and TV once and for all, and thereby to restore voter interest and participation—doesn't hold up. Since the 1940s Americans have increasingly stayed at home to be entertained, a trend fueled by demographics (the suburban migration), by improved at-home options (radio and television, and currently videodiscs and video tape recorders), and at least partly by fear (the rising crime rate). True, taking politics away from television would take campaigns outdoors again. But, absent other, broader social changes, most voters wouldn't follow.

No Spots, Please, We're British

Rather than abolishing polispots, some critics favor a move toward the British system: free television time, doled out in equal measure to all candidates; and longer blocks of air time than the thirty-second spots that dominate American elections. Among the consultants we talked with, Charles Guggenheim strongly favors the British model. Guggenheim worked for the Labor Party on the Common Market referendum, producing four ten-minute broadcasts. "That seems endless if you've been working in sixty-second ads," he says. It also required more thought than the shorter ads. "One reason why negative advertising is proliferating," Guggenheim added, "is because it's much easier to say something bad than something positive in such a short time."

But, as the 1987 British elections showed, some critics of the American way of political advertising have romanticized the alternative. When Britons turned on their televisions in May and June of 1987, many of them saw what London newspapers termed "presidential media"—not meant as a compliment to their American cousins. One ten-minute "party political," for instance, showed a military jet screaming across the screen. A wheeling gull materializes, white against the now-peaceful sky. As a couple strolls across the landscape, Brahms' First Symphony swells in the background. Then the closing graphic: "KINNOCK." It was several production values above the Bruce Babbitt ads that were airing at about the same time in Iowa—not surprisingly. "Kinnock" was the handiwork of Hugh Hudson, director of the film *Chariots of Fire*.

The paean to Neil Kinnock, the British Labor Party leader, emphasized his family, much like Rafshoon's 1976 work for Carter. (That emphasis, however, did not prevent a 1988 presidential candidate, Senator Joseph Biden of Delaware, from borrowing Kinnock's words about his roots—a wholesale plagiarism that, when discovered, forced Biden out of the race.) The Alliance Party ads featured the serious talking heads of its two leaders, the Liberal David Steel and the Social Democrat David Owen; the style was reminiscent of some of John Anderson's no-frills spots in 1980. The Conservative Party politicals for Margaret Thatcher emphasized patriotic footage that played on the same chords as Reagan's "Morning Again" spots —though the British versions were far less slick. The invasion of American styles generated criticism. The London newspapers scoffed at "Madison Avenue razzmatazz" and "media packaging." But people seemed to watch the broadcasts, and to remember them. According to a Harris poll, Kinnock gained eight points as a result of his TV work. But Kinnock's campaign made the same discovery that the John Glenn campaign made: television isn't everything. Kinnock won the TV campaign, but Labor lost the election. When a reporter asked Thatcher about Kinnock's TV efforts, she replied, "There's a lot more to life than slickness."

Television counted for less in the British voting for a number of reasons. The British parties are much stronger than the American ones. British elections concern themselves less with matters of the candidates' personalities than American elections do—the British, after all, have a royal family to revere. And there is campaign length. The British election began and ended while Biden, Michael Dukakis, Bruce Babbitt, George Bush, Bob Dole, and the other candidates were organizing and rallying, mostly in Iowa and New Hampshire—nine months before the first American party delegate would be selected, a year and a half before the voters would cast ballots in the general election. That difference has little to do with spots and much to do with the parliamentary system.

The 1987 British campaign showed one central similarity: British elections, like American elections, today exist primarily on television. British campaign money and the candidates' energies go into staging made-for-TV events like rallies, receptions, speeches, and motorcades. Both British and American TV news cameras like movement, crowds, and color. A balloon drop for one media campaign looks like a balloon drop anywhere else, and it's as likely to make the evening news on either side of the Atlantic. British campaigns cost much less than American ones—as would be expected with a smaller country, a shorter election period, and no paid media. But to reach the largest number of voters the most frequent number of times, British candidates go where American candidates go: to prime-time television.

To a significant degree, then, the British alternative is less alternative than variation. Moving toward it, or adopting some other approach to restrict polispots, is likelier to hurt than to help American voters. For now, at least, banning polispots would deprive candidates of a sometimes abused, generally worrisome, but ultimately irreplaceable means of communicating with the electorate.

Free Press and Paid Media

The Republican party officials who in 1952 turned down Rosser Reeves's proposal to test the effectiveness of his "Eisenhower Answers America" spots may have been shrewder than Reeves thought. From the start polispots and television campaigns have been entertaining and at times informative, but without magical powers. Spots can surprise, capture attention, engage interest; they may even put something past the audience, though not for long. As Joseph Napolitan says, "Something is new only once." Furthermore campaigns can't be reduced to simple formulas; the combinations and permutations of success and failure are too great.

Arguments about which is more powerful, free media or paid media, miss the point: both are important; each provides a different kind of information. In paid media, candidates have a natural incentive to present themselves and their positions in a way that will attract a maximum number of voters, while repelling a minimum number. But they also have to keep an eye on reality. Voters have a sense—not always a precise sense but a strong, general sense—of what can and can't be done. The voters' good sense, moreover, isn't the only constraint operating. Candidates must also think about how their opponents will respond, in person and in spots, to blue-sky claims. And the press increasingly publicizes and criticizes dubious spots as a part of its campaign coverage. But just as a candidate's polispots present an incomplete picture, campaign press coverage highlights only selected aspects of the campaign. "Left in the hands of just the free media, you'd get a slanted picture of the candidate," Michael Kaye told us. "Paid media is important to give a balance."

News coverage often focuses more on the metacampaign —who's up and who's down—than on issues. Most campaigns slight issues too, but there are exceptions. In Edward Koch's 1977 campaign for mayor of New York, David Garth told us, "We issued thirty position papers, at least fifteen pages a paper; I think there were two reporters in New York that read them." Three years later, Garth added, John Anderson issued a 419-page platform, "a brilliant guide to his positions, and no one wrote about it."

When the press does cover matters of substance, it tends to select a particular kind of issue. News accounts usually emphasize clearcut, controversial, divisive issues: Is the candidate for or against the contras, AIDS testing, abortion, the ERA? The press serves the electorate by trying to highlight divisive topics. It sometimes goes too far, as when a mayoral candidate's position on, say, the nomination to the U.S. Supreme Court of Robert Bork—something tangential to the governance of a city —becomes a focus of coverage. For their part, candidates, via spots and speeches, prefer what Thomas Patterson terms "diffuse issues": opposition to government waste, high taxes, crime. A candidate's choice of even diffuse issues tells us something about his or her priorities. It shouldn't be the *only* information that voters get, but it should be part of the mix—and it's a type of information that polispots convey most effectively.

Finally, some studies suggest that press coverage may be slanted against a party or candidate. After examining CBS's and NBC's coverage of the 1984 party conventions, William C. Adams concluded that the networks repeatedly forced Republicans to address the issues they wanted to avoid, particularly arms control, but almost never pressed the Democrats on their least-favorite issue, Reagan's healthy economy. Looking at coverage of the general election (excluding stories about the candidates' electoral prospects), Maura Clancey and Michael J. Robinson found that Reagan got ten times as much negative network coverage as positive coverage; Bush got considerable negative coverage and *no* positive coverage; and Mondale and Ferraro each received slightly more positive than negative coverage. A large proportion of network stories were rated neutral, and this undercut the Clancey-Robinson argument somewhat, as did the sizable coverage of the Republicans' favorable electoral chances.

Even going along with the subjectivity of the study—one viewer's "negative" may seem to another "neutral"—the explanation is more benign than sinister. Political journalism tends to focus its scrutiny on the frontrunner, regardless of his or her party, and throughout the 1984 campaign Reagan remained the frontrunner. In 1987 similar scrutiny led to Gary Hart's temporary exit from the race and, tellingly, a scramble among the remaining candidates to *avoid* the frontrunner label. The larger point is that, for a variety of reasons, press coverage gives voters a detailed, crucial, but often incomplete picture of the campaign. Polispots provide additional information that helps voters decide.

Information is not the whole message. People do watch TV emotionally. As Rogers Ailes told us, "You can present all the issues you want on the air, and if at the end the audience doesn't like the guy, they're not going to vote for him." Viewers of the 1980 Carter-Reagan debate, Ailes contends, remember four things: Carter's reference to his daughter Amy; Reagan's line, "There you go again"; Reagan walking over to shake hands with Carter at the end; and Reagan in general looking comfortable, while Carter "looked constipated." None of these memories has anything to do with issues.

But voters, as the political scientist V. O. Key concluded in the early 1960s, are not fools. The John Connally who persuaded Democrats to vote for Nixon in 1972 spots couldn't persuade anyone to vote for John Connally in 1980 spots. In the eight intervening years, he had been accused of various Texas-size wheelings and dealings; over $12 million in campaign expenditures netted him exactly one delegate. Tony Schwartz's Daisy played on emotions but had an intellectual subtext. As Schwartz, the wizard of feelings, says, it made people ask themselves, "Whose finger do I want on the trigger?" In point of historical fact Johnson committed a half-million American troops in Vietnam, but he never pulled the atomic trigger. Who is to say the voters of 1964 were wrong?

For the future the media managers have plans for more high-tech advertising that will test the intelligence and good sense of voters. The Republican consultant Eddie Mahe anticipates that cable television channels will be used in concert with direct mail. "I may decide, if I have a message I think you as a nurse or doctor are interested in—medical insurance—that the best way to get my message to you is to send you a mailgram saying, 'Watch channel 42 at 8 o'clock tonight. I have a message of specific interest to you, on federal medical insurance.' Bingo! I've got your attention." Cable will also let national campaigns further narrowcast their television appeals, as they frequently do now on radio.

Robert Squier scared some listeners when he described a kind of invasion of the mind-snatchers: "At the beginning of the evening, you would get a short, simple quiz on your interactive cable system. You would be offered an opportunity to see a free movie if you'd answer a few sports questions, some other questions, a lot of political questions. We wouldn't have to ask a lot of demographic questions, because if you were a cable subscriber for more than a year, we would have all we needed to know about you from other quizzes. We would know how much you vote, how you vote, what kind of programs you watch, how many times you switch over to the X-rated channel. Then you'd take the test. The system would determine your particular brand of undecidedness, based on previous polling in the population. The computer would then select the particular tape it needed to persuade you. It would have been pretested in focus groups. Then it would play on your TV that night, on everything you'd watch on cable. Later in the evening you'd be given another test, asking some of the same questions. If we've persuaded you, we'd know it right then." Every technique Squier described, he adds, "is now in existence."

Although Squier's vision is likely to remain a fantasy for a while, candidates did take advantage of new technologies as the 1988 campaign began. The most visible—and notorious—use of technology occurred in late September 1987; the Dukakis campaign put together an "attack video," consisting of Neil Kinnock's party political tape juxtaposed with a video clip of Biden mouthing the same words without crediting Kinnock. The material was put in the hands of political reporters. Biden was gone within two weeks. More routinely, videotapes became the feature attraction at house parties sponsored by several campaigns in Iowa and New Hampshire—more living-room politics, bringing the candidates to the voters rather than the voters to the candidates. The National Council of Senior Citizens produced its own tape, collecting the remarks of the declared candidates on the issues of concern to its membership. Candidates also used satellites to send their messages directly to local television stations, bypassing the campaign trail, the boys and girls on the bus, and in-person campaigning itself. Like the Woody Allen character in the automobile society of Southern California, the candidate's feet never had to touch the ground.

Research techniques also moved forward. Many consultants said that they planned to employ an instant-response mechanism to test longer advertisements. A sample of viewers would hold electronic dials as they watch something on television. They would move the dial upward when interested or amused, and downward when bored or offended. The device has been used to test product advertisements since the early days of television. Consultants used it to monitor responses to presidential debates in 1976 and 1984, and they expect to use it more heavily in 1988 and beyond.

In the end, still, we are willing to leave the polispots and the media campaigns to the knowing judgment of the audience. The typical thirty-five-year-old American has been watching television for three decades now and has been through more than a dozen political campaigns as a television consumer. The majority of the audience belongs to the party of skeptics, and not just about political promises; a 1977 Harris poll showed forty-six percent of those surveyed assenting to the statement that most or all ads on TV are "seriously misleading." Narrowcasting on cable and high-tech testing systems will not alter that balance of doubt.

The media managers line up with us on this point. "As politically unsophisticated as voters are, they are extremely sophisticated as TV viewers," says Ken Swope. David Sawyer concurs: "There's no way you can manipulate the voters. There's no way you can go back now and talk about a government as decent and beautiful as the American people. There's no way you can go back now and show the candidate wandering down the beach, with his jacket over his shoulder and a dog running by his side. Those are the clichés from the period when political television was naive. People now are looking with sophistication at your messages. Put out a message to con them, and they'll figure it out like that." Of course it is still possible to run unfair, or scurrilous, or racist campaigns on television—just as it has always been possible to run them in newspapers, leaflets, and speeches. Political television does not manipulate the electorate in a new, pernicious way; it mainly spreads the candidate's message more widely and more efficiently. The message still must travel past watchful eyes—the press's, the opposition's, and the voters'.

In the aftermath of Richard Nixon's victory in 1968, reporter Joe McGinniss concluded that the new Nixon was the product of the "adroit manipulation and use of television" by Roger Ailes, Harry Treleaven, and the other image makers. As McGinniss recorded Ailes, the hyperenergetic young producer, at Nixon's election-eve telethon: "This is the beginning of a whole new concept. This is it. This is the way they'll be elected forevermore. The next guys up will have to be performers." In 1983 an older, fleshed out, bearded—and calmer—Ailes offered a different conclusion: "The TV public is very smart in the sense that somewhere, somehow, they make a judgment about the candidates they see. Anybody who claims he can figure out that process is full of it." In the future we are sure the media managers will continue their search for the key to the voter's decision process. Just as surely they will fail to find it. The creation of political advertising will remain a problematic art.

SOURCE NOTES

Our major source is the Television Archives of the News Study Group, in the Department of Journalism at New York University. This collection, begun in 1972 at MIT, now numbers over 850 television commercials, as well as other political television materials, including campaign news coverage, candidate debates and forums, news conferences, and interviews with candidates, media managers, and political consultants. All of this material is on videotape and available for study and analysis.

In addition to the News Study Group archives, the following collections of television advertising were important to our work:

The Lyndon B. Johnson Library, Austin, Texas. Democratic presidential commercials, 1956–1964.

The John F. Kennedy Library, Dorchester, Massachusetts. Miscellaneous presidential commercials, 1952–1968, in the Victoria Shuck collection. Large collection of Kennedy films and commercials from 1960, and several Stevenson spots from 1952 and 1956, and the library's own collection. Also collection of works of Charles Guggenheim.

The John F. Kennedy School of Government, Harvard University, Cambridge, Massachusetts. Collection of Kennedy commercials from 1960.

The Republican National Committee, Washington, D.C. Republican party advertising from 1980 and 1982.

The Smithsonian Institution, Washington, D.C. Small collection of polispots, presidential and lower-level, in the Museum of American History, organized by Larry Bird.

The University of Rhode Island, Kingston, Rhode Island. Stephen C. Wood, director of the debate program, owns a complete set of the "Eisenhower Answers America" spots from 1952. L. Patrick Devlin, chairman of the speech communication department, has a large collection of polispots, mainly from presidential campaigns, covering 1952 through 1980.

In addition we talked with several collectors (including one who charges fees) but did not make use of their materials for this book. The National Archives contains spots donated by the Republican and Democratic national committees, available for viewing only with the permission of the national party committees. The Rosser Reeves archives, Wisconsin State Historical Society, Madison, Wisconsin, contains newspaper clippings, letters, and memorabilia, as well as the "Eisenhower Answers America" spots themselves. The Dwight D. Eisenhower Library, Abilene, Kansas, contains a number of longer campaign films as well as several polispots from the Eisenhower campaigns of 1952 and 1956. Finally, among the most important collections are the materials of Kathleen Jamieson at the University of Maryland, College Park, Maryland.

Chapter 1

The 1984 spots for Glenn, Hart, Mondale, and Reagan can be found in the NYU News Study Group archives and at the Kennedy School of Government at Harvard. NYU also has the Babbitt spots from 1987. On the Glenn campaign, we interviewed David Sawyer and Scott Miller, together and separately, five times. Barry Nova talked to us about the earlier Glenn races for the Senate, and James David Barber

explained to us his role in the New York Democratic forums. We also
attended several of the candidates' debates prior to the New Hampshire primary in February 1984. In addition one of us has been a
Glenn watcher since the Mercury astronaut days of the 1960s, and
interviewed Glenn for the first time for magazine articles and,
eventually, a book about the space program (Edwin Diamond, *The Rise
and Fall of the Space Age*, Garden City, N.Y.: Doubleday, 1964). Also
helpful about Glenn the man was Frank Van Riper, *Glenn: The
Astronaut Who Would Be President* (New York: Empire Books, 1983). We
learned about the Reagan campaign from Douglas Watts, Reagan's
media director. David Garth and David Sawyer told us about the
Mondale campaign. As the 1988 presidential race got underway, we
began a series of interviews with several consultants, including Daniel
Payne (Dukakis) and Roger Ailes (Bush). The principal books on 1984
are Jack W. Germond and Jules Witcover, *Wake Us When It's Over* (New
York: Macmillan, 1985); Peter Goldman and Tony Fuller, *The Quest for
the Presidency 1984* (New York: Bantam, 1985); and Jonathan Moore,
ed., *Campaign for President: The Managers Look at '84* (Dover, Mass.:
Auburn House, 1986). On the 1986 campaign, see Jerry Hagstrom
and Robert Guskind, "Selling the Candidates," *National Journal*,
November 1, 1986; and John F. Nugent, "Positively Negative,"
Campaigns & Elections, March–April 1987.

Chapter 2

Rosser Reeves, in our interview with him in the fall of 1983, talked
of TV advertising and the 1952 race. He also supplied us with valuable
materials. His book, *Reality in Advertising* (New York: Knopf, 1961),
outlines his theories of persuasion in detail. See also a profile of Reeves
by Thomas Whiteside, "Annals of Television: The Man from Iron
City," *New Yorker*, September 27, 1969.

Chapter 3

A complete set of "Eisenhower Answers America" spots is in the Wood
collection, University of Rhode Island. Stevenson spots are in the
Devlin collection, University of Rhode Island, and the Shuck collection,
John F. Kennedy Library. Our account of the Eisenhower spots comes
from our interview with Reeves. See also Noel L. Griese, "Rosser
Reeves and the 1952 Eisenhower TV Spot Blitz," *Journal of Advertising*,
1975; John E. Hollitz, "Eisenhower and the Admen: The Television

'Spot' Campaign of 1952," *Wisconsin Magazine of History*, autumn 1982; Stanley Kelley, Jr., *Professional Public Relations and Political Power* (Baltimore: Johns Hopkins University Press, 1956); Martin Mayer, *Madison Avenue, U.S.A.* (New York: Harper & Row, 1958); Vance Packard, *The Hidden Persuaders* (New York: Pocket Books, 1958); and Charles A. H. Thomson, *Television and Presidential Politics* (Washington, D.C.: Brookings, 1956). Stephen C. Wood gives the fullest account—and transcribes the complete set of Reeves's commercials for Eisenhower—in his paper, "Eisenhower Answers America: A Critical History," mimeo, Department of Speech Communication, University of Rhode Island, Kingston, R.I., n.d. Other accounts of the 1952 advertising campaign can be found in Robert F. Bradford, "Republicans and Sinners," *Harvard Business Review*, July–August 1956; Walter Goodman, "From Glad Hand to Greasepaint," *New Republic*, May 2, 1955; and Joseph J. Seldin, "Selling Presidents Like Soap," *American Mercury*, September 1956. *The Reporter* also published several analyses, among them Gordon Cotler, "That Plague of Spots from Madison Avenue," November 25, 1952; William Harlan Hale, "The Politicians Try Victory Through Air Power," September 6, 1956; and William Lee Miller, "Can Government Be 'Merchandised'?", October 27, 1953.

Chapter 4

A copy of the Checkers speech exists in the News Study Group archives. Bradford, "Republicans and Sinners," analyzes Checkers, as does Paul Seabury, "Television—A New Campaign Weapon," *New Republic*, December 1, 1952. Good sources, of course, are Richard Nixon's two books, *Six Crises* (Garden City, N.Y.: Doubleday, 1962) and *RN* (New York: Grosset & Dunlap, 1978). See also Garry Wills, *Nixon Agonistes* (Boston: Houghton Mifflin, 1969).

Chapter 5

Spots from the 1956 race are at the John F. Kennedy Library; the Devlin collection, University of Rhode Island; and the News Study Group archives. On two occasions in the summer and fall of 1983, Charles Guggenheim talked with us, in part about his involvement with the Stevenson campaign. A helpful reference for this final, pre-Theodore White presidential election is Charles A. H. Thomson and Frances M. Shattuck, *The 1956 Presidential Campaign* (Washington, D.C.: Brookings, 1960). See also Packard, *The Hidden Persuaders*. Among the articles we found useful are "The Electronic Election,"

Newsweek, November 19, 1956; "Neighbor to Neighbor," *New Republic,* October 22, 1956; and "Television and the 1956 Campaign," *Editorial Research Reports,* 1955.

Chapter 6

The best collection of Kennedy 1960 media materials is at the John F. Kennedy Library. Other spots can be found at the Kennedy School of Government, Harvard, and at the News Study Group archives. For the most detailed account of the campaign, see Theodore H. White, *The Making of the President 1960* (New York: Atheneum, 1961). A brief account, which includes information on TV in the campaign, is Stanley Kelley, Jr., "The Presidential Campaign," in Paul T. David, ed., *The Presidential Election and Transition 1960–1961* (Washington, D.C.: Brookings, 1961). Of the several books written by Kennedy aides, we relied especially on Kenneth P. O'Donnell and David F. Powers, with Joe McCarthy, *Johnny, We Hardly Knew Ye* (Boston: Little, Brown, 1970); on the Nixon side, Nixon's own books, *Six Crises* and *RN,* were useful, as were Herbert G. Klein, *Making It Perfectly Clear* (Garden City, N.Y.: Doubleday, 1980); and Gene Wyckoff, *The Image Candidates* (New York: Macmillan, 1968). The *Saturday Evening Post* editorial, "No, Madison Avenue Hasn't Taken Over Our Political Parties," ran on January 17, 1959. See also Marshall McLuhan, *Understanding Media* (New York: Signet, 1964). Two articles of help in both the 1960 and 1964 campaigns are Tom Wicker, Kenneth P. O'Donnell, and Rowland Evans, "TV in the Political Campaign," *Television Quarterly,* winter 1966; and Lawrence W. Lichty, Joseph M. Ripley, and Harrison B. Summers, "Political Programs on National Television Networks: 1960 and 1964," *Journal of Broadcasting,* summer 1965.

Chapter 7

We interviewed Tony Schwartz a half-dozen times in the summer and fall of 1983 about his work. We also viewed his spots in three other visits to his studio. See also his books, *The Responsive Chord* (Garden City, N.Y.: Doubleday, 1973) and *Media: The Second God* (New York: Random House, 1981). The materials on the changes in advertising over the last three decades come from the files of *Advertising Age* and *Adweek*; in particular, the editors and writers of *Adweek* were helpful to us.

Chapter 8

Besides our interviews with Tony Schwartz, we also interviewed Bill
Moyers; Paul E. Schindler, Jr., talked with Stuart Spencer on our
behalf. The best collection of Johnson spots can be found at the
Lyndon B. Johnson Library. Goldwater spots are in the Devlin
collection, University of Rhode Island; the Shuck collection, John F.
Kennedy Library; and the News Study Group archives. Besides
Theodore H. White, *The Making of the President 1964* (New York:
Atheneum, 1965), see Milton C. Cummings, Jr., ed., *The National
Election of 1964* (Washington, D.C.: Brookings, 1966), particularly the
article by Stanley Kelley, Jr., "The Presidential Campaign," and that
by Charles A. H. Thomson, "Mass Media Performance"; and Robert
D. Novak, *The Agony of the G.O.P. 1964* (New York: Macmillan, 1965).
Two Republican memoirs are also helpful: Barry Goldwater, *With No
Apologies* (New York: Morrow, 1979); and F. Clifton White, with
William J. Gill, *Suite 3505* (New Rochelle, N.Y.: Arlington, 1967). See
also Wyckoff, *The Image Candidates.* Lou Cannon, *Reagan* (New York:
Putnam's, 1982), tells the story of Reagan's televised address for
Goldwater.

Chapter 9

Our interviews with Raymond K. Price, Jr., David Garth, Tony Schwartz,
and David Sawyer helped clarify our understanding of the changes
of the 1960s. See also Theodore H. White, "The Making of the President
Ain't What It Used to Be," *Life*, February 1980.

Chapter 10

Roger Ailes, Raymond K. Price, Jr., Charles Guggenheim, Joseph
Napolitan, Robert Squier, and Arie L. Kopelman were interviewed
about their roles in the 1968 campaign. Kopelman also gave us
internal memoranda from Doyle Dane Bernbach's work for Hum-
phrey. The Devlin collection, University of Rhode Island, and the
News Study Group archives contain commercials from the campaign.
For Humphrey's campaign, see Napolitan's book, *The Election Game*
(Garden City, N.Y.: Doubleday, 1972). For Nixon's campaign, see Joe
McGinniss, *The Selling of the President 1968* (New York: Trident, 1969),
and, more sympathetically: Nixon, *RN;* Klein, *Making It Perfectly Clear;*
Raymond Price, *With Nixon* (New York: Viking, 1977); William Safire,
Before the Fall (Garden City, N.Y.: Doubleday, 1975); Stephen C.
Shadegg, *Winning's a Lot More Fun* (New York: Macmillan, 1969); and

Richard Whalen, *Catch the Falling Flag* (Boston: Houghton Mifflin, 1972). See also the general accounts in Theodore H. White, *The Making of the President 1968* (New York: Atheneum, 1969); and Lewis Chester, Godfrey Hodgson, and Bruce Page, *An American Melodrama* (London: Penguin, 1970). See also "Admen Join the Race," *Business Week,* July 6, 1968.

Chapter 11

Our interviews with Price, Guggenheim, Schwartz, and Squier helped our understanding of the 1972 media campaign. The Devlin collection, University of Rhode Island, has a large collection of 1972 commercials. The Nixon administration memoirs, cited in the previous note, were also helpful, as was Jeb Stuart Magruder, *An American Life* (New York: Atheneum, 1974). Presidential campaign advertising is discussed specifically in several articles: Dom Bonafede, "New Hampshire, Florida Primaries Highlight Powers and Limitations of Media," *National Journal,* March 18, 1972; L. Patrick Devlin, "Contrasts in Presidential Campaign Commercials in 1972," *Journal of Broadcasting,* winter 1973–1974; "The GOP Admen Have the Edge," *Business Week,* August 5, 1972; Andrew J. Glass, "Effective Media Campaign Paved Way for McGovern Win in California," *National Journal,* June 10, 1972; and "On the Spot," *Newsweek,* October 2, 1972. Besides Theodore H. White, *The Making of the President 1972* (New York: Atheneum, 1973), see Ernest R. May and Janet Fraser, *Campaign '72* (Cambridge, Mass.: Harvard University Press, 1973).

Chapter 12

In our three interviews Gerald Rafshoon described for us the Democratic media campaign of 1976. On the Republican side we talked with John Deardourff, Malcolm MacDougall, and Stuart Spencer. Spots can be found in the Devlin collection, University of Rhode Island, and in the News Study Group archives. MacDougall's book, *We Almost Made It* (New York: Crown, 1977), contains additional information, as does Gerald Ford, *A Time to Heal* (New York: Harper & Row, 1979). A good study of the 1976 presidential commercials is L. Patrick Devlin, "Contrasts in Presidential Campaign Commercials of 1976," *Central States Speech Journal,* winter 1977. General campaign accounts include Elizabeth Drew, *American Journal* (New York: Vintage, 1978); Jonathan Moore and Janet Fraser, eds., *Campaign for President* (Cambridge, Mass.: Ballinger, 1977); and Jules Witcover, *Marathon* (New York: Viking, 1977).

Chapter 13

For our accounts of the 1980 race we talked with Gerald Rafshoon (Carter); David Sawyer, Tony Schwartz, and Charles Guggenheim (Kennedy); Robert Goodman (Bush); John Deardourff (Baker); Eddie Mahe (Connally); David Garth (Anderson); and Stuart Spencer (Reagan). The Devlin collection, University of Rhode Island, has a large collection of 1980 spots; others can be found at the News Study Group archives. We also used L. Patrick Devlin's articles, "Contrasts in Presidential Campaign Commercials of 1980," *Political Communications Review,* 1982; and "Reagan's and Carter's Ad Men Review the 1980 Television Campaigns," *Communications Quarterly,* winter 1981. See also Elizabeth Drew, *Portrait of an Election* (New York: Simon & Schuster, 1981); Jack W. Germond and Jules Witcover, *Blue Smoke and Mirrors* (New York: Viking, 1981); Jonathan Moore, ed., *The Campaign for President* (Cambridge, Mass.: Ballinger, 1981); and Cannon, *Reagan.*

Chapter 14

In addition to the interviews cited previously, we talked with Michael Kaye, Daniel Payne, and Ken Swope about their media work. Nicholas Lemann's articles on polispots were helpful: "No; Seriously; I Want You to Look at the Camera and Say, 'Ride With Me, Wyoming!' ", *Washington Monthly,* July–August 1980; and "Barney Frank's Mother and 500 Postmen," *Harper's,* April 1983. James Perry recounts the 1966 Rockefeller campaign in his *The New Politics* (New York: Potter, 1968).

Chapter 15

Besides the interviews previously cited, Curtis Gans and his assistant, Becky Bond, talked to us about production values in political advertising. We also consulted Gans's testimony and supporting evidence offered to Congress. Two specialists in political applications of the new media technology, John Florescu and Andrew Litsky, talked with us; Robert Squier, Eddie Mahe, and David Garth were also helpful on the subject. David Sawyer provided copies of internal campaign memoranda, focus group findings, and polling data from the Jane Byrne campaign.

For our understanding of the political science literature on advertising effects, we are indebted to the reviews in Leslie Jane Smith, "Political Advertising: A Rising Force in American Politics," bachelor's thesis, Department of Government, Harvard College, 1983; and Kay Israel,

"The Interaction of Political Attitudes with the Preference of Format of Televised Political Commercials," Ph.D. thesis, Department of Political Science, MIT, 1983. Other effects studies we consulted include: Shearon Lowery and Melvin L. DeFleur, *Milestones in Mass Communication Research: Media Effects* (New York: Longman, 1983); Charles K. Atkin, Lawrence Bowen, Oguz B. Nayman, and Kenneth G. Sheinkopf, "Quality versus Quantity in Televised Political Ads," *Public Opinion Quarterly*, summer 1973; Bernard Berelson, "Communication and Public Opinion," in Wilbur Schramm, ed., *Communications in Modern Society* (Chicago: University of Illinois Press, 1948); Thomas R. Donohue, "Impact of Viewer Predispositions on Political TV Commercials," *Journal of Broadcasting*, winter 1973–1974; Gary C. Jacobson, "The Impact of Broadcast Campaigning on Electoral Outcomes," *Journal of Politics*, 1975; Herbert E. Krugman, "The Impact of Television Advertising: Learning without Involvement," in Wilbur Schramm and Donald Roberts, eds., *The Process and Effects of Mass Communication* (Chicago: University of Illinois Press, 1971); Michael L. Rothschild and Michael L. Ray, "Involvement and Political Advertising Effect," *Communications Research*, July 1974; and John Wanat, "Political Broadcast Advertising and Primary Election Voting," *Journal of Broadcasting*, fall 1974.

On the cost of campaigning, Herbert Alexander has written a number of helpful books, including *Financing Politics* (2nd ed.; Washington, D.C.: Congressional Quarterly, 1980) and *Financing the 1980 Election* (Lexington, Mass.: Lexington, 1983). Also useful is "An Analysis of the Impact of the Federal Election Campaign Act, 1972–1978," a study by the Campaign Finance Study Group, Institute of Politics, Harvard University, commissioned by the Committee on House Administration, U.S. House of Representatives, 1979. We also consulted David Adamany, *Financing Politics* (Madison: University of Wisconsin Press, 1969); Delmer D. Dunn, *Financing Presidential Campaigns* (Washington, D.C.: Brookings, 1972); Alexander Heard, *The Costs of Democracy* (Garden City, N.Y.: Doubleday, 1962); Max McCarthy, *Elections for Sale* (Boston: Houghton Mifflin, 1972); and Twentieth Century Fund, *Voters' Time* (New York: Twentieth Century Fund, 1969).

On polispots' information content, see Thomas E. Patterson and Robert D. McClure, *The Unseeing Eye* (New York: Putnam's, 1976); Walter DeVries and Lance Tarrance, Jr., *The Ticket-Splitter* (Grand Rapids, Mich.: Eerdman's, 1972); and Thomas E. Patterson, *The Mass Media Election* (New York: Praeger, 1980). Two helpful voting studies are V. O. Key, Jr., *The Responsible Electorate* (New York: Vintage, 1966); and Sidney Verba and Norman H. Nie, *Participation in America* (New York: Harper

& Row, 1972). For perspectives on the proposal to ban polispots, see Leslie A. Tucker and David J. Heller, "Putting Ethics Into Practice," *Campaigns and Elections*, March–April 1987, pp. 42–46; and "The Clean Campaign Act of 1985: A Rational Solution to Negative Campaign Advertising," *Journal of Law and Politics* 3 (1987), p. 727. Studies of press coverage in the 1984 election include William C. Adams, "The Media in Campaign '84: Convention Coverage," *Public Opinion*, December–January 1985, p. 43; Michael J. Robinson, "Where's the Beef: Media and Media Elites in 1984," in Austin Ranney, ed., *The American Elections of 1984* (Durham, N.C.: Duke, 1985), p. 166; and Maura Clancey and Michael J. Robinson, "The Media in Campaign '84: General Election Coverage," *Public Opinion*, December–January 1985, p. 49. For this chapter we also consulted F. Christopher Arterton, "Communications Technology and Political Campaigns in 1982," mimeo, the Roosevelt Center for American Policy Studies, Washington, D.C., 1983; Steven H. Chaffee and Jack Dennis, "Presidential Debates: An Empirical Assessment," in Austin Ranney, ed., *The Past and Future of Presidential Debates* (Washington, D.C.: American Enterprise Institute, 1979); Derek Shearer, "Fewer Americans Vote Than Ever, But There Are Some Clear Remedies," *Los Angeles Times*, June 14, 1987, p. V-3; and George H. White, "A Study of Access to Television for Political Candidates," report to the Campaign Finance Study Group, mimeo, Institute of Politics, Harvard University, 1978.

General Sources

Books Several authors have explored the rise of political consultants, media and otherwise, including Sidney Blumenthal, *The Permanent Campaign* (rev. ed.; New York: Simon & Schuster, 1982); David Chagall, *The New Kingmakers* (New York: Harcourt Brace Jovanovich, 1981); Kathleen Hall Jamieson, *Packaging the President* (New York: Oxford, 1984); Dan Nimmo, *The Political Persuaders* (Englewood Cliffs, N.J.: Prentice-Hall, 1970); David Lee Rosenbloom, *The Election Men* (New York: Quadrangle, 1973); and Larry J. Sabato, *The Rise of Political Consultants* (New York: Basic Books, 1981). We found several general books on TV and politics helpful, among them Edward W. Chester, *Radio, Television, and American Politics* (New York: Sheed & Ward, 1969); Robert MacNeil, *The People Machine* (New York: Harper & Row, 1968); and Sig Mickelson, *The Electric Mirror* (New York: Dodd, Mead, 1972). See also Robert E. Gilbert, *Television and Presidential Politics* (North Quincy, Mass.: Christopher, 1972); and Robert Spero, *The*

Duping of the American Voter (New York: Lippincott & Crowell, 1980). A valuable general reference on presidential politics is Eugene H. Roseboom and Alfred E. Eckes, Jr., *A History of Presidential Elections* (4th ed.; New York: Collier, 1979).

Articles   Samuel L. Becker and Elmer W. Lower cover much ground in "Broadcasting in Presidential Campaigns," in Sidney Kraus, ed., *The Great Debates* (Bloomington, Ind.: Indiana University Press, 1962); and a sequel, "Broadcasting in Presidential Campaigns, 1960–1976," in Sidney Kraus, ed., *The Great Debates: Carter vs. Ford, 1976* (Bloomington, Ind.: Indiana University Press, 1979). Lewis Wolfson's three articles, "The Men Behind the Candidates," provide valuable background information on political media consultants; the articles ran in *Potomac*, the Sunday magazine section of the *Washington Post*, on February 13, February 20, and March 5, 1972. Three general articles proved helpful: John Carey, "How Media Shape Campaigns," *Journal of Communication*, spring 1976; Robert E. Kintner, "Television and the World of Politics," *Harper's*, May 1965; and Richard L. Worsnop, "Television and Politics," *Editorial Research Reports*, May 15, 1968.

Index

Mezvinsky, Edward, 303
MGM Studios, 37, 40
Mike Douglas Show, 153, 155,
 168, 169
Mikulski, Barbara, 30
Miller, Scott, 3–13, 25, 279
Miller, William, 137, 145
Milton Biouw agency, 46
"Minute Men," 36
"Mistakes" (Lindsay), 321–323
Mitchell, James, 81
Mitchell, John, 162, 181, 219
Mitchell, Martha, 196
Mitchell, Steven A., 48
Mobil Oil, 275
Mondale, Walter, 342, 360, 391
 and Carter, 238, 249, 288
 v. John Glenn, 3, 5, 6–7,
  10–11, 17, 18–19, 23
 and McGovern, 196
 v. Gary Hart, 19–23
 v. Reagan, 24–28, 310, 373
Monday Night at the Movies
 (CBS), 129
"MonDole" (Carter), 248, 333
Moore, Arch, 331, 376
Moore, Mary Tyler, 314
"Morning Again" (Reagan), 26,
 27, 388
Morris, Howard, 38
Morrison, Bruce, 326
Moyers, Bill, 121–122, 127,
 129, 132
Moynihan, Daniel Patrick, 302,
 379
Mudd, Roger, 196, 275, 282,
 354
Muskie, Edmund, 176, 178,
 180, 185–188, 190, 193,
 221, 259

Napolitan, Joseph, 153,
 170–171, 172–175, 176,
 180, 183, 389
National Association of Broad-
 casters, 132
National Broadcasting Company
 (NBC), 35, 61, 67, 69,
 164, 286, 391
 political spots on, 24, 94, 129,
  132, 143, 144
National Council of Senior
 Citizens, 393
National Education Association,
 3
National Educational Television,
 153
Nelson, Gaylord, 196
Neustadt, Richard E., *Presi-
 dential Power*, 284
Newman, Paul, 183
"Newspaper" (McGovern), 215,
 218
Newton, Carroll, 61, 78, 100,
 102, 382
New York Herald Tribune, 43, 51,
 55, 68, 154
New York 19 (Schwartz), 118
New York State Draft Stevenson
 committee, 283
New York Times, 4, 177, 260
Nielson ratings, 24, 38, 61, 74,
 150, 240
Nine from Little Rock (documen-
 tary), 160
Nisei for Eisenhower-Nixon, 65
Nixon, Julie, 67
Nixon, Patricia, 67, 69, 71, 74
Nixon, Richard, 42, 51, 116,
 122, 123. *See also*
 Checkers speech
 aides of, 149, 262